Tales of Christmas

T0188717

Chicken Soup for the Soul: Tales of Christmas
101 Stories of Holiday Joy, Love and Gratitude
Amy Newmark

Published by Chicken Soup for the Soul, LLC www.chickensoup.com
Copyright ©2024 by Chicken Soup for the Soul, LLC. All Rights Reserved.

The publisher gratefully acknowledges the many individuals who granted Chicken Soup for the Soul permission to reprint the cited material.

Front cover illustration of snow background courtesy of iStockphoto.com/Rustic (©Rustic), illustration of Chritsmas gifts courtesy of iStockphoto.com/Yuliya Derbisheva (©Yuliya Derbisheva), illustration of Santa courtesy of shutterstock.com/Ekaterina Popelniak (©Ekaterina Popelniak), illustration of reindeer courtesy of shutterstock.com/wacomka (©wacomka)
Back cover and interior illustration of Christmas tree courtesy of iStockphoto.com/maroznc (©maroznc)

Photo of Amy Newmark courtesy of Susan Morrow at SwickPix

Cover and Interior by Daniel Zaccari

Publisher's Cataloging-in-Publication data

Names: Newmark, Amy, editor.
Title: Chicken soup for the soul : tales of Christmas : 101 stories of holiday joy, love and
    gratitude / Amy Newmark.
Description: Cos Cob, CT: Chicken Soup for the Soul, LLC, 2024.
Identifiers: LCCN: 2024941202 | ISBN: 978-1-61159-117-0 (paperback) | 978-1-61159
    352-5 (ebook)
Subjects: LCSH Christmas--Literary collections. | Christmas--Anecdotes. | Holidays-
    Literary collections. | Holidays--Anecdotes. | BISAC RELIGION / Holidays / Christmas &
    Advent | SELF-HELP / Motivational and Inspirational | SELF-HELP / Personal Growth /
    Happiness
Classification: LCC GT4985 C45 2024 | DDC 394.2663/02--dc23

Library of Congress Control Number: 2024941202

29 28 27 26 25 24   01 02 03 04 05 06 07

Tales of Christmas

101 Stories of Holiday Joy, Love and Gratitude

Amy Newmark

Chicken Soup for the Soul, LLC
Cos Cob, CT

Changing your life one story at a time ®
www.chickensoup.com

Table of Contents

1

~Ready, Set, Gobble~

2

~Tales of the Tree~

❸

~The Spirit of the Season~

❹

~Santa's Helpers~

❺

~Best Gift Ever~

6

~Holiday Hijinks~

7

~Creative Christmas-ing~

⑪
~Favorite Traditions~

Ready, Set, Gobble

Chicken Soup for the Soul

The Tiny Turkey

Thanksgiving, man. Not a good day to be my pants.
~Kevin James

Thanksgiving is a big deal in our family. We always have a huge gathering with all my husband's brothers and their wives and adult kids. One particular year, my brother-in-law and sister-in-law, Steve and Pat, were hosting the whole family. Pat was making a traditional roasted turkey and several side dishes. Everyone else was bringing their contributions to round out a huge family feast. My husband Tom was asked if he would do a smoked turkey as he had in years past. Everyone loves the smoked turkey, and he never minds doing it.

A week or so before Thanksgiving, we went to the grocery store to get our turkey. In the meat department, we picked out a large turkey and added it to the buggy. Tom picked up a Cornish hen and said, "I think we should just do this one," laughing at his suggestion. And then an idea hit me, so we bought the Cornish hen, too.

We got up early Thanksgiving morning to put the turkey on the smoker. We prepped both the turkey and the Cornish hen in the same way, coating them with a tasty spice rub. We put on the turkey but waited a while to add the Cornish hen since it was much smaller and would overcook in the time the turkey needed. Both would end up done about 11:00 a.m., and we were headed to our family gathering at noon.

When the birds came off the smoker, we decided how to arrange our prank. We carved up the big turkey, placed all the slices on a large platter, and covered it with foil. Then, we put the small Cornish hen in the middle of our traditional big turkey platter. We garnished around it with fruit and herbs as we usually did the smoked turkey. Then, we covered it with foil but domed and shaped the foil so it appeared that a full-sized turkey was under there.

We loaded up the car with the food, including a few desserts I had made. We put the turkey in the back seat instead of the back of the SUV where all the food was because we knew that, when we arrived, Steve would come out and help us bring everything in, and we didn't want him to see it. Sure enough, Steve helped us unload the foods, and Tom made sure that he carried the prank turkey platter himself so the weight wouldn't be a giveaway. After everything was inside, except for the real turkey, we greeted everyone and joined the party.

A few minutes later, Tom slipped out to the car and got the tray of real turkey. He snuck back into the house through the laundry room and left the platter of carved turkey back there. He rejoined the party, and no one was the wiser while the prank platter sat on the kitchen counter.

We visited with the family for a bit and helped Pat with some last-minute tasks in the kitchen. It was nearing the time to put the food out on the table. "We need to carve the turkey," Tom said. "Steve, do you have an electric knife?" Steve said he did and rummaged through a kitchen cupboard to pull it out. He was installing the blades on it when Tom said, "Would you go ahead and carve it, please, Steve?"

"Sure," Steve said, and he slid the platter in front of him. Of course, a lot of the family gathered around for the carving of the turkey, waiting expectantly to see the golden-brown bird.

"I'm not really sure why, but the turkey seemed to shrink up a little this time on the smoker," Tom said casually as Steve pulled at the edges of the foil and lifted it off the platter. What was revealed was a golden-brown bird — but not the one everyone expected to see. The Cornish hen looked tiny in the middle of the platter, and Steve and the whole family burst into laughter. It was fun to hear the genuine, deep belly laughs from everyone.

"It shrunk a *little* bit?" Steve asked. "That's a *lot*-a-bit! Pat, it's a good thing we cooked that other turkey. This one isn't going to go very far."

As the laughter died down, we owned up to having the real turkey platter, and I went to get it. Steve and Tom decided to cut up the Cornish hen, too, and we piled those pieces on top of the sliced turkey.

The table was set, the family was seated, and Steve's adult son Jeff said grace. He made sure to thank God for the provided food — especially for the Cornish hen. The family enjoyed a wonderful Thanksgiving meal together that year and many years afterward. And the story of the tiny turkey comes up as a fun memory almost every year.

— Kim Cook —

My Thanksgiving Family

Thanksgiving is a time of togetherness and gratitude.
~Nigel Hamilton

My tears flowed when the commercial came on again. It seemed like the station was playing this commercial every fifteen minutes, and I couldn't bear to see it again. I don't know what the ad was trying to sell, but a large, lovely family was gathered around a long table laden with a bountiful Thanksgiving dinner. Everyone was talking, laughing, and beaming happily at one another.

That was my family once. I came from a large, close-knit family. I was the oldest daughter, so when Mama got older, I gladly took over hosting our Thanksgiving dinner.

Those were such happy times, and I never thought about the inevitable time when they would be just a memory. As the years passed, and we all grew older, our family gatherings became smaller and smaller. Kids grew up and moved away or just lost interest, and we lost the older generation one by one. When my sister Alice died, my brother Jim hugged me after the funeral. "It's just the two of us now, sis."

For the past three years, there has only been me. This Thanksgiving, I planned to open a can of soup and sit alone at my kitchen table again. It would just be me and my memories.

The next morning, I went to the supermarket to pick up a few things. Most of the other shoppers were putting huge turkeys and hams in their carts, preparing for Thanksgiving Day. I stood in the aisle looking at the cans of soup while people with carts laden with all kinds of wonderful things passed me. I sighed. "You can do a little better than this," I said to myself, scowling at the array of soups.

I made my way over to the frozen food and stared at the prepared dinners. If one could judge by the pictures on the packages, they all would be quite delicious. I chuckled. They wouldn't taste like a homecooked Thanksgiving feast, but they should certainly taste better than a can of soup. I chose a turkey dinner and tossed it into my cart.

On my way out of the store, I stopped by the bulletin board where people posted things for sale, odd jobs they needed done, babysitter want ads, and so forth. I paused in front of the bulletin board as an idea formed in my mind. Before I could talk myself out of it, I fished around in my purse for paper and pen. There was a bench nearby, and I sat down to carefully compose my note. It had to sound sincere. My heart raced as I wrote it:

Are you going to be alone on Thanksgiving Day? So am I. But we don't have to be. Let's get together and share a meal, some conversation, and some companionship. Everyone who is interested is encouraged to reply. No restrictions of any kind. Any age, sex, race, religion, etc. If you, like me, don't look forward to being alone on Thanksgiving Day, please call.

I scolded myself all the way home. "Who do you think wants to have Thanksgiving dinner with strangers? You're a foolish old woman. What if some unsavory person shows up at your door?" It was all I could do to keep from returning to the supermarket and snatching my note off the bulletin board.

I didn't hear anything for two days. Then, on the third day, I got a call from a retired schoolteacher. On the fourth day, I got three more calls. By the end of the eighth day, I had twelve people eager to be a part of the communal Thanksgiving dinner. I decided that it was time to take down the note before my expectations got out of hand. As I was taking down the note, I heard a small sigh and glanced up to see a young woman with two small kids standing next to me.

"Am I too late?" she asked.

I looked into her tired face and shook my head. "Not at all. How many are you bringing?"

"It's just us," she said softly. "Just us."

I looked at the two little girls at her feet. "It will be nice to have children," I said, smiling down at them.

I baked a huge turkey with dressing, and everyone else contributed what they could. I looked around at the people gathered around my dining room table and the overflow table in the kitchen. There were six retired women, three retired men, a construction worker, a nurse's assistant, a fellow who had just gotten out of the army, and the young woman with the two little girls.

We were a motley group. The only rule I made was that we would not ask questions of one another. People were free to tell us as little or as much as they wanted to about themselves and their circumstances. Although the atmosphere was a little stiff at first, soon everyone was laughing, talking, and having a good time. I glanced around and smiled. Once again, I had people gathered around my table at Thanksgiving, and my house was filled with chatter and laughter.

We made a pact to keep in touch and make the gathering our new Thanksgiving tradition. By the next Thanksgiving, we had lost a few and gained a couple of new people by word of mouth. It has been eight years now, and seven of my original guests are still members of what we simply call "The Thanksgiving Group." We have become friends and see one another at other times, too. We still have an open invitation to anyone who will be alone on Thanksgiving Day. Word gets around, and I have never had to place an ad again for someone to share Thanksgiving with me. The eight of us enjoy it tremendously, and it is always fun to see who will be joining us for Thanksgiving dinner.

— Elizabeth A. Atwater —

Chicken Soup for the Soul

Giving Thanks

Recognizing and leaning into the discomfort of
vulnerability teaches us how to live with joy.
~Brené Brown

I was thrilled when I graduated from flight attendant training and received my silver wings. I had been excited that, at fifty years old, my secret dream had come true. Thanksgiving was in two days, and I wanted to rush home and celebrate with my daughters and friends after the intense three-week program that I'd just completed.

I hadn't even boarded the short flight from Virginia to Philadelphia when my phone beeped. The welcome message from my new manager ended with a final sentence that melted away my joy.

"Work Assignment: Thursday, November 23. Flight 768, PHL-YOW, terminal D. 6:00-9:48 a.m." The message was followed by a three-day schedule and the captain and copilot's names.

I read it in shock. I had to work on Thanksgiving Day? Harsh realities replaced my fantasies about the glamorous flight attendant life. This was my first taste of a typical rookie flight attendant's day. Instead of working 9 to 5, I could work as many as eighteen hours a day and as many as five flights in a day.

I couldn't remember which city the airport code, YOW, stood for. I had no idea where I was going.

Fear sluiced through my body. Worry dogged me through the flight home.

I wasn't ready. I'd planned to review my notes and practice the safety speech. The fifty-seater Bombardier aircraft required only one flight attendant. I would be working alone, without a seasoned FA to share the in-flight responsibilities. Somehow, over the next day and a half, I got organized.

I hid nervousness behind my smile. Fortunately, I didn't make too many mistakes.

The pilots, who lived in the Raleigh-Durham area, left me at the hotel pickup zone with a cheerful "Happy Thanksgiving, Karla. See you in the morning."

Despondently, I waited for the hotel van, shivering as the cold breeze snuck under my navy overcoat.

"Don't be silly," I told myself. "This isn't the first time you've worked on a holiday." But it would be the first time I'd miss Thanksgiving with my family. I called my daughters, glad that they were enjoying the holiday with friends.

Twenty minutes later, I checked into the Holiday Inn Express. As the motherly reservation agent handed me a key card, I was tackled from the back. I rocked on my heels and looked over my shoulder. I expected to find that a clumsy dog or kid had collided with me. "Hey, if you don't mind," I said. My eyebrows lifted in shock. I knew this young woman. We were wearing the same navy uniform. What a great surprise!

"Shawnie?" Laughing, I turned around fully and returned the short brunette's hug.

"Karly, I'm so glad to see you," squealed her familiar Southern voice. Her muted makeup and neat updo were completely different from the vivid fashions she preferred. "We made it through our first day. Look at us, all professional and styling."

My heart lifted at seeing a friendly face. "Am I glad to see you!" I had been too shy to socialize with most of my younger classmates. But our twenty-five-year age difference hadn't made a difference to this young woman. We had eaten lunch together a few times. We took the elevator together, talking excitedly about our first day. We both got off on the third floor. Her room was near mine, so we made plans to meet in a half-hour to have dinner together.

I changed out of my uniform into a pair of jeans and a pink sweater. Finding Shawnie had restored my good mood. I had someone to share Thanksgiving with! Though we both had an early wake-up call, I was much happier. We met at the elevator and rode down to the lobby, talking non-stop. Her day had been as exciting as mine.

I paused at the reception desk. "Excuse me, can you tell me where's the closest restaurant?"

The lady's eyes twinkled. "Got a hot date for you. You two are invited to dinner at the Cracker Barrel restaurant. The hotel shuttle bus will drop you off."

I exchanged a surprised look with my friend. I shook my head. "You're kidding me, right? I don't know anyone here."

Shawnie giggled. "Hot grits and honey, I'm all for a surprise." She winked. "Is he eye candy? That's all I need to know."

On the way there, we still hadn't figured it out. My life had certainly gotten more interesting. I had met so many strangers that day that it didn't occur to me to be scared. Worse comes to worse, I told myself, we could ditch any undesirable company and treat ourselves to pricey hotel food.

I had never been to a Cracker Barrel, and their charming gift shop made me want to start Christmas shopping right away. We followed the delicious smells that made me realize how hungry I was. The hostess led us to a long table. I hesitated, sure that there had been a mistake. A hot date meant one person, not ten strangers.

A stocky man came forward and shook our hands. "Happy Thanksgiving, fellow crew members. I was in the lobby when you checked in. I'm Captain Clark with United. You're rookies, right?"

"Yes, first day, in fact," I said, marveling that I was surrounded by flight crew members. After the introductions, we sat down and ordered. The other pilots and flight attendants were friendly and included us in their conversations.

Feeling bold, I ordered catfish with a side of hash-brown casserole and a small salad. For dessert, I had delicious chocolate cake made with Coca Cola. It wasn't a typical Thanksgiving meal, but then again, nothing about the day had been typical.

Before dinner ended, the captain stood and raised his glass. "I'd like to welcome the newest FAs, Karla and Shawnie, to our airline. Whether you're flying regional or mainline, we're a family. We look out for each other. Dinner is on me. Everyone, have a happy Thanksgiving and fly safe tomorrow."

I raised my sweet tea and toasted "Fly safe!" with my new airline family. I laughed with everyone instead of revealing how his words had touched me, but I was actually a bit teary.

It was the perfect ending to an amazing day.

I hadn't missed Thanksgiving, after all.

— Karla Brown —

A Hot Tub Thanksgiving

I cook with wine, sometimes I even add it to the food.
~W.C. Fields

My Thanksgiving nightmare began when I realized one of my turkeys had been stolen from my back porch, aka the auxiliary refrigeration system. I noticed bear footprints leading away from the scene of the crime.

Of course, it was the day before the big feast, when scores of people were due for dinner. I threw on my clothes and headed to the local store, hoping to find a turkey that was the right size at the last minute.

Thirty minutes later, at store number four, I found one. But my pleasing, portly poultry, weighing a luscious twenty-four pounds, was frozen solid. There was no way this birdzilla would thaw out overnight.

After hours of giving that creature a cold-water bath to coax it to thaw, I had a flash of genius. Could I pull off this devious plan without poisoning my guests? Oh, what's a little stomachache among friends, right?

At 3:00 a.m., under the cover of darkness, I crept to the hot tub, placed "Tom" into a fishnet I had used as a pool-house decoration, and then tossed it into the warm, rushing waters. I figured the plastic covering around the turkey would act just like an oven-baking bag.

After an hour, during which time I joined Tom in the hot tub, I dried off and pulled out the turkey. Then I snuck the nicely warmed bird back into the kitchen. I pulled off the plastic wrapping and gave the turkey its next warm bath, in the sink. Then I removed the once-frozen giblets from their cavity, now soft and warm, and gave the great bird another rinsing.

I made a delicious chestnut-and-cranberry stuffing, with chopped onions, croutons, and a nice hunk of Irish butter. It was sauteed with love and shoved into that roomy cavity. It was getting close to 5:00 in the morning, a perfect time to get both turkeys into the extra-large oven. I could differentiate between the two birds because one had meat stuffing while my "quick-thaw" bird had chestnut stuffing.

I set the oven to 300 degrees and headed off to bed for a few hours. I fell asleep as soon as my head hit the pillow, thanks to the spiced eggnog I had taste-tested for everyone while keeping the turkey company in the hot tub.

When I woke up, the turkey already smelled wonderful. I had pulled it off, averted disaster, and no one was the wiser.

Later that day, our guests sat down for the holiday feast. The blessing said at the table by one guest had a bizarrely special meaning to me. He said Thanksgiving is a time to feel blessed for all experiences, the usual ones and unexpected ones, too. My husband carved the majestic birds, although the hot-tub turkey almost slipped off the bones. Guests actually "oohed" at its succulent meat.

During the meal, I noticed more people favored the hot-tub turkey over the original roast. My curiosity took over; I decided to try some. Now, I understood the guests' "oohs." This turkey was the moistest, sweetest-tasting bird I had ever eaten. It truly melted as soon as I put it in my mouth. Swallowing that tender, juicy flesh, I felt like a Thanksgiving explorer who had discovered a secret the rest of mankind didn't know. By the time I finished my first helping, hot-tub Tom was picked clean. I scraped a few remaining pieces from the carcass but craved more.

Friends and relatives asked me what I did differently to that particular turkey to make it so yummy. I told them it was my new and special recipe that I could never ever divulge.

That stays between us, okay?

— Venus Velvet —

Giving Thanks for My Alternative Thanksgiving

*Entertaining doesn't need to be a difficult or daunting
process.... It just requires a little thought,
creativity, and heart.*
~Maury Ankrum

I suppose you could call me a "Thanksgiving Scrooge." While I'm a huge believer in the importance of gratitude — and have a daily gratitude practice that I never miss — something about the Thanksgiving holiday itself has never clicked with me.

My first problem: the dishes.

As a mom who held down an extremely demanding job while her children were growing up, I always felt the word "holiday" should imply a break from setting the table, clearing it, running the dishwasher, washing pots, wiping everything down, and sweeping up the crumbs. Thanksgiving, let's be honest, requires *a lot* of cleanup, even if everyone helps, as they do in my family.

My second problem: the food.

Turkey and mashed potatoes are not dishes I would choose on my own, never mind odd Thanksgiving classics like candied yams or cranberry relish. Also, lots of folks in my extended family have food issues. My husband and a dear family friend are both gluten- and lactose-free, so pies, stuffing, rolls and a host of other traditional dishes are troublesome. One son insists mashed potatoes be made with butter and cream, so two versions must be created in order to provide for the lactose-free crowd (more prep work and more dishes).

One sister and her husband are vegetarians and need a separate main course (more dishes). My father can't have chocolate or nuts. Both sons insist on gravy, but no one wants to make it. Disappointment and guilt ensue.

I hear you saying that we should go out to eat for Thanksgiving. But my father has Alzheimer's and is hard of hearing, so restaurants are tough for him.

I hear you saying that we should order in our next Thanksgiving dinner. But it's been challenging to find a place that can accommodate all our complex dietary restrictions.

What I don't hear you saying is: "Order Chinese food."

But that's exactly what I did five or six years ago. We didn't endure the mad rush at the grocery store that week. Thanksgiving Day itself was so relaxing. I think I went for a long walk. We slept late. Maybe we watched some football on TV. There was no endless fussing in the kitchen. It was lovely.

When my extended family came over that evening, there were plenty of options for everyone's dietary needs. Since there was zero cooking and almost no cleanup, we had time to sit around the fire, talk, and play games.

Isn't that really what Thanksgiving is about? Gathering with our loved ones, relaxing, and enjoying each other's company? I assure you that I was quite thankful. Leading up to the holiday, when friends and co-workers learned of my Chinese-food Thanksgiving plans, many of them (mostly women) said, "Oh, I wish I could do that!"

In subsequent years, we went traditional again: the turkey, pies, etc. I understand I can't have my way all the time. But then last year, I said to my husband, "Can we please do something different?"

He said, "How about Rome?"

I found cheap flights. Europe doesn't observe Thanksgiving, of course, and late November is not a heavy time for tourism. Rome wasn't especially crowded, and the weather was still pleasant. I found an inexpensive place to stay. It was a special treat to be away with our young adult sons, who have their own lives now. It was wonderful to have pasta and pizza on Thanksgiving.

And no dishes.

This year, we'll probably go back to the traditional Thanksgiving meal. My husband and boys do like the food, despite my own disinterest. And I'll go happily along with the plan because I think we're going to celebrate with my sister-in-law's family... who lives in Berlin.

I'm so thankful for my alternative Thanksgivings. They make me anticipate — instead of dread — the holiday. If you love the traditional Thanksgiving, right down to the last spoonful of gravy or crumb of apple pie, I say, "Godspeed, enjoy, and that's wonderful." But if you're like me — weary of all the planning, shopping, cooking, and cleaning, and eager to truly have a "holiday" — I hope my story inspires you to do something different.

You'll be thankful you did!

— Laura Knoy —

I Never Cooked a Turkey

When women support each other,
incredible things happen.
~Cher

How hard can it be to cook a turkey? After all, I watched my grandma and mom cook them for as long as I can remember. They would place the turkey in the roaster and pop it in the oven. And, just like that, every year a perfectly golden-brown, roasted bird graced our Thanksgiving table. I never paid much attention to the process. My focus was only on the feast.

I remember the year that things would be different. Although my dear grandma had been gone for several years, this was the first holiday when my mom would be gone, too. She had passed away on November 19, 1997, at the age of 74. Her funeral took place just six days before Thanksgiving.

Facing that first Thanksgiving without my grandma or mom, I quickly realized that not only had I suddenly become the matriarch of our family, but I was next in line to reign over the Thanksgiving dinner. This was a bequest I did not want. I felt sad and nervous. After all, I had never cooked a turkey.

It had been a few harrowing weeks of anticipating the death of my mom, so planning for this feast was a diversion that I sorely needed. It had been difficult to accept that her death was inevitable but more difficult watching her suffer. I was determined to fix a nice holiday dinner for my husband and our two teenagers. They had been close to their Grandma Ruth and missed her, so I wanted to make this Thanksgiving special for them, to ease their grief at least for a bit.

I headed to our neighborhood Kroger where I spotted an ad for turkeys at thirty percent off. I felt like this was a good start. It was in the early morning hours of a beautiful November day. The sun was bright. The usual Midwest gloominess was replaced by a sapphire-blue sky and crisp, cold temperatures. Large, lacey snowflakes glistened in the sun.

The energy that morning in Kroger was contagious. Holiday music was playing softly overhead, and fall decorations seemed to take over the store. Gourds and pumpkins, flower-filled cornucopias, tins of decorated cookies, and bags of candy corn were on display everywhere.

The grocery store was packed with wall-to-wall shoppers, mostly women, pushing carts brimming with all the holiday fixings. The atmosphere was festive, and I was trying my best to enjoy this bittersweet experience. So far, so good, until I got to the turkey aisle.

Staring down into the bin of frozen birds, I could feel my emotions bubbling up inside me. I started to panic. So many different sizes, so many different brands, so many different emotions, so many different memories.

The tears started flowing, slowly at first, until the sobbing took over. The lady next to me looked worried and asked kindly, "Are you okay?"

I felt myself starting to have a meltdown right there in the frozen-turkey aisle of Kroger.

I whispered through my sobs, "No, I am not okay. My mom just died, and she always cooked the turkey."

I was now fully engulfed in the ugly-cry. As my shoulders started to shake and the sobs gained momentum, a fellow customer hugged me when she overheard me say, "I never cooked a turkey."

By now, I was causing quite a stir. Several women were alerted by my sobs. They lovingly surrounded me, grabbing tissues from their purses. I could hear faint whispers, "Poor thing just lost her mom… funeral was days ago… never cooked a turkey."

I also heard louder voices giving well-intended advice, "Use a cooking bag, rub the turkey with oil, stuff the turkey, don't stuff the turkey, find the bag of gizzards inside the cavity, throw it away, cook it for the dressing."

The whispers of compassion and the voices of guidance spoken by the unlikely support group of women in the frozen-turkey aisle in Kroger that day was, to me, the language of love.

"You'll be okay… You can do it… I'm here for you if you need help… Your mom would be proud."

These compassionate ladies were there for me, just when I needed them. They lined up to embrace me. Some gave me telephone numbers on slips of paper to call for help if needed.

Some shared stories of their own mother's passing, while others, with tears in their eyes, admitted they were also having a hard time facing the holidays.

These sympathetic strangers gave me comfort and confidence that I would somehow make it through this first Thanksgiving without my mom.

As I walked out of Kroger that morning, frozen turkey in hand, I heard someone shout, "Have a happy Thanksgiving!" I smiled, thinking about our family tradition of sharing what each of us is thankful for.

This year, I knew I would share that I was thankful for the loving ladies I met in the frozen-turkey aisle of Kroger.

— Karen Kipfer Smith —

Surprises of the Human Kind

True hospitality consists of giving the best of yourself to your guests.
~Eleanor Roosevelt

We'd always had a traditional Thanksgiving dinner with our parents and siblings. But one year, my sister Karen warned us she would be late because she had to work a shift at the restaurant where she was a part-time waitress. We waited and waited, nibbling on carrot sticks and worrying as the food cooled.

Finally, Karen arrived at 5:45 p.m. and she was not alone.

Inside the doorway, towering over her, was a scruffy-faced guy wearing torn jeans and a flannel shirt that stopped two inches short of his wrists. He gave a hesitant smile and raised his hand to wave "hello" at the four of us. Karen cheerfully explained that David was someone she had met a few days earlier when leaving work. He was going through hard times and sometimes stood outside her workplace asking for change for meals.

My parents looked skeptical. Karen started talking faster. "You said one time that we could invite a friend to Thanksgiving dinner."

My dad harrumphed and sat down at the table. My mother started asking when she could have possibly said that, but then she stopped and said, "Well, um… never mind. Let's all sit down!" And then she started asking questions.

David turned out to be a college student who struggled to find enough work to cover tuition and rent. With loan payments pending and rent due, he'd given up his apartment and was living out of his car. Between gulping down large spoonfuls of cranberry sauce, he answered every question and repeatedly thanked my parents for letting him eat with us.

My older sister and I eagerly watched the back and forth between our mom, David, and our little sister, Karen. We were fascinated by this situation, and wondered how much trouble Karen would be in with our parents after our surprise guest left. And we also wondered if he was going to eat all the cranberry sauce!

Finally, the interrogation ended when my dad said, "Bette, let him eat."

We all ate in silence for the next couple of minutes until my dad put down his fork and cleared his throat. The quieter of my two parents, he had only one question — an inquiry about how well David's car was running.

"Sir, there is a little rattle, but I'm thinking the undercarriage is okay for now. It's kind of you to ask."

I noticed my dad sit up a little straighter.

"David, let's check that out before you leave so you are safe on the road."

By the time dinner was over, David's presence went from being an outlandish display of Karen's spontaneous nature to a wonderful memory of how my parents respond to unexpected surprises. Even better, they started a new tradition.

In subsequent years, each of us was encouraged to invite someone to join us for Thanksgiving dinner. It was a welcome new tradition for our family: the act of sharing not only food but also ourselves and our blessings.

My folks' only request was that they get some kind of notice so they could make enough food for everyone, especially enough cranberry sauce.

— Susan Bartlett —

Let's Talk Turkey

The only real stumbling block is fear of failure. In cooking,
you've got to have a what-the-hell attitude.
~Julia Child

Ye gads! What did he say?
Told his family I'd host Thanksgiving Day?
Please tell me that wasn't what I heard.
Side dishes, pies and a 20-pound bird. Absurd.
Only married a year but what's to fear?
Just a critical mother-in-law and cousins galore.
He knows my go-to meal is pizza,
Delivered to my door.
But, hey, I love a challenge. An optimistic woman strong.
With YouTube and Food Network,
What could possibly go wrong?
I accept my assignment with vigor and joy.
Every trick of TV chefs I will employ.
And I delve into cookbooks. What the heck is brine?
You put the turkey in a bag?
This calls for wine (in me, not the bird).
Don't forget to remove the innards.
Put your hand in where? Pull out the gizzards,
The neck, the heart and, oh no, there's the liver.
My husband will soon learn, I'm not a forgiver.
But I look on the bright side. Call in the forces.

Grandma Brown and Auntie Jo, two strong resources.
They've cooked many a fine turkey in their day.
Too bad they're a thousand miles away.
And who knew so many decisions to make.
Do I deep-fry this bird or simply oven bake?
My husband's proclamation is driving me wild.
I'm no Martha Stewart or Julia Child.
Now the day is drawing near, done research galore.
The traditional green-bean casserole and so much more.
I'm feeling quite smug—but then comes the tweet,
Of all the foods his family won't eat.
John's a vegan, Liz can't have gluten, Dan's allergic to whey.
I suggest they make a reservation at the nearest buffet (but not out loud).
There were just a few mishaps—a bit of a chore,
When the raw bird dropped and slid across the kitchen floor.
Had mother-in-law seen this she might have been cruel.
I grabbed Tom Turkey by his legs… and called the five-second rule.
I did the math, twenty minutes per pound,
But after allotted time, it wasn't even brown.
The little red button stayed buried deep in his chest.
I called the Butterball Hotline (who knew?) totally stressed.
They said, "Sometimes, the button doesn't rise or fall."
Why did I get the one turkey on faulty-parts recall?
"Now, remove the foil, slap more butter on the breast,
Turn your oven up high… and hope for the best."
But after the last of the pumpkin pie,
They all gave me kisses and hugs goodbye.
Perhaps I'll host it again next year.
I know now there's nothing to fear.
I can handle this rowdy bunch.
My most secret recipe—I kept spiking the punch.

—Violetta Armour—

Talking Turkey in a Foreign Language

Food, in the end, in our own tradition, is something
holy. It's not about nutrients and calories. It's about
sharing. It's about honesty. It's about identity.
~Louise Fresco

Peeling the spuds for Thursday's mashed potatoes, I had the feeling that something was off. I was about to celebrate the most important American holiday in its country of origin, the weather was appropriately brisk, my tablet was pouring out seasonal music, and a turkey dinner at a relative's house was on the calendar.

But it didn't feel the same as my holiday preparation in Europe (Italy and France), which I'd been doing for more than three decades. It didn't feel as meaningful. The question was "Why not?"

The answer is multi-layered.

When we moved to Italy, my kids were young and absorbed local culture easily. Thanksgiving had been a way to preserve some American identity, so I was conscientious about preparing a traditional holiday meal on that day.

Advance planning was needed: I had to remember to pick up cranberry sauce and stuffing while visiting the U.S. during the summer. Finding a proper-sized turkey involved trial and error. The menu had to be re-jiggered.

When I was a child, we always started Thanksgiving meal with soup. In Italy, I tried pasta. But once the pasta dish was done, nobody wanted turkey, much less potatoes or stuffing. I soon abandoned that for antipasto. I realized that people didn't eat salad alongside the main course, so I stopped serving that. People didn't know what cranberry sauce was, so I had to explain it. People didn't seem to know that you put potatoes and stuffing alongside the turkey and then put gravy on top of everything, so I had to explain that, too.

As for the guests, the first year or two in Italy, I invited Italian family members. That's why everything had to be explained. To keep things interesting for my sons, I started inviting one or two of their Italian friends and their parents. Our table capacity was about ten people, which focused the guest list considerably.

When we moved to southern France, we had more space so a lot more flexibility. Now we could have a table exclusively for our sons and their friends, and another for us and the parents of those friends. But I was meeting all kinds of people through my work, and they were all curious about Thanksgiving. New people meant fresh perspectives and an opportunity to introduce non-Americans to our most beloved holiday. We had the space, and extra tables and chairs. One thing led to another, and we wound up with three tables and up to twenty-four people.

The meals were sit-down, with china, linens, and crystal wineglasses, but the service was buffet. That gave me the opportunity to explain about cranberry sauce and how to approach the meal.

What made it interesting was the linguistic challenge. English, French, and Italian were a given, but not everyone spoke every language. And then there were the outliers: Swedish, Spanish, Hungarian, Farsi, Arabic. The years we lived in France, we averaged six to eight languages spoken at Thanksgiving. It took time to map out the seating arrangements to make sure that each person at a table could speak to at least one other person.

I started developing informal guidelines. Almost no one was invited two years in a row — to keep the guest list fresh. I tried to invite guests who ran in separate circles so that no one knew anyone else. Spouses or partners were seated at separate tables to keep things lively. I varied each table by ages and occupations — the banker by the dog trainer, the professor by the child psychologist, the doctor by the artist.

I took care of the basics: turkey, gravy, stuffing, mashed potatoes, and cranberry sauce. Those didn't change from year to year, but the rest of the menu did. Everyone was asked to bring something to eat or drink. Since the guest list changed every year, so did the contributions.

One year, we wound up with three quiches and no vegetables, so after that people had to choose within categories. However, certain categories had to be specific to the guest's social behavior. I learned that lesson the year a woman from Parma promised to bring prosciutto. She did, and it was delicious, but she was habitually late and arrived after we had passed from antipasto to the main course.

I learned that I needed to prepare a redundancy for every course — always an appetizer or two, a side dish, and a dessert, just in case people who promised to bring those items didn't show up. Sadly, there were no-shows almost every year. So, I had to overbook, like an airline, to ensure that my tables remained full and vibrant.

I learned that one's turkey supplier is fundamental. No supermarket Butterballs in Europe. All the years we lived in France, the turkey varied in quality. The one year I ordered in advance from a *fournisseur* (supplier) was the year of a nationwide trucking strike. No turkey anywhere. I made a mad dash across the border to Italy the day before Thanksgiving to pick up as many turkey breasts as I could find. Another year, the guests arrived, and the turkey was still in the oven because it was an odd size and consistency. That was the year I learned the wisdom of cooking the bird the day before.

By the time we moved back to Italy, our children were grown and gone. But the idea of sharing Thanksgiving traditions with non-American friends and acquaintances had taken hold, and I decided to continue.

I found an excellent turkey supplier and always ordered a female because they are more tender. The butcher didn't label them as free-range turkeys, but that's what they were — obscenely expensive but consistently fantastic. I would stuff the bird on Tuesday, roast it on Wednesday — savoring the aroma as it permeated every square meter of our apartment—and bring it to the butcher that evening so he could slice it professionally. Then, I would arrange the white meat on one platter, the dark meat on another, and have everything ready to re-heat on Thursday.

Since just about all our guests in Italy spoke Italian, I printed up menus and explanations of the Thanksgiving holiday for everyone. Instead of relying on volunteers for various bottles of wine, I found a source and bought Amarone in bulk. A local bakery prepared a cornucopia of breads, most of which weren't consumed during the evening, but they made a lovely centerpiece for the buffet table. Tables, actually: one for the appetizers, one for the mains, and one for dessert. Just before the main course buffet was ready, I would ring a dinner bell and say a prayer.... Well, more like a mini-speech than a religious exhortation, describing the holiday and thanking our guests for joining us.

What I remember most about these Thanksgivings (aside from the exorbitant amount of work, mostly in logistics) was the vibrant buzz at mealtime. Some years, the tables almost seemed to levitate from the joy of strangers coming together for a uniquely American yet universal celebration of camaraderie. It's different from the vibe of a family gathering because families are defined by blood and tradition, while my European gatherings were assembled by choice and volition.

Isn't the latter almost closer to the core idea of Thanksgiving? Gratitude for friendship and new opportunities? Hope for a future of undiscovered promise?

Maybe that is why I miss my Italian and French Thanksgivings so much, despite my gratitude at being with my family this year.

—Claudia Flisi—

Chapter
2

Tales of the Tree

Oh, But There Was a Creature Stirring

*'Twas the night before Christmas, when all through the
house, not a creature was stirring, not even a mouse.*
~Clement Clarke Moore

We would be spending our first Christmas in the rural Texas countryside. After living in a one-bedroom city apartment, my mother had decided that only a rustic holiday would do. I'm not sure if it was the thrill of living on thirteen acres, the coyotes, owls, and frogs screeching into the night, or a gravel road that would pop your truck tires if you weren't careful, but she was determined to have a country Christmas.

What she lacked in budget, she more than made up for in creativity. The wooded landscape happily provided a small cedar to serve as our tree, along with enough greenery to make our own door wreath from scratch. We even had real mistletoe after she knocked a few clusters of it from a scraggly hackberry tree. She did have to splurge on a can of fake snow to flock the windows, as that was one thing the central Texas landscape certainly was not going to provide. With a few strands of lights from the five-and-dime store, our little tree glowed.

We had a few hand-me-down stockings that she'd proudly given a facelift with some fresh glitter, and she touched up a few faded glass ornaments. But if there were to be any funds remaining for gifts, that would have to be it for decorating.

I remember watching my mother stare at our small tree as she tapped her fingers to her chin. Something was still missing.

"Ah!" she said, her face brightening with the solution. "We need to find something for garland."

A trip back to the store for beautiful but pricey garland was out. A short experiment with the last of the glitter proved to be a failure. The cedar fronds did catch a little sparkle but didn't resemble the drapey loops of garland that my mother craved. She scoured the house as she experimented and then eliminated décor options before finally landing in the kitchen.

"That's it!" she screeched in delight, pulling a bag of popcorn kernels from the pantry. In no time, she had two large mixing bowls overflowing with fluffy popcorn. She swatted my hand away after I grabbed two large handfuls and attempted to jam them in my mouth.

"That's for the tree," she chided me.

Confusion turned to curiosity as she dug out her small sewing kit and needle and carefully began stringing popcorn along a length of thread. Popcorn and thread went a long way. In no time, she'd formed several feet of budget-friendly, puffy popcorn garland.

I was impressed!

There was more than enough popcorn garland to string around the tree several times. If you squinted and pretended, you'd almost believe it could be snow. I remember our small family gathering around the television that evening as we admired our little country Christmas tree.

The next morning, I popped out of bed before my mother woke up and hurried out to the living room to work on my Christmas list for Santa in the glow of our tree. I stopped short.

Our rustic, little loops of popcorn garland were gone! Every last kernel had simply vanished.

My mother rounded the corner from the small hallway to catch me standing in front of the tree, with my mouth open in shock.

"Kristi Lynn!" she scolded. "Tell me you did not sneak in here and chew all my garland off this tree!"

Pleas of innocence were met with a skeptical glare as she surveyed me and our tree. I was every inch my mother's daughter and a crafty little soul. She saw the flash of excitement dawn on my face. The only reason I hadn't eaten the garland off her tree was that the idea just hadn't crossed my mind yet.

"Maybe it was Dad?" I offered. "I can't even reach the top branches."

She mulled over the idea, knowing that I was quite capable of climbing furniture, especially if it meant securing secret snacks, like the time I used our living room ottoman as a ladder to reach chocolate on the top pantry shelf. "Maybe..." she said.

Undeterred, out came the bag of popcorn kernels again. In no time, she was threading more popcorn garland. We looped the fresh garland on the tree branches and gathered around its warmth once more that evening after supper.

My mom tucked me in to bed and wagged a finger at me. "Don't you eat that garland," she warned before turning off the lights.

I fought sleep and strained my six-year-old ears, trying to listen for the telltale signs that my parents had gone to bed. But drowsiness overpowered me and, in a flash, warm morning sunshine glowed through my curtains.

The tree!

If I were quiet, maybe there was still a chance I could sneak out and snatch a few pieces of popcorn off the tree before my mother woke up. Just from the back side, I reasoned. No one had to know.

My mother had anticipated my antics, though. I was momentarily disappointed to find her already poking around the kitchen until I realized she was making pancakes. I plopped down in front of the Christmas tree, eagerly awaiting her announcement that breakfast was ready when I heard a faint rustling.

Followed by the unmistakable sounds of chewing.

I slowly got up and squinted into the dark recesses of the tree, only to see a pair of beady, little eyes staring back. I clapped a hand over my mouth in shock and slowly backed away from the tree.

"Momma!" I hissed, arm outstretched and pointing at the tree.

She turned on one heel, realizing something was wrong, and tiptoed toward me. Spatula still in hand, she bent down and peered in the branches before letting out a shriek and swatting at the tree!

Two small mice squeaked and fell out of the tree, scurrying along the wall and quickly out of sight. We took one look at each other and howled with laughter. "I told you I didn't eat the garland!" I said, proudly declaring my innocence, as we now had undeniable proof. She hugged me tight and brushed the hair away from my forehead as we held each other and laughed.

Later in the season, we gathered at my grandmother's home on Christmas Eve, where she would read the iconic poem, "The Night Before Christmas." It didn't take long for us to start laughing as she read.

That fateful Christmas, there had definitely been a creature stirring, to bring us a story we'd never forget.

— Kristi Adams —

11

The Peace Tree

The perfect Christmas tree? All Christmas trees are perfect!
~Charles N. Barnard

A s a college professor, December was the time of year when my duties and responsibilities were already way over-the-top, but one year the Universe decided to help me out for the holidays. I had suggested to my husband, Gabe, and fifteen-year-old daughter, Dana, that we should just skip the Christmas tree that year. Our plans were to spend both Christmas Eve and Christmas Day out of state with my family. We wouldn't even be home to enjoy a tree.

Besides, I reminded them, it was always a challenge to coordinate our schedules to pick out a tree and schlep it up three flights of stairs to our New York City apartment. Gabe, of Jewish heritage, applauded the notion of going treeless, but Dana, whom I had trained to be a Christmas enthusiast, protested. She did, however, agree to downsize from our typical tree, which I pointed out, as she rolled her eyes, would keep us right in step with the economic trends of the time.

So, preparing to trudge down the street for food shopping on a chilly, busy mid-December day, I was fully in sync with my inner Grinch. A few steps away from our apartment in Greenwich Village, I noticed a medium-sized Christmas tree lying at the curb beside a parked car. I grumbled to myself, *I guess someone is unloading in preparation for taking that tree inside. Lucky them, with a car. They probably have an elevator, too.*

On the way back with the groceries, I was surprised to see that the car was gone, but the tree was still there. A small object glittering in the sun caught my eye. Peeking through the branches of the prone tree, I noticed that a colorful Christmas orb with a peace symbol on it had been left on one of the branches. Apparently, on December 15th, outside my door on a busy street in Greenwich Village, there was an abandoned Christmas tree, the needles still soft and fragrant.

New York City is a great place to find all manner of treasures on the street, but the understood rule of acquisition is that the offering must be procured from the curb immediately or *fuggedaboutit* — the coveted item is long gone. It was, therefore, unusual that, at a peak time in the Christmas season, the tree was still there at the curb. I fantasized about dragging it home, but I was laden with groceries. Besides, I could not be assured that Gabe or Dana would agree to keep my "find."

As I entered my apartment with the groceries, I noticed that my husband was working at home. I began unpacking the groceries, but then, impulsively, intruded upon Gabe, hard at work at his computer, to tell him about the tree. Typically grumpy about such interruptions, he was surprisingly amenable to taking a look. We quickly grabbed our jackets although I thought the tree was surely gone already.

But it was still there! We righted the tree to examine it carefully: no roaches, no broken branches. The tree was fine, beautiful, and perfect! We easily carried it upstairs, rummaged in the closet for the tree stand, and set it up for our daughter's approval.

At first glance, Dana made one of those "How tacky can you be?" faces. But after considering the story, she began to admire the tree, as well as the way it was "delivered" to our family. We agreed it brought to mind a favorite E. E. Cummings poem that begins, "Little tree, little silent Christmas tree." Tentatively, I proposed that we make the little peace ornament it had come with to be the exclusive decoration on our tree. Gabe and Dana agreed.

Suddenly, I had found my Christmas spirit. I began inviting friends and family to drop by to honor the holidays, meditate on peace, and celebrate our foundling tree, our most memorable gift that season.

— Karen Beatty —

12

Our Dancing Christmas Tree

Christmas tree. Taking nature to the next level.
~Author Unknown

One sunny Saturday in December, my family headed out to a nearby tree farm to find our perfect Christmas tree. After traipsing around a sprawling field, we finally settled on a little Scotch pine, perfect for our living room. Back home, we set the tree in its stand and watered it. The next day, we decorated it with six strands of dazzling lights and dozens of cherished ornaments.

Monday came, and the kids headed off to school and my husband to work. That afternoon, as sunlight flooded the living room, I grabbed a cup of coffee and beelined to the sofa to enjoy the beauty of our festive pine. Immersed in my Christmas reverie, I sat quietly, mesmerized by the beauty of the ornaments shimmering in the sunlight. But a moment later, as my gaze shifted to the wintry scene outside, my peripheral vision caught an unexpected glimpse of arboreal movement. Had our Christmas tree just wiggled?

My eyes darted back to the pine, but all was as it should be. Not a single branch moved. Nervously hoping I'd imagined the movement, I glanced away, but it happened again! Without question, our Christmas tree had just shimmied.

Heart pounding, I rose stealthily and approached the tree, which, once again, stood dutifully dormant. Slowly, my laser-focused eyes scanned the branches, daring them to move yet terrified that they'd do just that. For a few long moments, nothing happened as I stood there, motionless, baffled by the creepy event I'd just witnessed — or had I?

Just as doubt began trickling into my wired brain, it happened again. As if on cue, several branches broke out dancing as dozens of strange, worm-like creatures abruptly rose from their roosts and began swaying rhythmically to and fro.

Repulsed by their choreographed madness, I emitted a horrified screech. Our beautiful Christmas tree was infested! With what, I didn't know. But whatever-it-was was definitely alive and kicking. I'd noticed nothing unusual the day before while decorating the tree. But I suspect the warmth of our cozy house had caused our uninvited holiday guests to hatch overnight.

Grossed out yet spellbound, I stood watching the show. The movements of those creepy-crawly critters — which, upon closer inspection, resembled pudgy caterpillars — were perfectly synchronized as if an invisible conductor were directing their dance with a golden baton. Simultaneously, as one, they arose from their respective branches, gyrated fluidly for a few seconds, and then dropped back down to await their next cue.

This mind-blowing dance routine continued every few minutes as my very own Larval Rockettes treated me to performances as smooth and practiced as anything Radio City Music Hall had to offer. Although my skin crawled at the thought of our house being overrun by these plump, no-doubt-squishy interlopers, their harmonious moves were nothing short of riveting. And since their synchronized routines far exceeded my own clumsy dance skills, I couldn't help but give them a grudging nod.

I groaned when it hit me that every last ornament and light would need to be removed from our Christmas tree — and carefully, too, to avoid knocking the little buggers off their perches. It took me hours to undress that poor tree. Later that night, after my husband had hauled it outside, I spent another hour scouring the carpet for dislodged creepers. The next day, we purchased a precut tree of a different variety, and the painstaking process of decorating began all over again after examining every branch.

Our family's unforgettable "two-tree Christmas" was one I vowed never to repeat. The following year, we purchased our first artificial tree. It was a difficult adjustment for all of us. But my disappointment was soothed by the knowledge that the Larval Rockettes would never again be dancing in my living room.

—Wendy Hobday Haugh—

Barbie Looked Mean at Me!

One of the most glorious messes in the world is the
mess created in the living room on Christmas Day.
~Author Unknown

"Look, Daddy. My Barbie doll has blond hair, just like mine and yours," said Linda, stroking the long, blond tresses and admiring Barbie's red-and-white dress. Just a few minutes earlier, my two big sisters and I had gotten out of bed and rushed to the Christmas tree to find matching wrapped gifts. Each box was the size and shape of the Barbie doll boxes we'd seen at the store.

There were three of us girls. Linda was eight, and Sharon was seven. Both of them were blond like Dad. I was four and had dark hair like Mom. A few years later, there would be a fourth sister, Ruth Anne, who was blond, so Mom and I were outnumbered.

That Christmas, Mom had enjoyed shopping for blond Barbies for Linda and Sharon, and a brunette Barbie for me. So, when she saw how happy Linda was to get a Barbie that matched her own hair color, Mom couldn't wait to see Sharon's happy reaction to her own blond Barbie. But when Sharon opened her package, her doll had brown hair, and mine had blond hair.

Uh-oh, thought Mom. She'd been very careful to wrap and mark the boxes correctly, so what had happened? She and Dad looked at each other, bracing for Sharon and me to have meltdowns. They were already thinking of how to negotiate a switch. But, to their surprise, Sharon was fine with brunette Barbie. Me… I didn't know I was supposed to be upset, so I opened my Barbie and fell in love with her. In fact, I immediately named her Ricky Ricardo, for reasons I don't remember.

"Teresa," said Mom gently. "I think your Barbie and Sharon's got mixed up. See, your Barbie should have brown hair like yours, and Sharon's should have blond hair, like she does. Wouldn't you two girls like to switch?"

"No!" we both screeched in unison, clinging fiercely to our dolls.

Again, Mom and Dad looked at each other, wondering what had really happened.

"I think I'll just toss some of this trash," Dad said. He picked up the Barbie doll boxes, which still had some of the wrapping paper on them, and carried them into the kitchen where he and Mom took a closer look. Even with the paper mostly demolished, they could see that the boxes had been opened on one end and rewrapped like a child might do. That's when Mom and Dad started to put two and two together.

"Remember Sharon's birthday?" Dad said. A few months earlier, as Mom was carrying Sharon's birthday cake to the dining room, Dad noticed that all the gifts on the table seemed to have been opened and clumsily rewrapped. It turned out that Sharon had found them and opened them all. She'd done a pretty good job of hiding her crime — until then.

So that Christmas morning after Mom and Dad figured out that Sharon had most likely opened the presents early, Dad looked at Mom and winked. He knew that Sharon competed heavily with Linda. Back in the living room, he said, "I'll bet Linda was the first one awake this morning. She's the oldest, so I'm sure she was the first one up, even before me and Mom."

Sharon quickly piped in to say, "Nuh-uh. I was awake before anyone, when it was still dark."

Mom joined the questioning. "But how did you see if it was dark? Did you turn on the big lights?"

"Nope, I used my little flashlight," Sharon said, as she continued putting tiny, plastic high heels on Barbie.

Dad said, "Oh, that little flashlight is too small for you to see much except the way to the bathroom."

"I saw all the way to the Christmas tree," said Sharon, not realizing she was tattling on herself.

"Good thing there weren't any presents under the tree for you to see," said Mom.

"There were Barbies!" said Sharon. "Two blond ones and one dark one and…" She suddenly got quiet, realizing that she'd blown her cover.

Mom wanted to laugh but instead asked gently, "Did you switch Barbies with Teresa?"

Sharon started sobbing and crawled into Dad's lap. "I wanted to see all the Barbies. Linda's Barbie had a pretty smile and so did Teresa's Barbie. But my Barbie was scary," Sharon said, as the sobbing grew sadder. "Barbie looked mean at me. I don't want a doll that doesn't like me." Our wonderful dad snuggled her in closer until she felt better.

I never saw the mean look on my Barbie, the one Sharon thought was mean. I was four years old, and to me my doll was pretty and blond, like most of the family. There was no way I wanted to give up my Barbie. None of us could see the mean look that Sharon saw, but it was very real to her. At that time, she was the middle child, and maybe she was extra sensitive about that.

Whatever the case, Mom and Dad navigated the rough waters of childhood emotions with us easily that morning. They salvaged our family's Christmas with their kindness and a lot of hugs. After the Barbie problem was declared solved, we girls spent several happy hours dressing and undressing our grown-up dolls. The mean look that caused such angst was never mentioned again for as long as Mean Barbie "lived."

— Teresa Ambord —

14

If Ornaments Could Talk

Some Christmas tree ornaments do more than glitter
and glow, they represent a gift of love
given a long time ago.
~Tom Baker

I had a scheduled surgery around the holidays, so my family helped get the house ready for Christmas. In no time at all, the tree was standing with lights and ribbon in place, awaiting the ornaments. My husband brought out my carefully stored, highly coveted box labeled, "Tree ornaments and Grandma's nativity set." This ordinary box doesn't look like anything special from the outside, but the inside is filled with treasures from years gone by.

Ever since my kids were small, I would gather them around the tree and tell them the story behind each ornament as they picked a special place to hang it. They were all teenagers with busy work and sports schedules now, but I still wanted to hold tight to our family tradition and decorate the tree together. It took three ridiculously long weeks for that day to come around. When did this get so difficult to arrange? With eager anticipation, I got everything out, put on the Christmas music, got the hot chocolate ready, and plugged in all the twinkly lights.

Just as I was ready to call everyone in, our youngest son said basketball practice got moved up. My daughter texted that she might have to stay late at work. And, of course, one of our kids came home not feeling well. (Sigh.)

I turned off the music while everyone scattered. Giant fail.

I was annoyed that our plans fell apart after waiting for so long to pull them together. As I grumpily sulked over my dinner, I heard a *ping* on my phone. My son texted that practice was cut short due to incoming snow. *Ping!* My daughter was on her way home from work at the regular time after all. I called my oldest son at the gym, and he said he'd cut his workout short and head back. Everyone would be home within the hour after all. Yay!

I announced to the family that we would try this again when everyone was finished eating, but it was not met with the excitement I had hoped for. When they groaned in reluctance and said they just wanted to do it another time, I felt like Clark Griswold as I heard myself saying, "We WILL decorate these trees tonight, and you WILL like it because we are making a family memory!" I realized how ridiculous I sounded when they looked at me as if I had finally traded the Polar Express for the Crazy Train. I turned the music back on and stood next to the tree as they looked at one another in bewilderment. Realizing that this was going to happen, they got up from the table and made their way over to me.

I held back tears as my children came near, and I was hit with a moment of clarity. The truth was, my outburst really wasn't about the tree at all. I had panicked. This was the first year they weren't all here together. Our oldest lives out of state and, in a few months, her sister will follow. Our son could be deployed with the Army at any moment. Another will be graduating high school next year. The youngest two weren't so young anymore. Time with our kids under one roof was quickly slipping away, and the loss of it felt palpable. I had such a short window of time left. Instill the values! Root them in love! Make the memories! Spend the time!

As everyone hesitantly gathered around the box, I wondered if they would ever realize how deeply I loved them and how special these simple family moments really are. I carefully unrolled the tissue-wrapped ornaments as each of my grown children leaned in to see which ornament the paper revealed. As I told them the stories behind each one, they got excited when it had a special meaning to them.

If only these ornaments could talk! They would tell the stories of our family and how the ordinary moments in life end up making the fondest memories. Every ornament has a story, and together they tell what matters most to us — faith, family, friends, and a bond that grows stronger with each passing year.

Later that night, as everyone was getting ready for bed, I reflected on our family tradition and hoped it wasn't just for me. I didn't really know if it made an impression on the kids or not, but my heart was full. Just then, my oldest son stopped me in the hallway and gave me a long, meaningful hug.

"Mom," he said in my ear as we embraced, "thank you so much for doing the Christmas ornaments. It means a lot to me."

There it is.

— Denae Jones —

15

One Shiny Bulb

*The best Christmas trees come very close
to exceeding nature.*
~Andy Rooney

I n the Pacific Northwest, we often have stretches of "dark days" during the winter. I usually try to get out of the house at least once every day during those times — a walk to the mailbox, trip to the grocery, visit to the senior center — but as the Christmas season approached, a stretch of bad weather and a bad cold had kept me indoors and added to the gloom. The lingering pall of Covid still hung over the world.

Then, in early December, one shiny silver bulb appeared on a blue spruce near the entrance to my neighborhood. Surprised by the decoration and wondering who had put it there, I smiled and drove on by. Days passed, and I noticed a miniature, gold-colored reindeer perched on a branch near the bulb. As the week progressed, more and more ornaments adorned the tree — a shiny red ball, sparkly plastic icicle, bit of tinsel. With each addition, my delight grew, and the dreary winter days seemed a little brighter.

One Friday afternoon, my granddaughter Bailey came to visit and helped me decorate the Christmas tree in my living room. We played our usual game of hiding the elf in the branches and taking turns finding him. We loaded the tree with ornaments collected over the years and added a few new ones — some handmade, others purchased as travel souvenirs. In a burst of inspiration, Bailey festooned the fireplace mantel with a garland of greenery, added candles and tinsel, and created a festive tableau.

The house was starting to feel Christmas-y, but my holiday spirit still hadn't kicked in. Then, I suggested an excursion. We gathered supplies in a tote bag, donned jackets and gloves, and headed out the door.

Together, we added two ornaments to the tree at the neighborhood's entrance: a glittery, silver ball and a giant, plastic snowflake. A long-handled "grabber" helped us reach high branches where, after several tries and impeded by laughter, we looped the ornaments' hooks over the spruce's needles. When we stood back to admire our work, cars drove past, people waved, and more than one driver gave us a thumbs-up. We waved back and threw kisses their way. I'd found my Christmas spirit at last.

Days later, my neighborhood friend Nan picked me up for lunch. On the drive to our favorite restaurant, I shared my tree-decorating experience.

"I wonder who started that," I said.

Nan gave an enigmatic smile.

I laughed. "It was you, wasn't it?"

She nodded and admitted that she and her husband Joe thought we all needed some cheer. If she hadn't been driving, I would have given her a hug.

As Christmas Day approached, more and more ornaments filled the tree's branches, bringing delight to everyone who drove past. A feeling of community and "joy to the world" permeated the neighborhood and increased with every new decoration.

I have since sold my house in that subdivision. But when I drove past my old home this past Christmas, I smiled to see bulbs, stars, and plastic snowflakes adorning the blue spruce's branches once again.

— Sandra R. Nachlinger —

16

The Jewelry Tree

Jewelry is like the perfect spice — it
complements what's already there.
~Diane von Furstenberg

As I turned each page, the glossy photos left me in awe! Christmas magazines typically offer a range of easy and affordable DIY projects, but this particular article was purely for inspiration.

The legendary jewelry team at Tiffany & Co. had decorated a fifteen-foot-tall Christmas tree in the atrium of a New York City museum. It was breathtaking! White twinkle lights graced the branches, giving the evergreen an ethereal glow. Shiny presents tied with wide ribbons were artfully tucked around the base.

But the stars of the show were the ornaments. Unlike most Christmas trees, there wasn't a Santa, elf, or angel to be seen.

Instead, the entire tree was draped in Tiffany & Co. jewelry!

Diamond tennis bracelets, emerald earrings, and ruby brooches dripped from the branches in decadent abundance. The richly colored jewels, set in opulent yellow and white gold, caught the light like midnight stars. It was glamorous, extravagant, and over-the-top in the most enchanting way. My sparkle-loving heart swooned at the photos. Oh, to be able to see it in person!

The jewelry tree planted itself deeply in my imagination. Every few years, I'd remember it and get excited all over again. What would it be like to see such an amazing creation?

One year, I looked at my own growing collection of costume jewelry. I didn't have anything from Tiffany, and certainly nothing that could even come close to the riches displayed in those photos, but what if I tried to create my own humble version of the bejewelled tree?

I knew I could never cover a fifteen-foot fir, but I thought I might be able to stretch my collection over a tabletop tree. I bought an artificial 4-foot imitation spruce, thinking the wired branches would hold up well under the weight of the "ornaments."

I chose brightly colored lights to suit my personality and positioned the tree on a card table in the corner of my living room. A festive tablecloth woven with gold thread served as my shiny base.

Next, the decorations. This is where it got fun!

I emptied my jewelry box and put every single piece on a very large tray. For years, I'd been picking through flea markets and collecting vintage treasures. I was shocked at how many pieces I'd acquired!

I decided to use wire hooks to hang brooches and rhinestone earrings like ornaments. Bracelets could be looped on the ends of branches. Finally, I opted to drape strings of pearls and beads over the entire tree like classic beaded garlands.

I made myself a hot chocolate, turned on the Bing Crosby Christmas album, and set to work! My little tree didn't have the height or expense of the Tiffany creation, but that didn't matter, because the more I worked on the tree, the more emotional I became. To be honest, it caught me off-guard.

As I lifted each piece, I realized I wasn't just hanging jewelry on a tree. I was telling the story of the women in my family.

There was the enamelled bracelet that Sandy, my mother-in-law, had bought me that time she visited us in Nashville. It was one of her favourite stories to tell when she reminisced about that trip.

There was the flower brooch worn by Aunt Maggie, my great-aunt who taught me how to buy annuals for my garden.

There was the cross given to me by Nana on the day of my confirmation. It was simple and gold, and she'd given it to me out of her own jewelry box.

And there was the bracelet Mom gave me when I graduated from high school — my first and only real pearls. I remember feeling it was a gift beyond my years, something I would treasure forever.

Each glint of gold and flash of silver flooded my heart with memories.

As young women, we fight for our own identity, completely convinced we'll make it on our own. But as I touched each gleaming treasure, I was reminded of the gentle and loving way these beautiful women had shaped my life. I felt deeply rooted and lifted up, grateful to know I had come from a long line of caring, creative, and compassionate souls.

When all the jewelry had been placed on the tree, I turned out the lights. I had intended to admire my handiwork, but I found myself admiring something else. I saw a tribute, a story, a legacy.

Over the holidays, everyone wanted to see my jewelry tree. They marvelled at the creativity and teased me about my immense collection of paste jewels! But as I told them the story of the tree and of the women whose lives graced its branches, they stood in awe. In turn, they shared memories of their own moms, aunts, and grandmothers, oftentimes gently fingering the ring or necklace that was part of their own legacy.

I still think of the Tiffany tree every once in a while, but when I want to remember something truly spectacular, I think back on my own humble jewelry tree. That moment when I realized my tree wasn't just about necklaces and earrings, that it was about so much more, will stay with me forever. I've decorated a lot of trees since that year, but not a Christmas goes by without taking a moment to give thanks for the women in my life and praying that, in some small way, I too might carry on this grander story of love.

— Allison Lynn Flemming —

17

Chicken Soup
for the Soul

Chaos Under the Christmas Tree

Truly wonderful the mind of a child is.
~Yoda

I like to believe that I was a charming child, but I'm not sure that my Grandma Brandt saw things that way. I knew she was aggravated with me as we drove up the hill from my house to the highway. I was bouncing around in the back seat of my grandma's blue Nova as she glared at me through the rearview mirror.

"You have to behave yourself," she said sternly.

"Yes, Grandma," I said while standing on the vinyl seat with my little four-year-old arms braced against the ceiling. (This was before seatbelt laws and child-safety seats.)

"Please, sit down," she said, her voice exasperated. I want to believe I sat down, but I may have ignored her.

I was too excited. It was just a week before Christmas. The house was decorated, and there were so many things going on. On top of it all, it was snowing, the first snow of the season. Big snowflakes were drifting down from the gray skies. I made my way over to the window, rolled it down and, despite the cold air, stuck my mittened hand out to catch a snowflake.

"Close the window," my grandmother snapped.

As we got to the top of the road, before we turned onto the blacktop, Grandma stopped the car.

I climbed over the back seat to sit next to her.

"You have to behave today," she said sternly. "I have to get the shopping done for Christmas, and I need you to be good for Aunt Gertie and Aunt Lizzie."

I was trying hard to listen and sit still, but when she said that I would be staying with my great-aunts, I started jumping up and down. I loved staying with them.

Grandma did not appreciate my enthusiasm.

"Don't touch anything," she said. "Some of their Christmas decorations are very old. Promise me you won't touch anything."

I'm sure I promised her that I would not touch anything.

My great-aunts were waiting for us. I gave Grandma a quick kiss and bounded out of the car and up the steps.

Aunt Lizzie and Aunt Gertie wrapped me in big hugs, and they hurried me inside.

The house looked amazing. There was sparkly garland hanging in all the arched doorways, and smiling Santas, sparkly angels, reindeers, snowmen, and every Christmas decoration imaginable filled the small house. I'm not sure anything matched, but none of that mattered. It was just beautiful.

I was drawn to the bay window of the living room. A coffee table with three small cedar trees in gallon cans served as a Christmas tree. The trees were decorated with twinkling lights and beautiful glass decorations in different colors. They had thrown a white sheet across the coffee table and set up the nativity stand under the trees.

Nativity sets were one of my all-time favorite things about Christmas, even at four years old. I was too little to set up the nativity scene at my house, but I knew it was arranged the exact same way every year.

Not this one. My four-year-old brain could barely comprehend the chaos under the tree. My great-aunts must have emptied out their Easter baskets, because the area under the tree was covered in plastic Easter grass in a mix of pale yellow, green, blue, and pink. On top of the mess, they had put two different stables. While there was only one Mary and Joseph statue, there were numerous cows, donkeys, horses, sheep, and shepherds in all different colors and sizes.

This just wouldn't do.

I forgot my promise not to touch any of the Christmas decorations. There were some things about Christmas that needed to be done correctly, and this was one of them.

I dragged a crochet blanket off the couch and spread it on the floor. Then I carefully took each figurine off the table and sorted them into piles, laying each one carefully on the blanket so it wouldn't break. Then, I set the stables on the blanket and started the long task of sorting out the different colors of the Easter grass. That took a lot of patience, but soon I had piles of the different colors sorted out.

The first problem was the pink Easter grass. It did not fit into my ideal nativity scene at all. I mounded it around one of the gallon cans that was holding the Christmas tree to hide the bottom of the bucket. Then, I put the two stables in front of the bucket, side by side. I figured that although most nativity scenes had only one stable, it made sense that a town as big as I imagined Bethlehem to be would have more than one.

I took the yellow Easter grass and spread it around the bottom of the stables so it would look just like the barn at our farm when I helped spread the straw out for the calves. I added Mary and Joseph and the manger to one of the stables and a cow and donkey behind them. I grabbed some Lincoln Logs out of the toy box and built a fence around the other stable. Then, I filled the stable and the pen with all the other animals. I spread the green Easter grass out below the other Christmas trees, even pooling the blue grass to make a pond and stream behind the stables.

Aunt Gertie had a basket of small pebbles and shells on one of the side tables and I used them to make a road for the kings to travel on. I bunched the sheep and goats into little herds with the shepherds spread all around them taking care of them. I crawled as far back under the tree as I could to place the three kings since they still had days of travel ahead of them.

I worked all afternoon to sort out the nativity scene and make sure it was just right. I was rearranging one of the shepherds when I heard the door open.

"WHAT ARE YOU DOING?" Grandma shouted.

I looked up from underneath the tree. I had totally forgotten that I had promised not to touch any of the Christmas decorations. I looked around the room, and there in their favorite chairs sat Aunt Gertie and Aunt Lizzie.

"Oh, Annie, hush," Aunt Gertie said with a big smile on her face. "Look what a lovely job this girl has done."

They had sat and watched me rearrange their decorations all afternoon and hadn't said a word.

"It's the best nativity scene I've ever seen," Aunt Lizzie said, ushering Grandma to the couch.

I never got in trouble for touching the Christmas decorations. I love nativity scenes to this day, and I am forever thankful that Aunt Gertie and Aunt Lizzie let me get lost in the story of Christmas that afternoon.

— Theresa Brandt —

Chapter 3

The Spirit
of the Season

18

The Real Christmas Story — A Walk Through

Blessed is the season which engages the
whole world in a conspiracy of love.
~Hamilton Wright Mabie

"I have an idea" might be one of my favorite sentences. It usually leads to wonderful things, but when my dad says it, it always leads to something fun and creative.

"I have a vision of a drive-through nativity!" he exclaimed, his eyes sparkling with inspiration. "Visitors can drive around the church grounds in their cars, meeting actors playing different characters from the first Christmas."

My imagination started to dance with ideas, but my practical, internal voice started to worry.

Outdoor theatre? In Canada? In December? What are we thinking?

"I'm a little nervous about cars and actors in an icy parking lot," I replied. "But what if we look at the mystery plays of the Middle Ages? They used a series of stages to tell Bible stories, with each stage hosting its own scene. The audience walked from stage to stage to experience the full story."

And so, "The Real Christmas Story — A Walk Through" was born!

We chose seven moments from the first Christmas and wrote a short scene for each that could be performed by a few actors on a simple stage. The audience would start at one end of the churchyard and travel in small groups. Upon entering the gate, they would meet the prophets Isaiah and Jeremiah, with their predictions of the coming Christ Child. As each scene ended, the audience would move on to the next stage, while a new group started behind them.

Along the way, they would meet angels, shepherds, and wise men. Finally, an excited citizen of Bethlehem would intercept them on the path and bring them to the front of the church. There, they would witness Mary and Joseph sitting by the manger. More citizens (our cleverly disguised church choir!) would surround the family, singing carols and marvelling at the newborn child. Finally, a volunteer would bring the audience to a reception area for hot cider and cookies.

The script felt solid and the vision clear, so now came the real challenge: how to execute it. This was going to be a massive undertaking!

We decided to stage the play for one night only, walking multiple audience groups through the route over the course of the evening. That way, hundreds of people could see the story, and we only needed to risk one night of potentially inclement weather. But keeping a cast of actors and singers outside for four freezing hours wasn't realistic.

That led to our next big decision: We double-cast the show! In other words, we needed to find two actors for every role, rehearse two full casts, and make sure we had enough singers for two choirs. On the night of the show, we would rotate the casts on and off the stages in thirty-minute shifts to make sure no one stayed outside too long. All in all, we needed about fifty actors and singers to make the whole thing work.

Dad and I shared the idea with the congregation.

"We have a vision for a dramatic telling of the real Christmas story. It'll be our gift for the community. Oh, and we'd like to do it outdoors — in December!"

Everyone giggled. Then, they realized we were serious!

We posted a sign-up sheet and were immediately swamped with teens and adults who wanted to sing or act a part.

A man named Warren approached us. "I've spent decades building sets and costumes for Gilbert and Sullivan operettas. I think I can help."

Warren recruited a whole new team of volunteers to build stages, paint backdrops, and apply make-up. He solicited donations of fabric and old jewelry to create stunning costumes, roomy enough to be worn over much-needed winter jackets.

Volunteers appeared in droves.

"I can put together a team to help people find parking."

"Our ladies' group will make the cider and cookies."

"We'll need tour guides to lead the audience groups through the stages. I'll take care of that!"

In total, we amassed a cast and crew of over 100 people to tell our story!

As rehearsals progressed, Dad made a confession. "You know, I wish we could have a real baby for Jesus. A doll will work, but a baby would be magical."

So, we put out the word. "Would anyone like to volunteer their baby to be Jesus in the outdoor nativity? We'll need the parents to play Mary and Joseph. Also, we really want two babies so no one needs to stay outside the whole time."

A week before showtime, two families shyly volunteered. Neither were comfortable about performing in front of people but they both hinted how much it would mean to the baby's grandparents. We were pretty sure there had been a bit of familial coercing involved!

Finally, the big night arrived. The weather was clear. We gathered the cast and crew together for final instructions. We lifted a communal prayer of gratitude that Dad's parking-lot vision had become a fully produced, seven-stage play! We were shaking with excitement. This was so ambitious, so different from any other theatre in our area. Would people like it? Would they understand what we were trying to do?

We were about to find out.

The first cast of actors took their places, and we gave the signal to begin. The debut audience group made their way through the gates to meet the prophets. I stayed in the shadows, nervously searching for any reaction. I followed them as they witnessed the angels, shepherds, and wise men. I saw them smile and even laugh.

Finally, they arrived at the stable. And that's when I saw it: awe. They hung on every word, sang the carols, and marvelled at the baby. A little girl whispered to her mother, "Is baby Jesus real?"

What a question to ask, and what a question to answer! This little girl understood the true heart of the story, better than any of us could have ever described.

Without knowing it, we'd started a Christmas tradition. Our play ran one night each year for ten years. In total, over 5,000 people saw the live performances! One year, Vision TV Canada filmed a documentary about our production, which ran for five years, reaching a national audience of over 100,000 homes.

We lost count of the thousands of people who experienced "The Real Christmas Story — A Walk Through" either as actors, singers, volunteers, or audience members.

And, after that first year, we never had trouble finding a real baby Jesus again! Couples eagerly approached Dad with the news, "We're due in November. Can our baby be part of the play?"

When I think of those years, I think of family: Dad inviting me into his idea. Mom serving cider and cookies to the cast. My boyfriend volunteering as a tour guide. My friends singing harmony in the choir. Our church family creating something beautiful for our community. And young families offering to share their newborn babies with us all.

Family, community, art and music all came together to tell the great story of Christmas. I can't think of a better idea.

— Allison Lynn Flemming —

19

Chicken Soup for the Soul

A Tradition of Days Long Past

The best way to spread Christmas cheer
is singing loud for all to hear.
~Will Ferrell, Elf

"But I don't like singing," I whined to my husband.

"It's supposed to be a big group of people. You can just fake it if you want."

I pursed my lips and debated. Should we accept the invitation to go caroling with our friends, or should I let embarrassment get the better of me and decline?

"Fine," I conceded and went to look up a recipe so I could bake cookies to bring to our host.

When we arrived at the caroling party three days later, the house was decorated with Christmas lights, a large tree, and stockings over a mock fireplace. It smelled of delicious warm food ready to eat. The house was packed with guests. Some mingled while snacking on food. Others had the printed-out songs in front of them and were practicing in preparation for when everyone would go outside and serenade the neighborhood.

Too nervous about singing, I went for the kitchen. Amber, our friend who was hosting the party, greeted me as soon as I entered.

"I'm glad you came," she said with a warm smile.

"Thank you for inviting us. I admit, I'm a bit nervous about singing."

She waved away my fears. "Oh, don't worry. This is about having fun."

"What made you decide to do this?" I asked, especially since I'd hardly heard of anyone caroling anymore.

"I've just always loved the nostalgia of Christmas caroling. It takes me back to days long past when life was simpler."

My head instantly filled with nostalgic images of carolers from the 1900s and 1800s. I hadn't thought about it that way.

"When we moved here," Amber went on, "the neighborhood felt like the perfect place to start the tradition."

"A lot of people certainly agree," I said as I looked around the crowded house at everyone's excited faces.

"Okay, everyone!" Amber's husband called from the front door. "We're going to be heading out soon."

My husband, with his stomach now full, arrived by my side with a printout of the songs we would be singing. "Are you ready for this?" he asked, the twinkle in his eye making it clear that he was teasing me over my fear of singing in front of people.

"Maybe," I admitted. Talking with Amber had gotten me excited about going around to the neighbors' houses to spread Christmas cheer. However, I was definitely still very nervous about singing.

As we reached the first house, I stationed myself toward the back of the group. My head dipped low as I buried my face in the piece of paper. Like a quiet mouse, I started singing. Or did I?

My mouth was moving, and I was definitely singing, but I couldn't hear myself or how off-key I might have been over everyone else's singing. Looking up, I saw that no one else noticed either.

Well, I thought, *if I can't even hear how bad I sound, maybe I can get away with singing a little louder.*

So, I did. And, still, I couldn't hear whether I was off-key or not.

By the fourth house, I found myself smiling and letting the songs fly from my mouth. I was having too much fun to worry if I sounded good enough or not.

"You seemed to enjoy yourself," my husband said when we were driving home.

"I did."

"Do you want to go caroling again next year?"

"Definitely!"

Insecurity out. Christmas spirit in.

— Katrin Babb —

20

The Power of Love

*Christmas is the spirit of giving without a thought of
getting. It is happiness because we see joy in people.
It is forgetting self and finding more time for others.*
~Thomas S. Monson

"Boys!" I called to our three children just before
Christmas. "We're having a special guest for a few
days. Let's play Twenty Questions to see if you can
guess who it is!" Suggestions flew fast and furiously.

"Is it Grandma?" She lived too far away.

"Is it Uncle Ed and Auntie Heather?" No, that's two people.

They went through a list of possible choices and then went on to
animals. First, the ordinary ones.

"Is it a kitten?" We'd had cats before, but they always disappeared.

"Are we getting a puppy?" Nine-year-old Chris thought that would
be the fulfillment of his secret dream. Then, the guesses got more bizarre.

"Is it an anteater?" said Nicky, the five-year-old.

I laughed out loud.

In the adult Sunday School class the previous Sunday, the pastor
had talked about hospitality over the Christmas season, tying it in with
the story of Mary and Joseph looking for a place to stay in Bethlehem,
when there were no places available. He challenged us to think of
someone poor and lonely with whom we could share our home and
hearts. My own heart was stirred. I felt as though I was on the verge
of something significant.

"Someone poor and lonely," I mused. "I don't know anyone poor or lonely."

My husband Terry and I had always tried to be hospitable, inviting people over for meals, even at the spur of the moment, and opening our home to people who needed a place to stay for one reason or another, even if it meant moving the children around or having them sleep on a mattress on the floor. In the bustle of the season, the possibility of a poor and lonely guest was temporarily forgotten.

Then the phone call came. "Would you be able to take a two-week-old baby for a few days?" said the voice on the other end of the line. It was the social worker we had dealt with when we took in two little girls the previous summer. They had stayed more than a month, but it was summertime then and much easier to incorporate two extra children into our family. My husband and I were both teachers, and we were both available and relaxed in July and August. Now it was December, and we were recovering from the stress of teaching children and teenagers every day.

But a newborn baby? Waking up for nighttime feedings was a thing of the past. I had nursed my children and didn't know much about schedules anymore or even how to deal with baby bottles. I wrestled with my thoughts. "Let me talk it over with Terry, and I'll call you back."

"Terry! Hilary wants us to take a newborn for a few days! Should we do it?"

"As long as you are the one to get up at night, you can do it," he immediately replied. Then I remembered the "someone poor and lonely" part of the pastor's pre-Christmas lesson. *We have to do this*, I thought. It was if everything fell into place in my mind. *Okay, Lord, I'll do it.*

What have I done? I asked myself as I dialed the social worker. I was excited at the way this opportunity seemed to fall into our laps, but I was also nervous.

"We'll do it," I told Hilary. She filled me in on the details. The mother had been one of Terry's students. Barely sixteen years old, she had dropped out of school. Now, only two weeks after the baby's birth, the reality of motherhood was harder than she had imagined. She decided to give up her baby boy. We would be the interim placement before he went to his forever home. How could we refuse someone in need?

The children still didn't know who was coming to share Christmas with us. "Our guest is coming in a few minutes!" I called out. The boys were beside themselves, running to the window every time they heard a car. At last, one slowed down and pulled up.

"Who is it? Who is it?" the boys clamoured. We opened the door to the social worker carrying a blue bundle. The boys crowded around. "Ohhh... It's a baby!" They jumped up and down and danced around the room. Then, they were stunned into silence as we unzipped the baby from his — yes, it was a boy — grubby, blue bunting bag. One corner was damp from a small bottle of milk tucked into it. That's all he had in the world — the faded sleeper he was wearing, a damp bunting bag, and a half-full bottle of milk. This definitely qualified as "poor."

What the boys didn't notice was the look on the baby's face. It was totally blank. Only two weeks old, and already he had given up on this unfriendly world. *Here is a child who definitely needs love and attention. Why, he's lonely!* The thought was startling. Was it possible to fix? We would try.

I got into the routine of getting up at night as regularly as clockwork. I even went back to bed after the 6:00 a.m. feeding. It was still dark, unlike when my babies were little. None of us needed to be up that early. When we were all up, the boys were eager to help. They were glad to take a turn to feed him, talk to him, and hold him up to see the coloured lights on the Christmas tree. At bedtime, the boys prayed from their hearts for him. Five-year-old Nicky prayed, "Help his belly button get better."

Seven-year-old Stephen prayed, "Help the baby feel at home and help him not to be afraid." Their prayers were right-on.

Three days passed. The social worker made arrangements to pick up the baby. I noticed his face again. To my astonishment, it had changed! Baby K had become alert instead of withdrawn. I realized that his eyes were fastening onto our faces instead of being vacant. His mouth would move, and he was beginning to make little sounds. The change from the empty look on his face when he arrived was astonishing. I was floored. Our actions, inspired by the Christmas season and a Sunday School lesson, had seemed so small. But to Baby K's life, they were huge. Now, he was ready to go to his forever home. I had learned about another facet of hospitality: the power of love.

—Alice Burnett—

21

Chicken Soup for the Soul

Black Friday

*Once again, we come to the Holiday Season, a deeply
religious time that each of us observes, in his own way,
by going to the mall of his choice.*
~Dave Barry

Most of my life, I avoided Christmas shopping right after Thanksgiving. I'd heard the stories of shoppers fighting with each other over the latest doll or video-game console on Black Friday. However, a dozen or so years ago, my best friend, Kelly, invited me to Christmas-shop with her in the Chicago suburbs.

I hesitated, but Kelly can be very persistent. So began a Thanksgiving tradition. Sometimes, my wife Jen goes along; sometimes, one of Kelly's kids. Most of the time, it's just the two of us, but we're never alone.

For those who shop late on Thanksgiving evening or in the wee dark hours of Black Friday morn, a community develops. People are forced together in queues waiting for doors to open and reveal the season's bargains. Most of the time, those new acquaintances get along. Sometimes, they even demonstrate what the traditions of Thanksgiving, Advent, Hanukkah, Kwanzaa, or Christmas are all about.

In 2016, Kelly called me early in Thanksgiving Week.

"You're coming up on Wednesday, right?" she asked. "Target has a 70-inch TV on sale at 6:00 on Thursday evening. We need two — one for us and one for my mom. Can you stand in line with me?"

"Sure," I answered. "That's what Black Friday is all about."

Thanksgiving Day came, and, after an early dinner, Kelly and I drove to Target to wait in line for a chance to buy our TVs. The weather, which had promised to be cool, took a downward turn. As the sun receded in the west, the wind picked up. I'd dressed warmly according to the forecast, but I hadn't counted on the wind. The chill soon seeped under my jacket sleeves, up my arms, and all over. Fortunately, as the cold increased, so did the warmth of the crowd.

What had been a straight, single line became a huddled mass. It was orderly; everyone knew whose place was whose, but we weren't exactly in a neat queue. Still, the warmth of so many TV-seeking bodies was comforting.

From the back of the line, a little girl appeared. She couldn't have been more than seven or eight.

"Wanna hear me sing my multiplication tables?" she inquired.

Without waiting for a response, she began singing.

"One times zero is zero,

"One times one is one,

"One times two is two…"

She danced a little as she sang to our increasing applause.

Pretty soon, Dad appeared, apologizing for his daughter's forwardness and for letting her out of his sight for just a few seconds. We told him it was all right. We loved her song and dance.

As the clock moved slowly toward 6:00, the social interactions increased. The store next to Target opened for their Black Friday sale. The woman standing in front of us asked if we could hold her place while she went to buy her daughter a coat. The two disappeared into the newly-opened store and returned a little while later, the daughter wrapped in a new coat and scarf.

At 5:30, employees from Target walked through the orderly mob handing out presale tickets for the various specials. Kelly and I each got a printed guarantee that the TV we wanted would indeed be inside for us when the doors opened. Our wait had not been in vain.

With twenty minutes to go, the chill was running throughout my body. My distress must have been obvious because a young man came up and asked if I was cold.

"Maybe a little," I responded.

The man, a total stranger, took off his outer coat and placed it carefully around my shoulders.

"You can give it back when we get inside."

I thanked him, smiling to hold back my tears.

Kelly, never one to miss a photo op, said to everyone nearby, "Hey! Let's get a selfie!"

Following her lead, we gathered tightly around Kelly and her iPhone. Afterward, Kelly took phone numbers to send the photo to everyone who wanted one. I printed mine and keep it in my office desk to look at during the times when I forget the human race can sometimes be truly human.

Six o'clock finally came. Our new neighbors hugged goodbye as we filed through the doors. I returned my benefactor's coat and hugged him as well. Later, as Kelly and I checked out with our huge TVs, we ran into some of our queue mates. We smiled and said, "See ya," knowing we never would.

Christmas came early that year. No, the TVs stayed wrapped in their Santa-and-reindeer paper until the Big Day. But the greatest gift that year came long before the holiday candles were lit. It came in a cold, dark and damp parking lot where an impromptu family celebrated the best of a very holy season.

—Phil Baisley—

22

A Warm Christmas Welcome

Remember this December, that love weighs more than gold.
~Josephine Dodge Daskam Bacon

In the dim auditorium of the church, tears coursed down my cheeks. A sob caught in my throat as swirling emotions threatened to overcome me. I took a deep breath and fixed my gaze on the stage as the curtain parted for the first performance of the annual Christmas play.

The actors gathered around an enormous, shimmering Christmas tree. They hung ornaments on its boughs and chatted. Others curled up on a velvet couch nearby. Their dialogue flowed without a hitch. One petite actress captured my attention — and my heart.

That actress — my daughter Alyssa — had turned nine earlier in the year. When we moved to a new state for my husband's job, I called the local elementary school to enroll Alyssa. "She has Down syndrome," I said to the principal. "Her prior education plan placed her in a regular classroom."

"We put all the kids with Down syndrome in a special resource room," she answered. My heart sank. They didn't want to include Alyssa in a class with typical students.

With some persuasion, though, the principal agreed to the placement from Alyssa's previous school — but only temporarily. "I'll refer her to the school psychologist for testing, and we'll make a final determination based on his results," she said. Acceptance for Alyssa would be an uphill battle.

After that chilly welcome, I fretted about her performance every day when she went to school. I monitored communication from the teacher and responded to any negative feedback. Determined to keep Alyssa on track, I went above and beyond the scope of homework assignments. In a quest for acceptance, I drove Alyssa to be perfect. I exhausted myself, and I'm sure I frustrated her.

Around the same time, we began to attend a church that was big enough for us to get lost in the crowd. In October, the bulletin announced a sign-up for a Christmas musical with some parts for children. I turned to Jeff. "Do you think I should try to sign up Alyssa for this play?"

"Sure, why not?" he answered.

I wondered if they would accept Alyssa, a born actress, as part of the cast. I didn't know if I could bear another rejection of my child, especially from my new church family.

With the go-ahead from Jeff, I concluded we should take the risk. Before I could second-guess my decision, I filled out the interest form and tossed it into the offering basket as it passed by.

A couple of weeks later, I took Alyssa to the first practice. I don't think she noticed the wide eyes when everyone noticed she had Down syndrome. She took her seat with the other actors while I hung around at the back of the room—just in case.

After our experience at our new school, I worried about how she would be accepted at our new church. We had been burned before by leaders, teachers, and even friends who didn't understand how to embrace kids with differences. When Alyssa blurted out words during quiet times in practice, I fidgeted in my seat, willing myself not to rush over to shush her. When she wandered away from the group, I held my breath, hoping she would return on her own. In the back of my mind, I waited for the axe to fall.

As the weeks went by, the actors memorized their lines. They rehearsed movements on the stage. A crew designed and constructed the set. Alyssa worked right along with them. At home, we practiced slowing her speech so the audience could understand her lines. She memorized the songs until we all knew them by heart.

After a couple of weeks of practice, I checked in with the director of the Christmas program. "How do you think Alyssa is doing?"

"She's doing well," he answered. "Her memory is phenomenal. I think she knows everyone's lines." He chuckled and shook his head. "She prompts them when they forget."

I let down my guard a bit. But part of me stayed wary.

On the day of the Christmas performance, I obsessed over details. Did Alyssa know how to manage her costume? What should she take to keep herself occupied backstage? Would someone make sure she didn't miss her cues? Did she get a good night's sleep? Would she be able to communicate with the helpers? When I led her to the group, she smiled and waved me away. "See you later, Mom." Apparently, no jitters for her.

On shaky legs, I hurried to my seat next to Jeff among the audience. I clutched his hand and leaned forward, waiting. "Is everything okay?" he asked.

"She's great. But I have nerves for both of us." The church auditorium darkened, and the audience hushed. I let out a long, slow breath. "This is it."

I sat taller on the edge of my seat and craned my neck to see the action through a forest of heads. I had attended the dress rehearsal, so I knew what to expect. When Alyssa entered the stage and delivered her first line, a dam burst inside my heart. Relief, apprehension, joy, pride, gratitude, and more jumbled feelings swept through me. In the cover of darkness, I sniffled and dabbed at tears.

Jeff leaned over and whispered in my ear. "She's right where she belongs, isn't she?"

I beamed. Jeff was right. The rejection of Alyssa by her school had caused my faith in people to falter. Then, the cast and crew of the play embraced my girl and her differences. Under the light of affirmation, she flourished. Their gift of acceptance made us feel truly welcome in our new home that Christmas.

— Annie Yorty —

The Last-Minute Purchase

*Christmas gives us an opportunity to pause and reflect
on the important things around us.*
~David Cameron

Me work in a jewellery store? It was hard to imagine. I didn't wear any accessories, not even a watch. However, I was a teenager who needed money and the store had a help wanted sign in the window. They must have really needed help for Christmas to hire me, with my lack of experience.

My lack of interest in jewellery was reflected in my sales. After two weeks, George, my boss, brought out the sales figures. I was dead last. The only thing I was good at was selling aftershave. We had a nice one called British Sterling. I convinced the women who were buying it for their men that they were really buying it for themselves. It didn't matter if their husbands or boyfriends liked it. If it pleased them, it was the right one.

The closer we got to Christmas, the busier the store got. We braced ourselves for the big day, Christmas Eve.

True to form, many customers, mostly men, rushed into the store, desperate to find the perfect gift for their loved ones. Of course, we had just what they wanted, showing them the more expensive items and only showing lower-priced ones if they asked.

About a half-hour before closing, a young girl came into the store with a worried look. All the stores would be closing soon. I asked if I could help her.

"I want to buy a gift for my mom," she said. "It has to be something very special."

"What can you tell me about your mom?" I asked.

"She's beautiful," she replied.

My next question was how much money she had to spend.

"Six dollars."

Six dollars! Even though this happened way back when I was a teenager, that was still not much money.

"Does your mother wear earrings?" I asked.

"Yes, she does."

"Are her ears pierced?"

"Yes, they are."

Now we were getting somewhere. I knew that we had some earrings in her price range.

I patiently showed her several pairs. Nothing seemed special enough for the young girl's mom. The store was filling up, with wallets being flipped out like a shootout at the OK Corral. George kept glancing furtively at me.

Finally, like the star in the east, a pair of earrings appeared. The little girl gasped, "They're perfect. My mom will love these."

Quickly, we rushed to the cash register, and I rang up the sale. It came to $4.98. As I started to put the earrings in a bag, two big, brown eyes sparkled at me with great joy. Yes, the joy of the season was in her eyes.

I couldn't stop my next sentence. "Would you like them gift-wrapped?"

"Would you?" she squealed.

I went to the back of the store. George's eyes followed me like searchlights looking for enemy aircraft. He was scrambling to serve the many customers.

I got out one of the store's special boxes, wrapped the earrings in gold paper, put a red ribbon around it and asked, "Would you like a bow?"

"Oh, yes!"

I found a perfect red one. The gift looked beautiful, fit for the best mom in the world. She must have been the best mom in the world. What other kind of mother would raise such a wonderful child?

Head held high, the girl walked out of the store to her dad, who was watching the whole production in the store through the window.

It was one minute to 6:00. I turned around, and there was George with wide eyes staring at me. Let's just say he didn't wish me a Merry Christmas. In fact, he wasn't very merry at all.

"We had many customers who wanted to spend a lot of money, and you wasted a lot of time on a sale of $4.98. Not only that, you gift-wrapped her present. We only do that for purchases over $10."

Without hesitation or fear, I replied cheerfully, "Yes, there were many with lots of money, but this child knows the true spirit of giving. She gave most of what she had. All I did was thank her for showing me what Christmas is all about. It's not about money. It's about giving. Merry Christmas, George."

— John Stevens —

24

Chicken Soup for the Soul

A Christmas Angel

Let us keep Christmas beautiful
without a thought of greed.
~Ann Garnett Schultz

My mood was less than Christmasy two days before Christmas Eve. I had volunteered to help deliver food baskets to those less fortunate, but the day had started on a sour note. The doors had barely started to open when the crowd surged through like a tsunami. Some people fell and some were shoved as the mob leaped over and around them. Thundering down the aisle, they were headed straight to where we waited with the highly coveted toys fresh from the delivery truck.

As the crowd got closer, my first thought was that this could only get worse. Hesitating only a moment, we began grabbing the toys and throwing them as hard and far as we could. The pack dispersed, fighting to intercept the airborne toys. Any manners they may have had suddenly disappeared at seeing the toys, and we had to make fast decisions to avoid more falls and injuries. These people meant business. The toys disappeared within minutes. Disappointed, the crowd scattered, grumbling unhappily.

After the initial rush, those of us who had volunteered to deliver food baskets loaded up and left to deliver baskets of turkey or ham, sweet potatoes, rolls, and everything else needed for a perfect Christmas dinner. The names of those who had applied for food assistance during the holidays had been provided by area churches, and I was eager to help.

At the first home, a woman stared blankly at the basket and me.

"Merry Christmas!" I greeted her.

She continued to stare.

"Ummm... you signed up for a holiday basket?" I prompted.

"They didn't say the food was going to be raw," she replied.

My jaw dropped. My first impulse was to fling it through the door and walk away, but I had undertaken this chore hoping to refresh my heart with the real meaning of Christmas: love. When you work with the public as I did, it's easy to become embittered, watching as everyone else gets to enjoy the holidays, shopping, dining, and finding the perfect gifts while you are overwhelmed with work and demands. That year, I had resolved I wasn't going to fall victim to the same negative energy as years before when anger and resentment had built up within me.

No matter what it took, I was determined to carry the true meaning of Christmas in my heart all season long. But, all too quickly, my resolution began to fade. Resentment began to build when I pulled up to homes that were much nicer than mine, with newer cars in the driveways. I suspected that some were taking advantage of the giveaway, but I failed to consider that these folks may have fallen upon hard times or become victims of layoffs and factory closings.

Finally, though, I was down to two baskets. Despite double- and triple-checking my list, I kept coming up with one extra basket. I was tired and discouraged, and I just wanted to go home.

But sometimes God saves the best for last.

Grabbing a basket, I headed for the last house on my list, where a dim light glowed in the window. I knocked loudly on the door, and the porch light switched on. The door was opened by an older woman with a radiant smile. Quite a few teeth were missing, and she had wrinkles galore, but she had a beautiful smile and kind eyes.

"Oh! You're here, you're here!" she cried out happily, holding the door wide. "I was so afraid that you weren't coming."

The burden of resentment that I had carried all day began to slip away like snow melting on a metal roof as I followed her into the kitchen and hoisted the basket onto the table. Perhaps it was because she was the most grateful person whom I had encountered that day. Or maybe it was the childlike joy that just seemed to radiate from her. I don't know, but I hesitated as she eagerly began to rummage in the basket. I didn't want to leave.

Pulling food from the basket, she kept thanking me profusely.

"This means so much," she said. "Some of my neighbors are coming here for Christmas dinner. They haven't anywhere to go. Ohhh... this is so wonderful! Thank you! Thank you so, so much!" She smiled rapturously at the sight of a frozen pumpkin pie.

"How many will be coming?" I asked.

"Last count?" She paused to think. "Around seven or so."

I looked at the food spread out upon the table. There would be enough for dinner for everyone but nothing more. But I wanted there to be enough for second helpings and leftovers to be carried home and happily anticipated the next day.

Turning, I went to my car and returned with the extra basket to her surprise and delight.

Sometimes, it's not the food; it's who you share it with that brings the real joy. This woman understood the true meaning of Christmas. Rather than hoarding the contents of her basket, she chose to share her bounty with those who hungered not just for food but for the privilege of gathering together, creating an impromptu family of the heart.

This lady with her beautiful, gap-toothed smile would welcome her friends and neighbors into her home on Christmas Day, providing something far more nourishing than any food; she would be providing companionship. Instead of sitting down in front of a squawking television and eating a microwave meal, these folks would be sharing a meal, passing dishes hand-to-hand as they had as children, reminiscent of when the families of their past had sat down for a meal together.

Wearing my first real smile of the day, I prepared to leave but stopped and turned back for one last look. My only regret was that I wouldn't be there to see her and her friends all gathered together at the table on Christmas.

The only thing that home would lack that Christmas Day would be animals and a manger. It already had an angel.

— Laurel L. Shannon —

25

The Promise of Change

Wonder is the beginning of wisdom.
~Socrates

I trudged through the new house. How could I possibly be happy in a new place so far away from lifelong friends? How would we do Christmas without family? I struggled to put aside negative thoughts and remembered Ray's words. "Honey, the smaller community and country life will be so good for all of us. I can always transfer back if things don't work out."

When we'd left our home in the Scottsdale, Arizona desert, the twenty-foot saguaro cactus in front of our house, with its long, curved arms, seemed to reach out and beg us to stay. But Ray had taken a transfer to the northeastern part of Arizona.

Our new home was nestled between pastures — one to the side of the house and one in the back. Huge cottonwood trees lined the curved driveway. The air smelled crisp and clean, and I realized Christmas this year would not be the balmy seventy-three degrees it could be during December back home. It had not snowed yet, but we needed winter jackets.

Our young daughter seemed oblivious to the move and change. She loved the big trees, begged for a treehouse, and could hardly contain her excitement to have our barn finished so we could bring our horses to the new house. Our Saint Bernard and Golden Retriever loved the cool weather, and the cat made herself right at home.

When I finally pulled the Christmas decorations from boxes, we spent the evening stringing white lights, colored bulbs and special family ornaments on the live tree. Colored lights adorned the porch, and fresh greens graced the doorway. I breathed in the fresh pine scent and started to feel more comfortable about the move.

On Christmas Eve, we watched a DVD of the classic movie, *It's a Wonderful Life*, and the pellet stove warmed the house. Before the doorbell rang, we heard bells jingle. Oh, how I hoped we had carolers. We always loved to open our doors to them in Scottsdale.

A tall, older fellow stood at the door. He extended his hand. "Hello, I'm your neighbor, Wendell." He winked. "Thought you guys might like to celebrate Christmas Eve with your neighbors. We always have a hayride. It's lots of fun. How about it?"

Our daughter squealed, "Oh, Mom, Dad, could we? Could we?"

We piled into Wendell's truck and traveled down an old, narrow forest road for a short time before a sight I will never forget came into view. A campfire roared. It lit the dark sky, which was peppered with more stars than I had ever seen. Children scurried everywhere, some with browned marshmallows that dripped and sizzled. Groups of adults gathered around the fire drinking from steaming cups.

A horse-drawn wagon stood off to one side of the tree-lined road. Several young girls ran toward our daughter, asking if she wanted to go on the wagon with them. "Mom and Dad, you can come, too." Ray and I hurried to catch up and climbed on to settle ourselves on a bale of hay. The wagon master and the heavy-footed horses plodded forward.

Total strangers hugged us, and men shook Ray's hand and slapped his back. Youngsters on the wagon handed out cups of hot chocolate and warm donuts. A group of teens strummed guitars and sang "Silent Night," while a flutist whistled alongside them. I struggled to hold back my tears.

We arrived at a scene that took my breath away. A lit stable with a live nativity brought my trickle of tears to a flood. Three young ladies played violins with precision and calm grace. "Oh, Come All Ye Faithful" penetrated the still night. Baby Jesus cooed in the arms of a young Mary. That's when I knew we were right where we needed to be.

Yes, we were going to miss family and friends, but these people presented a promise of new friendship and memories that could last a lifetime.

— Alice Klies —

Chapter 4

Santa's Helpers

26

Our Encounter with Santa Claus

The greatness of a community is most accurately
measured by the compassionate actions of its members.
~Coretta Scott King

About ten years ago, our Christmas was looking rather abysmal. Being laid off from a lucrative position in November and having to pay for a broken water heater in early December seemed to ensure that our Christmas would be neither holly nor jolly. Having a six-year-old daughter in the full throes of Christmas fever was only adding to our stress level. With our budget shot full of holes like Swiss cheese, we needed to figure out how to keep our spirits high while our means were very low.

So, late one December night, the wife and I decided that perhaps planned distractions would help quell any potential disappointments for our Christmas-crazy cutie.

And so, it began. First, the wife decided we were all to have codenames for the season of holiday hullabaloo. She declared herself to be "Colonel Christmas," while dubbing me as "Captain Yuletide" and the daughter to be "Corporal Eggnog."

Next, using skills acquired by trial and error with a trail of dead laptops, the wife dove mind-first into the minefield that is online retail Christmas shopping.

Then, I was tasked with accompanying the daughter to every

Christmas-themed event in our small community.

The daughter and I went to a Christmas parade where we saw dancing Christmas trees and were pelted with small candy thrown by elves. We went to a production of *The Nutcracker*, which left the rarely quiet Corporal Eggnog speechless. We went to a "breakfast with Santa" and, oh boy, can St. Nick put away the pancakes!

Meanwhile, the wife, Colonel Christmas, was busy conjuring her own form of Christmas magic. By approaching the twelve days of Christmas as a military campaign (though her military education consisted of *M.A.S.H.* reruns), the wife managed to create a tree-and-present pile that suitably impressed our six-year-old.

And so it came to pass that Christmas Eve arrived right on schedule. Traditions were observed: the reading aloud of *'Twas the Night Before Christmas* and *How the Grinch Stole Christmas*. Then, the drinking of eggnog and the opening of a single present.

I was preparing the daughter for her long winter's nap when she stopped the proceedings with panic on her face and cried, "Wait! What about the reindeer food?"

"Reindeer food," it turned out, was a bag of oats lightly laced with glitter given to the daughter by her teacher. It included instructions indicating that we were to spread said "reindeer food" across our lawn on the night of Christmas Eve, which we did.

After that minor drama had been dealt with, Christmas Eve quietly and slowly slipped into Christmas morning.

As dawn cracked the morning sky, the family enjoyed our tradition of cookies and eggnog for Christmas breakfast. After our morning munchies and before the presents, the daughter announced that we MUST go outside to see if the reindeer had eaten their food. I grudgingly followed her as she opened the door to the porch. It revealed a sight that left us speechless.

A thirty-gallon trash bag filled to the spillage point with brightly wrapped gifts waited to be discovered. The daughter screamed, the wife gasped, and, I must admit, I may have staggered.

Chaos and confusion ensued. Where and from whom had this come?

After the tinsel settled, we discovered ten gifts labeled to the daughter and an envelope addressed to the missus and me. The gifts ranged from a homemade set of knit hat, scarf and mittens to random but age-appropriate toys. Opening the envelope, we found a card with a crisp one-hundred-dollar bill inside and the simple handwritten message "Merry Christmas and good luck" signed "Santa."

A decade has passed, and I never did find out the identity of the person or persons who gave our family that Christmas morning miracle. After some time, I realized I had been searching in vain because I was looking in the wrong places.

It had been Santa.

Santa Claus is not a rotund old man dressed in red velvet selling soda pop. Santa is the spirit of Christmas who wishes to give to and for children without care for thanks or recompense. At Christmas, we should all hear the call of Claus and wish to be a Santa. Having seen firsthand that spirit in action and its effects, when asked if I believe in Santa's magic, the answer is and always will be "Yes!"

—Steve Coney—

27

Chicken Soup for the Soul

The Year of the Skinny Santa

*Mother is she who can take the place of all others
but whose place no one else can take.*
~Author Unknown

What happens when Santa doesn't show up for the school Christmas party? If you're lucky enough to have had a mom like mine, the answer to that question can be both embarrassing and hilarious.

Every year, the students at St. John's Grade School looked forward to the Christmas party, held on the last day of classes before the holiday break. We gathered in the gym, where long tables were decorated with paper coverings, Christmas plates, cups, and napkins. We could always count on pizza, pop, chips, and an assortment of Christmas cookies, all compliments of generous parishioners.

The highlight of the afternoon was always the appearance of Santa Claus. Because the real Santa was busy getting ready for the big event on Christmas Eve, one of his helpers would show up at the party to take his place. Usually, it was a jolly-looking gentleman with a real beard who did his best to entertain us in the absence of the boss himself.

We kids knew the drill. The music teacher, Sister Inez, would play Christmas carols on the upright piano, and we kids would sing "Jingle Bells," "Frosty the Snowman," "Rudolph the Red-Nosed Reindeer," and other kid-friendly tunes. The finale was always "Santa Claus Is

Coming to Town." On the second go-around of the song, Santa himself would walk in, complete with jingle bells and a bag of gold-wrapped chocolate coins, which he would distribute to us kids as we filed out the door at the end of the party.

The year when I was in fourth grade, events took an unexpected turn. About halfway through the party, a buzz started among the older kids. What trickled down from the seventh- and eighth-grade tables was this disturbing piece of information: Santa's helper was a no-show.

By the time that message got to us fourth-graders, a near panic had ensued. The sisters tried their best to calm us down.

"Don't worry," Sister Eleanor kept saying. "It will all work out."

I knew my mom was volunteering in the kitchen that day. Suddenly, I had the urge to see her and speak to her. Even a fourth-grader can get worried around Christmas when Santa's helper doesn't show up.

I raised my hand and asked permission to go to the kitchen and talk to Mom.

"Make it quick," Sister told me.

The fact that my mom was volunteering at all was something of a Christmas miracle. She had rheumatoid arthritis and wasn't always able to help out. But this year, by the grace of God, she was well enough to show up for a party that she knew meant so much to us kids.

When I got to the pass-through window that opened into the kitchen, I looked for Mom. For a moment, I thought it was odd that I didn't hear her. She had a wild sense of humor and a voice that carried a long way. Whenever she volunteered at school, I felt anxious about her saying and doing something that would embarrass us. This time, I didn't see or hear her. Mom would have been easy to spot, too. At five feet, ten inches tall and well-built, she would have stood out among the other moms.

"What do you need, honey?" one of the ladies in a Christmas apron asked when she saw me at the window.

"I need to talk to my mom," I said.

She exchanged looks with another woman, who was getting out more bottles of pop for the kids.

"I think she had to go to the bathroom," she told me. "I'll tell her you were looking for her. Now, go sit down."

Back at my seat, I couldn't help worrying. I wondered what was going to happen when we got to Santa's entrance cue and there was no Santa. Sister Inez played the introduction to "Santa Claus Is Coming to Town." When we got to the crucial part of the song, there came Santa, right on cue, ringing his sleigh bells — or, I should say, *her* sleigh bells. Underneath Santa's red suit and beard so-snowy-white was my mother. She was ho-ho-ho-ing in her best alto voice, shouting "Merry Christmas, boys and girls!" and ringing those bells like crazy. Her RA gave her a very distinctive walk, making it even more obvious who Santa's helper was this year. The girl sitting next to me turned to me and said, "Hey, isn't that your mom?"

I was mortified. I guess my face showed it because my classmate said, "Don't be embarrassed. I think it's cool! I wish my mom would do stuff like that."

Pretty soon, every kid at the table had caught on, and I started hearing things like, "It's Mrs. Provenzano!" "Elizabeth Ann, it's your mom! Cool!" "Man, she sounds just like Santa!" The little kids were oblivious, but the older students thought it was great. Here was my mom, dressed like Jolly Old St. Nick, having a blast. And everybody loved her! Suddenly, I saw her in a new light. Now, she wasn't just my embarrassing mom. She was a celebrity. Her flair for theatrics had saved the day and sealed her in my memory forever as my personal hero.

On the way out the door, as I stopped to get my treat from "Santa," I said, "Hey, you look familiar."

"Santa" winked at me, handed me a bag of candy, and said, "Move along, little girl."

I took the candy and gave her a hug and a smile. Then I ran off to get my bookbag for the trip home.

Over the years, I learned a lot of valuable lessons from my mother. That year, as an anxious fourth-grader at the Christmas party, I learned something that has served me well: Don't take yourself too seriously and always be willing to step up when Santa needs one more helper.

— Elizabeth A. Dreier —

28

Our Holey Christmas

Never ever doubt magic. The purest honest thoughts
come from children. Ask any child if they believe in
magic, and they will tell you the truth.
~Scott Dixon

Three weeks before Christmas, I was playing with our three young children in the basement when my husband, dressed in his puffy down coat, maroon pants, and work boots, came in from shoveling the driveway. Whispering, I asked him discreetly, since he already had on a coat, if he would go up to our drafty attic and retrieve our Christmas tree, ornaments, and holiday decorations.

I didn't want the children near the attic because it was a small, unfinished area between the roof and the ceiling of our second floor. Even though it was covered in pink insulation, it was always cold up there. The "walls" were wooden beams with exposed pipes and wires, and the "floor" consisted of a few planks laid across the joists. It wasn't a safe place for children, and since I was pregnant with our fourth child, I knew it wasn't a good place for me either.

Unbeknownst to me, our precocious five-year-old son, James, must have overheard my whispered request. I didn't notice his absence from the basement play area, but he sneaked quietly up the stairs to see what his father was doing. The rest of us continued playing until James suddenly ran back down the basement steps and screamed at the top of his lungs.

"Santa Claus has fallen through the roof!"

For a second, I considered that it wasn't time for Santa yet so he wouldn't be on our roof now, but seeing the panic in my son's eyes, I realized something was seriously wrong.

James was already racing back up the stairs by the time I managed to get to my feet. I told our daughter to stay in the basement with our youngest son, and I waddled as quickly as I could up the steps to the first floor.

Nothing seemed amiss on the first floor, and for a second, I wondered if James, who was a persistent punster and prankster, was playing some type of joke. Suddenly, I heard him talking loudly to someone on the second floor. So, once again, I waddled up the stairs. By the time I found him in the master bedroom, I was out of breath.

Following his pointed finger, I looked up to see a leg in maroon pants and a foot in a black boot dangling from our ceiling.

"Do you need help, Santa?" James was asking loudly. "Do you want me to call the police?"

Realizing the leg belonged to my husband and not Santa, I waddled — more rapidly this time — up the third flight of stairs to the attic. I found my husband on the floor — at least the top half of him — surrounded by pink insulation.

"What happened?" I shouted.

"My boots were wet, and my foot slid off the plank. I fell, and now I'm stuck. I don't want to move around too much because I'm afraid I'll fall through to the floor!"

By repositioning a few of the planks, my husband was able to use his arms and other leg to push himself up a little. Then, with considerable pulling and twisting on my part, we managed to free him from his predicament. We both were relieved to discover that he was not hurt during the incident — just a little embarrassed. Looking down the hole into our bedroom, we could see James calmly smiling back at us.

"I knew it was you, Dad," he whispered, looking up at us. "I just thought I was supposed to pretend so the other kids would think it was Santa."

When we got down to our bedroom, neither my husband nor I

knew what to say, but I knew James well enough to sense the wheels turning in his head. Before I could decide what to say, James added, "I thought it looked like your leg, Dad. Santa's leg would look bigger, and his pants would be red."

"I bet it's going to cost a lot of money to fix that hole," he noted, and he was right.

In fact, James was very matter-of-fact about the whole incident, and he seemed relieved we didn't dwell on it.

Of course, I worried Christmas wouldn't be the same, but it turned out that my worries were unfounded. That Christmas there was a special bond between myself, my husband, and James, and there was plenty of magic in that, too.

We ended up having a wonderful Christmas. When we asked our children what was their favorite part of Christmas, James said he was glad he could give out presents like Santa. He added that he was also glad that the real Santa never got stuck in a chimney — or a ceiling — like Daddy did!

James called that Christmas our "holey Christmas" because of the ceiling hole, and I think we all remember it as a special one. We learned there are many forms of magic in the world — and you just need to be open to discovering new ones. We also learned to store our Christmas tree and holiday decorations in the basement.

— Billie Holladay Skelley —

29

Santa Signs

*Sign language is the equal of speech, lending itself
equally to the rigorous and the poetic,
to philosophical analysis or to making love.*
~Oliver Sacks

Over thirty years ago, I decided that having to make noise with one's mouth was some sort of handicap. Thus, I began my study of ASL: American Sign Language. I studied for several years, starting at the College of Marin and later at City College of San Francisco.

I loved being able to connect to the deaf community. They love to party, and we would often shut down the disco at 2:00 a.m.

For Christmas one year, my deaf teacher made me a gift of a soft, stuffed garden glove with the two middle fingers sewed to the palm. This resulted in a permanent gesture featuring the thumb and the two outside fingers that means "I love you." (It is actually a contraction of three ASL letters: I, L and Y.) It was a treasured gift, and I eventually stuck it in the back shelf of my car so that it was visible from behind. Over time, I completely forget it was there.

One day, I was driving north on Highway 1 through Marin County. I was tooling along in the right lane. No hurry. Eventually, something caught my eye in the car next to me. A young boy in the back seat was up against the window, staring at me intently. To my surprise, his hands came to life in ASL. He asked me if I was deaf. In ASL, I replied that I was not and asked if he was deaf. He was.

The freeway conversation that ensued was interrupted repeatedly as he jumped between the front seats to relay my comments to his mother who was driving. Then it was back to the window to continue our discussion. I was starting to get nervous about being distracted while driving, so I said in ASL, "Nice to meet you," and hit the accelerator.

It took me a while to remember the stuffed glove I had long ago shoved in the back window. Then, it all made sense.

As years went by, I lost touch with the deaf community and eventually purchased a Santa suit to pick up work over the holidays. As an actor and cartoonist, it is "catch as catch can." I soon found myself holding court in a Nordstrom department store in Daly City, California one December. It was a typical day full of families with charming kids. Contrary to holiday clichés, I was rarely assaulted with wish lists. It was primarily a photo-op moment.

As another family approached, I was startled to see the father turn toward a young son and say something to him in ASL. I hadn't signed in years. A wave of panic flew through me. I took a deep breath and relaxed, signing "Merry Christmas" to the family. That boy's eyes were as big as saucers — almost as big as the grin on his face. He was summarily plopped onto my knee as the rest of the family gathered around me for their photo-op.

When it was all over, the family headed out of the mall down a long corridor. Every now and then, the boy would look back over his shoulder, and I would sign something to him. In that moment, all my years of study paid for themselves with interest. I just wished that I could see that little guy sharing with his deaf friends the news that Santa signs.

— Brian Narelle —

30

The Cat Lady Christmas

*Of course, there is a Santa Claus. It's just that no single
somebody could do all he has to do. So the Lord has
spread the task among us all.*
~Truman Capote

We'd just purchased a house in Italy and were moving
in. We loved everything about being in Italy and were
eager to get well-situated before Christmas and begin
meeting our new neighbors. All were friendly and kind,
yet some warned us about a reclusive lady who lived close by, saying
she was a bit eccentric and had a lot of cats.

Instead of being annoyed, we were intrigued by this elusive cat lady
whom we hadn't seen yet, although we knew which house was hers and
had met several of her cats as they cruised through the neighborhood.
We loved all animals and had a special affinity for cats, so we were
interested in getting to know her.

Busy with setting up our home, we relegated her to the back of our
minds for a while until the day we were walking down the street and
a ragtag old woman came out of her house, followed by a half-dozen
cats. We assumed she was our mysterious cat lady.

We introduced ourselves as best we could in our elementary Italian
and shook her bony hand. Neither she nor her cat brood had any fat to
spare. After making polite small talk, Maria requested an odd favor. She
asked if we'd send a letter to Santa for her. She said she'd do it herself,
but she didn't get out much and really didn't know where to send it.

Since we were from America, we were used to odd questions from Italians. For example, many wondered what peanut butter was like because they'd heard so much about it but had never seen or tasted it. But we'd never had a request for a letter to Santa before. Italians celebrated a much less commercialized Christmas, so we thought maybe the people there associated Santa more with America. We were interested in seeing her letter, though, and were hoping to help her out if possible.

Days later, her letter to Santa appeared in our mailbox. It was written in Italian in faint, convoluted handwriting, but we were able to figure it out. Basically, it was a letter asking for meager financial help and some cat-food supplies. My husband and I looked at each other, knowing that this would be our Christmas project.

When we mentioned the letter to some of our friends, all were eager to help out with supplies and cash donations. They told us that often the poorest people in Italy were the proudest and couldn't bring themselves to ask for help, even when desperate. This was a clever way to receive some assistance without actually asking for charity.

It wasn't long before we had an abundant hamper of food for our neighbor and her cats, along with woolly socks, mittens and scarves for her and blankets for the kitties. We stuffed the collected cash into an envelope with a Christmas card and left the whole caboodle on her doorstep, ringing her doorbell as we ran away giggling. We felt like children again, doing good deeds and being secret Santa helpers.

The next day, another letter to Santa appeared in our mailbox. In it, our neighbor Maria thanked Santa profusely for his generosity and lovely gifts. However, she stated that she had asked for 100 euros in cash, but there were only 90 euros in the envelope. She said she was sure that Santa had fulfilled her request completely but suspected that her American neighbors had slipped 10 euros out of the envelope for themselves for their trouble.

We found ourselves guffawing out loud and couldn't wait to tell our friends about Maria's response. What a wonderful, cat-filled Christmas we would all have in our new neighborhood in Italy.

— Donna L. Roberts —

31

Chicken Soup
for the Soul

My Grandmother
Would Be Proud

My grandfather was a wonderful role model.
Through him I got to know the gentle side of men.
~Sarah Long

It's hard to explain to a six-year-old why there's no Christmas tree in her living room while her classmates are talking non-stop about theirs. And let's not forget about the outside decorations on the houses and the huge Santa blow-ups on every neighbor's lawn. The menorah in the window never satisfied my thirst for the tree, lights, or chocolate-chip cookies and milk that my best friend Debbie told me they left for Santa on the kitchen table.

Being the only Jewish kid in my class made me stand out, and no more so in my young mind than during the holiday season when my peers made jokes about reindeer poop and waited excitedly for Santa. I did know that grown-ups were allowed to add other presents under the tree that didn't have to be delivered by Santa.

My Orthodox Jewish grandmother did not take kindly to my complaints about the absence of a Christmas tree. She insisted that I follow her legacy and be the proud granddaughter of a proud Jew. My grandfather, however, understood the yearning of a little girl's heart to be like everybody else at least once a year. He recognized that the lights and glitter seemed magical to me, and unlike my grandma, he knew that I'd someday come to honor and recognize my heritage and no longer need a tree to make me happy.

So, a week before Christmas when no one was looking, Grandpa snuck a Hanukkah bush into the corner of the attic. It was a tiny tree from our backyard that he cut down one afternoon while Grandma napped. He sprayed pinecones with white paint and tied them to the tree with twine. One strand of blinking white lights and a cardboard Star of David completed the magic. This way, Grandpa could claim it was a Hanukkah bush. Lucky for us, Grandma never ventured into the attic.

Grandpa didn't put any presents under the tree because he wanted to respect the ritual of Hanukkah by opening eight small gifts. I asked Grandpa if Santa would know about the Hanukkah bush and, if not, could he write a letter and tell him? I wasn't sure if Santa would be permitted to come to a Jewish person's home.

On Christmas Eve, Grandpa and I left a plate of cookies for Santa right under the Hanukkah bush, just in case he came. And I, like millions of other children around the world, couldn't sleep. I wanted to believe that Santa didn't mind if I was Jewish and that if he saw the lights twinkling in the attic as he flew by, he'd surely stop.

On Christmas morning, while my classmates unwrapped their gifts and then rode their new bikes down the driveway, I sat at the breakfast table, anxious to check on my Hanukkah bush. Grandpa winked at me and touched my hand under the table. We excused ourselves and, like co-conspirators, snuck upstairs.

There was a small box under the Hanukkah bush with a note attached.

Dear Lisa,

Thank you for the delicious cookies. I hope you don't mind that I shared them with some of my elves because we didn't have a chance to eat dinner. How much I loved your Hanukkah bush. It gave me a chance to explain your beautiful holiday to my reindeer and friends. They loved the story of the miracle of lights. You're so lucky you get to celebrate such a special time. I hope you like your gift.

Love, Santa

Like my grandma had hoped, I grew up to be a proud Jewish granddaughter of a proud woman whose heritage I hold close to my heart. But I still have the beautiful pewter ornament that shows a little girl holding her grandfather's hand, and I still believe in the magic of Christmas, too.

— Lisa Leshaw —

32

My Santa

There are three stages of man: he believes in Santa
Claus; he does not believe in Santa Claus;
he is Santa Claus.
~Bob Phillips

I can only imagine the look on my young face as my mother sat me down at the kitchen table to talk to me. I was still quite young, and she looked so serious that I sat down with some trepidation. She leaned down closer to my face as she spoke.

"You know how we see Santa Claus in the mall at Christmastime every year?" I nodded. "Well," she continued, "Santa is very busy at the North Pole getting ready for Christmas and can't visit with everyone, so he has helpers who visit the children for him in the malls and at church. Your daddy is one of Santa's helpers!"

I was confused, trying to grasp what Mom was telling me. For the next several beats, I barely heard her speaking for all that was whirling through my brain. Had she just told me that my daddy was one of Santa's helpers? That he played the role of Santa Claus on the real Santa's behalf? But he was just a man. He was my daddy, who went to work every day and watched the news before he went to bed every night.

When I realized that Mom was still talking to me, I pulled my focus back to her with some effort. Basically, she'd been explaining things in a little more detail, but I had missed most of it as I tried to grasp the reality of it all. It was so cool to think that my daddy was Santa's helper. I was sworn to secrecy, a pretty tall order for a little kid who'd just been given the news of the century, but I kept my promise and didn't tell anyone.

From that point on, I was allowed to watch the transformation of my daddy from "Ordinary Everyday Guy" to "Super Daddy Santa" as my mother skillfully applied the right combination of make-up to give Dad's face that weathered look and make it look like he had just come in from the cold. She used old-fashioned school paste and cotton balls for the eyebrows, and then Dad put on the bearded wig and the costume with just the right pillow. And *voila!* he was Santa Claus. And he was good at it — *really* good at it! He was so good that he'd been doing it for years and I never had a clue it was him! Apparently, though, I made the observation a time or two that Santa walked just like my daddy.

With all the preparations complete, it was time for Santa to do his duty and go visit the children. I remember driving over to my Aunt Pat's and Uncle Ben's house, taking such delight in watching the faces of the people glancing over as our car passed by. For a split second, their eyes would open wide and their mouths would drop open, and then big smiles would light up their faces. When we finally arrived at Aunt Pat's home, my dad would go into the house through the back door while we peered in through the windows, standing in the bushes in the dark of night.

My very small cousins were frozen in a state of awe as they saw Santa coming through the door into their living room. He bent down to talk with each of them, and they answered back. Then, he gave them each a candy cane and left the same way he'd come. Those treasured moments would become lasting memories in the years ahead, not only for the little girls and their parents, but for my dad as well! I was so proud of him.

As I got a little older, I realized that it was the one time each year that Dad could be someone else, someone special and magical. Someone who did more than go to work every day and go to bed after the 11:00 o'clock news each evening. He was always a nice guy, but his experience as Santa was different.

Over time, as an adult, I came to understand and appreciate what being Santa truly meant to my dad so long ago. Children looked at him in awe, and their parents smiled at him in appreciation. For as much as he gave to the children over the years, it meant just as much to him.

Life wasn't especially kind to Dad through the years that followed. Little by little, Santa just faded away. The joyful memories he left behind, however, were imprinted into the hearts of every one of those children.

—Gail E. Bierschbach—

33

Tales of Our Elf on the Shelf

What one loves in childhood stays in the heart forever.
~Mary Jo Putney

"When is the elf coming to our house?" my two-year-old daughter asked. I had no idea what she was referring to.

"Elves don't come to our house, sweetie. They make toys at Santa's workshop."

"Ella said her elf came to her house yesterday and then goes back to Santa at night."

I responded with a platitude like "That's nice" and redirected her attention elsewhere. I thought or rather hoped that was the end of the conversation, but I soon learned I was merely at the beginning.

This was in 2007, when Elf on the Shelf was becoming popular, and I was a naïve parent who thought that the elf was cute in a colorful, see-through box. But looks can be deceiving. The package should contain a large warning label stating:

I may look cute, but I require an immense amount of time and creativity that will last for the next ten years or so. I also come with a lot of specific rules that must be followed. If you are not up for the challenge, take your hands off the box and go buy a stuffed animal that only requires some occasional washing. Trust me, I'm not joking.

However, even if that warning had been posted, let's be honest, I would have bought it anyway because who would believe that a stuffed elf would be more work than caring for a hermit crab or newborn baby?

When my kids first met their elf, like any pet requiring oodles of time and money (yes, money—I'll get to that later), they had to choose a name.

I rattled off some suggestions of boy names that my husband had negated when we were pondering baby names. I was excited that I might finally get the chance to have my favorite name selected.

"How about Gavin, Reese or Aiden?"

They responded the same as their dad did.

"No way!"

After much deliberation, they settled on an extremely creative one: Elfie. Yeah, I wasn't too impressed either. I'm guessing that probably ranks in the top five for elf names.

After the naming ceremony, I was about to remove Elfie from the box only to hear my daughter scream in terror.

"NNNNOOOO, you can't touch him, Mom, or he will lose his magic!"

I wondered how I could create the same rule for my phone.

So, Elfie sat in the box, untouched, waiting to fly back to Santa to report on my children's behaviors.

Now, that sounded good to me—a tattletale elf who held a lot of power in the gift-giving department.

What didn't sound so great and ended up becoming an enormous amount of work (just what I needed during the holiday season) is that the elf needed to be moved every night when I was at my lowest functioning abilities. But not just moved, he needed to be posed in some funny or interesting manner like ziplining across the living room on a candy cane or inside a snowman made of toilet-paper rolls. (You're welcome, if those ideas are new to you.)

And then my kids wanted to buy Elfie accessories like clothes, sleeping bags and cooking utensils. At the beginning of the pandemic, you could even buy your elf a mask, hand sanitizer and toilet paper.

By the time we were done, Elfie had nicer PJs than I did. It was all getting a little out of hand.

Every year, my kids wanted Elfie to return earlier. I would roll my eyes and think of the extra work. But, like most mothers, I did it anyway.

Just like our pet hermit crab, Elfie grew on me over the years despite the extra time commitment. I tried to focus on my kids' excitement when they searched for him instead of how I spent hours scouring the internet for "Elf on the Shelf ideas."

Last year, my older kids barely uttered hello to Elfie, and they didn't dare search for him. It was then that I realized how much I was going to miss the guy when my youngest outgrows him.

I still think he should come with a warning label about the huge time commitment, but I would be willing to add a disclaimer saying, "Okay, I'll admit it. It's totally worth it."

— Cheryl Maguire —

34

Chicken Soup for the Soul

A Visit from Santa Claus

We are better throughout the year for having, in spirit,
become a child again at Christmastime.
~Laura Ingalls Wilder

From the time our granddaughter Olivia was born, we reserved the first Sunday evening in December for Santa. Our families met at the community center in our neighborhood where we enjoyed hot chocolate and Christmas crafts together. At some point during the evening, Santa arrived with a "Ho, ho, ho!" and took his seat on a platform flanked by two festive Christmas trees.

While cellphones snapped pictures, Olivia sat on Santa's lap and shyly whispered in his ear, telling him what she wanted for Christmas. Santa always gave her his complete attention, no matter how many other children waited in line.

The year Olivia turned nine, she was still just as excited about seeing Santa. But that December Sunday morning, her daddy called us. "We're meeting the doctor at the hospital this afternoon. He's going to do the C-section today because of complications."

Olivia's little brother, Daniel, wasn't due until New Year's Day, a month later. Amid excitement over the early arrival of this long-awaited baby and fears about the outcome, everyone forgot about Santa.

At the hospital, Olivia confided to me that she'd had a nightmare that something bad would happen to the baby. I couldn't guarantee that everything would turn out all right. But I tried to divert Olivia's attention by entertaining her with videos and games on my cellphone while we anxiously awaited news. We all breathed prayers of thanks when Daniel checked in at 5:39 p.m., weighing an even six pounds.

Olivia was one of the first to hold him. She came back out to the waiting room and said, "He's the most beautiful little human I've ever seen!"

However, despite his healthy birthweight, Daniel's lungs apparently weren't ready for this out-of-body experience. He began having respiratory issues before the rest of us could see him, and the nurses whisked him off to newborn intensive care. For the next two weeks, Christmas took a back seat as we visited our tiny elf in NICU and prayed for his lungs to mature. In mid-December, Daniel finally came home to a thrilled big sister.

Olivia's focus was on her baby brother, but I knew she was disappointed at not seeing Santa when she mentioned that Daniel was born on the day of the Christmas event. Her momma was disappointed, too, about not getting pictures with Santa, their longstanding tradition. Knowing Santa was busier the closer it got to Christmas, she held out little hope they would be able to see him that year, especially since their family couldn't leave the house with a preemie in tow. But she took a chance by calling the Christmas event leaders and explained the situation.

One evening, a knock sounded at Olivia's front door. When she answered it, there stood Santa, greeting her with a hearty "Ho, ho, ho!"

Olivia just stared at the same jolly elf she recognized from all those years at the community center, resplendent in his red suit and white beard. Her parents invited Santa in, and he again made Olivia feel as if she were the only one in the room. But she was happy to share the attention with her new baby brother, dressed in his own Santa suit. Pictures that year show a minuscule St. Nick and a big sister with a brighter smile than she'd ever worn when sitting on Santa's knee by herself.

A kind act in a busy season made that Christmas special for our family. After the stress and worry of the previous few weeks, a visit from Santa Claus was just what we needed.

— Tracy Crump —

35

Muddy Memories

*Spend Christmas with little children and old people.
One hasn't forgotten the true meaning of the season
and the other still remembers it's about love.*
~Toni Sorenson

Starry-eyed and hopeful are the best ways to describe the wonder I felt as a young boy the night before Christmas. It was really more of a knowing than a feeling. I knew, without question, that something special was about to happen.

It was not the gifts, the bulging stockings or even the surprise of it all. Those things were nice, especially at such a young age. But, as I look back, the memories I cherish most are less tangible. Magical really.

The piney smell of the small yet stoic tree that my mom brought home every year because she felt sorry for it since no one else would ever choose its dwindling needles. Or the look on her face when my dad gave her nothing but a large Rocky Road candy bar, which sat on the kitchen counter for over a week until the urge got the better of her and she unwrapped it — only to find an expensive harmonica that she had always wanted. And my young brother's scream of delight on Christmas morning as we both ran barefoot across a Lego-strewn floor at the sight of new bicycles, banana seats and all, beside the tree. And the smile on my dad's face.

Cookies and milk left beside the fireplace were also part of the equation… as was another very special imprint.

The glory of Christmas is forever etched on my soul — not because of the usual reasons you see in the movies, but for the connection to my parents and brother, all of whom I dearly miss, and the aforementioned memories they created. More importantly, those memories helped me to create more for my children — a special gift my kids can take with them into the future. And I, too, smile.

The night before Christmas brought with it something wonderfully special: the sound of reindeer on the roof! I can still hear them clomping and stomping, at least eight of them from my count, as I lay awake each year listening ever patiently. When would they fly away? Somehow, I always fell asleep before I found out.

The next morning, my brother and I would run, not to see what was under the tree, but to the front door and fling it open. There on the porch, along the front walk, on the car (ironic if you knew my dad and his feelings about said car), and on the side of the house below the kitchen window would be dozens of muddy reindeer prints! It never occurred to me why their muddy prints would be all over the place when they obviously landed on the roof.

As I grew older, I eventually learned the secret to the reindeer prints: a hoof-shaped stamp that my dad would carve from a giant russet potato and "ink" made from mud. It was an imprint for the ages, not just the season. Lastly, he created an elaborate rope, weight and pulley system for the landing area on the roof.

Did this knowledge disenchant me or dampen my magical memories? No, just the opposite. It emboldened me and brought me closer, in heart, to my parents, for they loved my brother and me enough to go to such an extent. Even an ill-shaped, mud-covered spud can be a vessel of love. It is also entirely possible that they got more out of it than my brother and me.

Having learned the recipe for this charming charade, I eventually started my own performance with my kids. Carving a reindeer hoof potato stamp is fairly easy. Easier yet is the muddy ink made from just the right ingredients in the backyard. Just add water. The harder part was thinking like a small herd of reindeer if they were to actually leave an overabundance of muddy prints throughout the front yard. As my wife put the kids to bed, they, too, waited patiently, or impatiently, for the arrival of the reindeer and the man in the red suit. And soon they fell asleep.

The stamping of the front porch was the fun part. The really fun part was the performance of the clomping of the hoofs. We lived in a two-story house. So as not to be too much of a method actor and break my neck, I used the trellis over the back patio as the stage. For a little extra spice, I usually threw in a couple of hearty, deep and lingering ho, ho, hos.

There's a thin line between the unbridled awe and bewilderment young children have and the moment when they "know" and go along with the loving ruse because they, too, want it to last.

One year, as my final performance approached, I carefully carved that year's stamp and began to imprint, both figuratively and literally, the muddy prints. I adorned the porch, driveway, front door, garage door, cars and sidewalk. Knowing it might be my last performance, I had made up an extra-large batch of muddy ink. The front of our house looked more like a herd of three dozen reindeer had visited rather than just eight.

It was late and dark, but there was still mud left over.

Louise, a neighbor across the street, had recently become a single mom with two small kids of her own. Of course, I thought I might as well vandalize her property too and share the gift, albeit with a muddy mess. I stooped down on her porch and began eagerly stamping the potato and flinging mud all around. And then the front door opened. Looking down, startled and flabbergasted as to what I might be doing, a smile of recognition slowly dawned on her face, and she quietly closed the door.

An imprint, paid forward like ripples in a pond, a muddy one at that. The spirit of Christmas worked through me as though I was an apparition of St. Nick, and I realized that he really does exist. Maybe not in the way I understood him as a young boy, but in a heart-centered, keep-the-torch-burning sort of way.

They say a picture is worth a thousand words. A print, even if made from a potato, after all, is just that… more powerful than words. Half-eaten cookies and an empty glass of milk were evidence of Santa's arrival, but muddy prints from his reindeer, never questioned, were proof that something magical had taken place.

Someday, my kids will remember those performances — among many others — and impart their own creativity on their own families. They will call upon these memories with fond recollection and make more of their own. And they, too, will smile.

It wasn't until years later that I realized how powerful acts of love, kindness and giving are when packaged in more abstract ways. A hug, a kiss, and a kind word or two are the oxygen of life, but the little, unorthodox things that show love in other ways are often what stay with us forever… even if imprinted with a muddy potato.

— Stan Holden —

Chapter 5

Best Gift Ever

36

Chicken Soup for the Soul

Patching Myself Back Together

For it is in giving that we receive.
~Saint Francis

I t was 2:00 a.m., and I couldn't sleep. Since the divorce, I had lain in bed every night thinking of all the things that could go wrong for my boys and me. To ease my insomnia, I tried taking over-the-counter and prescription pills, exercising in the morning, and then in the evening. I tried limiting my screen time after 8:00 p.m., cutting out caffeine, and doing meditation. Nothing worked.

I talked about it with my therapist. She said that there was no mystery about what was wrong. My ex-husband had spent a substantial part of the last five years of our thirteen-year marriage telling me I was worthless. Now, I was trying to take care of three little boys and put my life back together, and I had no faith that I could do it. Knowing what was wrong didn't change anything.

My therapist suggested that whenever I couldn't sleep, I needed to get out of bed and do something, anything, until I was tired. It had to be an actual activity, something routine that I could do to take my mind off whatever thoughts were racing through my mind.

I thought the idea was stupid, but I was exhausted and didn't have anything to lose. The next night, when I couldn't sleep, I got out of bed and grabbed some cleaning supplies. Within a couple of days, our very small home was spotless, and I still wasn't sleeping. I decided my next insomnia project would be unpacking the final moving boxes. I hadn't yet gone through my boxes of fabric.

I had been an avid sewer my whole life, and like everyone who sews, I kept every little scrap of fabric thinking that I could use it for the next project. Almost every project produces leftover scraps. My ex-husband always had a problem with my sewing. Nothing I ever made met his standards, and he would sneer when I didn't complete some of my projects. It was just another example of how I was a failure, at least that's what he said.

At first, I laughed off his comments. Everyone, especially crafters, has projects that they never finish. Everyone who sews keeps fabric scraps. My grandmother had a trunk of them at our house when we were growing up. Whenever the trunk got too full, we would go searching for fabric pieces in the right shape and color to make a patchwork quilt. Grandma called it "rooting." But, eventually, a little part of me started believing my husband.

I didn't have room to store all the fabric, but I couldn't bear to throw it away either. The next Saturday, I made my way to the craft store. There, among all the quilting supplies, I found a plastic template for a four-inch square. I had never made a quilt by myself. I decided to start with a nine-patch quilt, which was my grandma's favorite. She loved the pattern and always said it used up a lot of scraps.

The next sleepless night, I opened a box of fabric scraps and took out my brand-new template, a marker, and sharp scissors. I laid out the scraps and tried to cut as many blocks as I could from each piece. I stacked the little blocks in a box. Night after night, the stack of blocks grew.

As I cut the pieces, I remembered the project and people that went along with them. There were scraps from a black pencil skirt I had made in high school. There were pieces left over from the gingham curtains I had sewn for my first house. There were scraps of orange material from when I had the boys dress up like pumpkins for Halloween, and then grays and blacks from the multiple years my son had wanted to be Batman. There was pink material from a pillow I had made my niece.

Each piece came with a happy memory. Taking all the scraps and making them into something else was not at all sad, and it gave me purpose, too.

After several weeks, my boxes were overflowing with neatly cut blocks in all different colors. I got out my sewing machine and started turning the individual blocks into larger pieced blocks. It wasn't long before I was sewing them together into a quilt.

The stitches weren't perfect, but I refused to let that bother me. I just kept "rooting" through my boxes, cutting blocks and piecing them together into quilts. Eventually, those sleepless nights and project scraps amounted to over thirty quilts. I started sleeping better, and I worked on the quilts during the evenings and weekends. I had forgotten how much I loved to sew.

Christmas was coming, and money was scarce. I had always managed to give presents to everyone, though, and I hated to miss a year. So, I wrapped up my quilts and decorated the packages with ribbon a bit nervously. These were scrap quilts, so all the colors and the textures weren't perfectly matched, and my sewing wasn't perfect either.

I handed out the packages to all my nieces, nephews, and siblings after Christmas dinner. Every couple got a full-size quilt, and there were smaller ones for my nieces and nephews. For someone who had been told that they couldn't finish a project, watching thirty quilts get unwrapped on Christmas Day was an amazingly positive moment.

My oldest brother's wife, Connie, waved me over amid the chatter. She was running her hand over a piece of fabric in the quilt I had given them. I realized it was a leftover from a pillow I had made her daughter, Nicole, when she was a baby, and I was in high school.

"Where did you get all this fabric?" she asked.

I gulped.

Should I tell everyone that I had made their presents out of scraps from leftover projects?

I heard my ex-husband's voice in my head telling me that I was a failure.

For a minute, I couldn't say anything.

"You saved all this from all those years?" she asked, although she already knew the answer.

I nodded.

"It's like you gave us all parts of your life," she said with a smile. "I have no idea how you found the time, but what a wonderful gift."

I gave her the biggest hug.

I sleep better these days. I still see my quilts around, years later. They appear at baseball games, hayrides and camping trips. One has even been immortalized in my niece's engagement pictures.

My family still talks about that Christmas when I made everyone a patchwork quilt, and I remember regaining my sanity and my self-confidence one scrap of fabric at a time.

— Theresa Brandt —

37

Up in Smoke

A secret remains a secret until you make someone
promise never to reveal it.
~Fausto Cercignani

O n Christmas Eve, my brother-in-law had a sudden hankering for grilled pork chops. He trudged outside to fire up the grill and discovered an empty propane tank. He didn't really want to drive on the snow-covered roads that cold evening to fill it up, but he sure did want those pork chops.

So, he rushed inside, grabbed the keys and called out to his wife. "I'm going to the hardware store to fill up the propane tank!"

My sister hurried over, trying to act nonchalant. "It's really cold outside. Why don't you just wait until after Christmas?"

My brother-in-law was already heading toward the door. "No, I'm really craving pork chops."

Her heart dropped. She had saved money far too long for the surprise to be blown one day before Christmas. "Which hardware store are you going to?"

"I'll just go to Lowe's," he replied.

Whew. My sister relaxed and went back to making cinnamon rolls. Halfway through the recipe, she paused. She raised a brow. He wouldn't change his mind and go to the local Do it Best center, would he? For many years, her husband had dreamed of having his very own Traeger smoker. She had saved and saved, and this year went down to the store and purchased one.

"We'll order it, keep it at the store, assemble it and drop it off on the day after Christmas," the helpful salesperson had promised. "No charge!"

Perfect! My sister couldn't wait to see her husband's face when he realized he was getting that smoker.

My sister returned to her baking, not too worried. After all, even if her husband went to the local hardware store instead of Lowe's, why would he stumble upon the secret gift?

Meanwhile, en route to Lowe's, my brother-in-law's plans changed. Why not just head to Do it Best? It was a lot closer. Arriving there, he found out that the refilling tank had frozen.

"It will take about fifteen minutes to unfreeze it," said an employee. "Have any other shopping to do?"

My brother-in-law shrugged. Why not? He decided to wander through the store. As always, his steps led him to the smokers and grills. Right away, a tag on one smoker caught his eye. In big, bold letters it said: REBEKAH. Hmmm. That was the same way his wife spelled her name — and it was unusual. He leaned in closer. Under the name was a phone number.

His eyes grew big. He slapped a hand over his mouth. "No way!"

Jubilant about his Christmas gift, my brother-in-law snapped photos of the smoker with the tag. He forwarded it to his brother and best friend with a message: "Guess who's getting a smoker for Christmas!" The manager of the store ambled over and smiled. "Help you with something? Deciding which smoker to purchase?"

My brother-in-law turned, still not quite sure. "I think my wife already did."

A puzzled expression crossed the man's face. "What?"

He pointed to the tag. "That's my wife's name. And that's her phone number!"

Mortified, the manager's face paled. "Oh, no! I've been here ten years, and this has never happened. I'm so sorry. What are the odds?"

On the way home, my brother-in-law debated. Should he admit to finding out about the present? He decided to wait. He didn't want to disappoint his daughter. She was likely in on the gift, too.

On Christmas morning, he unwrapped a box that included wood pellets, seasonings and a picture of the smoker that said: "To be delivered on 12/26." His true excitement about the gift helped him feign surprise. But after the presents were unwrapped, and his daughter was upstairs, he pulled his wife aside.

"No way!" she exclaimed when he 'fessed up. "What are the odds of that?!"

They laughed all day — and especially the next day while eating pork chops cooked perfectly on their Christmas smoker.

— Lisa Mackinder —

38

Joke's on You, Dear

*I love Christmas. I receive a lot of wonderful presents
I can't wait to exchange.*
~Henny Youngman

My husband, Charlie, is not a great gifter. There have been many gifting mishaps over the years. From itchy clothing that's the wrong size to books I already have, it's all happened. One year, however, sticks out as the funniest in my memory.

That year, we had agreed to budget a certain amount for each of us to spend on one another while the largest chunk would be spent on the children in our lives. I took my part of the budget and got my husband five or six gifts that I knew he'd love because they were all based on his interests. To my utter shock, my husband had only one very large box for me.

Now, I gave him the benefit of the doubt. I wondered if it was one box containing several different things. Or maybe it would contain something very small. My imagination ran wild with what could be in that box.

On Christmas morning, we watched our son rip into his gifts with glee. He was so thrilled. Then came my husband's turn. He opened each gift, and, as he did, he got more and more sweaty. He thanked me profusely and said, "Wow, it's all my favorite things!" And I said, "Well, of course. I love you, and I pay attention." He began to fidget.

"Your turn, babe," he said. He hauled the large box to the center of the room.

I started to pick at the wrapping paper, while Charlie nervously ran his hands on his pants. When the paper was off, I laughed. It was a box for a hardwood-floor buffer!

"Well, hand me some scissors. I want to see what's inside!" I said. I reached out my hand, laughing.

My husband rubbed his head. "It's a hardwood-floor buffer."

"Now, quit playing, honey. What's in the box?" I asked, still thinking it was a joke.

Charlie looked at me like I had lost my marbles. It was then I realized he really had bought me a hardwood floor buffer. It was my only gift. My husband had used his entire gift budget on one item, and it was not really for me but for the home. It was a reminder that I did the cleaning as a stay-at-home mom. I was extremely disappointed, but, at the same time, I couldn't stop laughing.

"Well, I hope you saved the receipt!" I cackled.

"I'm so sorry this was a bad gift," Charlie said.

I laughed that much harder. Tears came to my eyes, and I nearly fell over. My son, William, smacked his dad on the leg.

"Daddy, I told you that you should have gotten her the K-Cup machine and the 'Best Mom' cup!" He looked at me. "You broke Mommy, Dad."

Charlie was visibly confused. So, I figured it was time to let him in on the joke.

"Honey… what is this thing again?" I sputtered between giggles.

"A hardwood-floor buffer. The lady at the store said it's the best one and that she loves hers," he explained.

I laughed again. His face started to turn red.

"I'm sure she does — but, honey, it won't work for me!" I snickered.

He tapped his foot. "Why not?"

"Because we have carpet all through the house!"

Now, in the years following the hardwood-floor buffer incident, my husband has become a better gifter (with the help of his son,

William). But, every year, I ask him if he got me a hardwood-floor buffer. He doesn't think it's funny, but I think it's my favorite Christmas gift-giving disaster.

— Brittany Perry —

39

A New York City Noel

Traveling — it leaves you speechless,
then turns you into a storyteller.
~Ibn Battuta

At some point during a casual conversation, it had made the travel wish list. Of all the places we wanted to go to, visiting New York City during the holidays was at the top of the list. I dreamt of visiting iconic places like the Empire State Building and the Statue of Liberty, and seeing the tree at Rockefeller Center in person, not just in a Christmas movie.

Finally, on a chilly afternoon in early December, our plane touched down at LaGuardia Airport, and the months of planning and dreaming were finally over. We were in New York City — at Christmastime!

My husband and I found our ride and loaded our luggage and ourselves in the vehicle, soaking in the sights of the city as we crossed the bridge from Queens into Manhattan. We checked into our hotel and then set out on foot in Midtown Manhattan. The city was dazzling, all lit up for Christmas. The festive lights of Fifth Avenue sparkled on the buildings and reflected off the windows of the passing yellow cabs as they whizzed by us on the crowded streets.

We stopped by Dylan's Candy Bar and then Serendipity 3 to taste their famous frozen hot chocolate topped with whipped cream. Stepping back into the chilly night, we walked toward St. Patrick's Cathedral. The peaceful serenity inside the church, with its gothic arches, stained-glass windows, and flickering candlelight, stood in stark contrast to the hustle and bustle of the city that never sleeps. I lit a candle and said a prayer, thankful to be in such a beautiful and majestic place.

The next morning, we took the subway to the Empire State Building. In the queuing area, famous movie scenes played out before us, reminding us of the myriad pop-culture references surrounding this iconic building — as if we could ever forget. Everywhere we looked felt like a scene from a movie — *King Kong*, *An Affair to Remember*, *Sleepless in Seattle*, and even *Elf* — were all centered around this epic skyscraper. After taking the art deco elevators to the 86th floor, we stepped onto the windy observation deck, squinting against the sun, to see amazing views of the city below. The towering Empire State Building cast a long shadow across the urban landscape beneath it. And, just off in the distance, I could see Lady Liberty standing proudly in New York Harbor.

Our next stop was Macy's on 34th Street, the location of the classic Christmas movie, *Miracle on 34th Street*. The holiday window displays were fun and festive. Mounted high above the entrance to Macy's, in sparkling white lights, was the word *Believe*. In front of the store, the Salvation Army bell ringer danced to Christmas music, enthusiastically ringing his bell as passersby dropped coins into his red bucket. His Christmas spirit was contagious.

We entered the store and made our way up the escalators to our destination. Finding Santaland, we two forty-something-year-old adults unashamedly stood in line to meet Santa Claus. When our big moment finally arrived, a worker dressed like an elf directed us to meet him. We felt like kids again, chatting it up with Kris Kringle at the Macy's on 34th Street in New York City! Our elf took photos to commemorate the occasion.

Later that day, we took the subway to Ground Zero where we paid our respects to those who had died on September 11th. We walked on the Brooklyn Bridge, grabbed a slice of Ray's Pizza in Times Square, and saw a Broadway show. We were exhausted but happy after a long day of sightseeing.

The next day, I finally saw one of the sights I had been most looking forward to on this trip: the tree in Rockefeller Center. Rows of angels, each holding golden trumpets, flanked the massive tree, which was sparkling with multi-colored lights and topped with a blazing star. Skaters bundled up in coats and hats glided across the ice, creating the perfect holiday atmosphere. It seemed surreal that I was actually seeing the tree in Rockefeller Center in person. This wasn't a Christmas movie; it was real life!

During our four days in New York, we crammed in as much as possible. We toured Madison Square Garden and saw the Knicks play. We boarded a boat to Liberty Island and saw the Statue of Liberty. We ate delicious food in Bryant Park, where we watched more skaters glide across the ice while Bing Crosby serenaded us with classic Christmas songs through the speakers. We ate at The Russian Tea Room, caught a glimpse of a *Saturday Night Live* rehearsal during our NBC tour, and went to the Top of the Rock to enjoy spectacular nighttime views of the city. The air itself was filled with excitement and a pulsating energy that cannot be fully articulated with words, only felt and experienced. It truly was a dream come true to be in New York City at Christmastime.

As we boarded the plane to head home, I thought back on our magical trip to New York. This long-anticipated holiday trip could finally be checked off our travel wish list. We had finally done it, and it had been truly wonderful. I remembered what Santa Claus at the Macy's on 34th Street had said to us.

With a twinkle in his eye, he had asked, "What do you want for Christmas this year?"

We looked at each other and smiled, both thinking the same thing.

We had already received the gift we most wanted that Christmas—a trip to New York City with each other.

— Suzannah Kiper —

Instant Gratitude

*It's not what's under the Christmas tree that matters
but who's around it.*
~Charlie Brown, A Charlie Brown Christmas

Recently, I ran across an ad online for a used Suzy Homemaker vintage oven for sale. The aquamarine plastic oven by Topper was selling for $149.60. In 1966, this toy debuted as a competitor of the Easy-Bake Oven, America's first working toy oven, which used a light bulb as its source of heat. At that time, the toy sold for a hefty $15.95.

As an eight-year-old girl, there was nothing I wanted more. I envisioned myself baking cakes and other treats with my little oven and surprising my family with homemade delectables. On a visit to Grandma's house, I found her Sears catalog, turned to the toy section and found a picture of the oven. I pulled out the page, folded it several times, and took it home in the pocket of my dress.

I showed the picture to my mother and told her about my plans to help the family by making lovely baked goods. She looked at the picture and then the price, and her interested look turned sad. She told me that we couldn't afford such an extravagant gift. I told her I would have Santa bring it, but she cautioned that Santa probably had many little girls who wanted the Suzy Homemaker oven, and he might not have enough for everyone who wanted one.

I wasn't too worried about Santa running out of stock. I hung the catalog picture on the refrigerator and joyfully counted the days until I would be able to see Santa. After my visit, I sent him a letter to make sure he wouldn't forget my oven. I was so excited about the Suzy Homemaker oven that I didn't ask Santa or my parents for any other gifts.

Soon, it was Christmas Eve, and I couldn't sleep because I was so excited to finally get my Suzy Homemaker oven. I wondered if Santa was in our neighborhood yet. When morning came I jumped out of bed, threw on my robe, made sure my parents were awake, and ran to our tiny Christmas tree that was perched on a table. I quickly opened my smaller presents: white socks with ruffles on them, a jump rope, pink mittens, and a Candy Land game.

And then I saw the box. "That must be it!" I said to myself. "That must be my Suzy Homemaker oven!" It was smaller than it looked on TV, but I couldn't wait to open it. My mom handed me the box and said she hoped I liked what was inside. I said that I knew I would as I tore off the colorful comic-page newspaper she used for wrapping.

I knew my mom and dad were watching me, so I tried to hide my disappointment as I saw that my gift was not a Suzy Homemaker oven at all; instead, it was one of my dad's shoeboxes. I opened the lid and looked inside. There was a bag of unpopped Jolly Time popcorn, a box of cherry Jell-O, a Jiffy blueberry muffin mix, and a box of instant chocolate pudding mix. There was a note from my mom saying that she would help me to make these items and also teach me how to make her lemon shortbread Christmas cookies.

At that moment, I forgot about the little aquamarine plastic oven and began to make plans. "Mama, can I make the Jell-O soon so it will be ready by lunch? And when can we bake the cookies?" My mother's face lit up as she said that we could get to work right away.

I thought about how silly I was to want something so badly one moment and not care about it at all the next. I guess Santa did run out of stock, and I hoped the other little girls loved their Suzy Homemaker ovens, but I really didn't miss mine at all.

— Laura McKenzie —

41

Stupid Old Bat House

Laughter is the language of the soul.
~Pablo Neruda

The wind howled around the house, and the gray sky added to the feeling that a winter storm was brewing. My mother lit the candles on the table already laden with trays of meat, cheese, crackers, and other snacks. "I wish your father would get home," she said.

Dad wasn't home yet for our Christmas Eve celebration. He loved to shop for our gifts at the last minute, often presenting them to us with no more wrapping than the shopping bag from the store.

Just then, the front door opened. "I'm home!" Dad burst in, loaded down with shopping bags. "Are we ready to celebrate?"

Anticipation mounted as he placed the bags in a corner before ambling over to snatch a bite from the table.

"It's all ready if you want to ask a blessing," Mom scolded, although she wore a smile.

After the food was blessed, my sister and I loaded our plates and made our way to the living room. Mom and Dad followed. As we snacked, we visited about the day, and then Dad read the Christmas story from the gospel of Luke.

"Everyone ready to open gifts?" His grin grew in a way that could only mean he had a fun surprise planned. He rose to grab his bags from the corner, handing them out with joy.

Everyone took turns opening their gifts. When Mom opened

hers, she looked puzzled. It was a piece of wood with a shallow box attached to it. It had a space at the bottom, as if made for something to enter it. It was far too small for most birds.

"What is it?"

"A bat house," Dad stood in front of her, grinning from ear-to-ear, "to keep down the mosquitos in the summer."

"You got me a stupid old bat house?" Her voice was filled with indignation.

Everyone stilled.

Then, a burst of laughter erupted from Dad. Mom's face slowly reddened. She'd let the first thing that came to her mind slip out. As she worked to recover her composure, he pulled his coat back on. He left through the front door without a word. When he reentered, he cradled a beautiful, wood bird feeder.

Mom's face glowed, both from joy and embarrassment.

On Christmas morning, I went downstairs to find her putting cinnamon rolls in the oven. As she turned, a beautiful pair of diamond earrings caught the light. When I commented, she blushed. She'd found them under her pillow.

Every Christmas, we'd laugh about the "stupid old bat house." It hung along a path near the creek, with signs of a thriving bat community calling it home. Just like our Heavenly Father, Dad really did know how to give the best gifts. We just didn't always recognize them at first glance.

— Wendy Klopfenstein —

42

A True Gift from the Heart

*Gratitude is the music of the heart, when its chords
are swept by the breeze of kindness.*
~Author Unknown

My husband Lee and I met in late 1983 through a personal ad I placed in a local San Francisco paper. Our first meeting was a blind date following a long phone conversation. We sat in a coffee shop and talked for hours. We were among the lucky ones, able to see eye-to-eye on almost everything: politics, religion, art, dogs, children. Quickly, a romantic relationship ensued. We lived happily for the most part until, in 2016, in his early seventies, Lee was diagnosed with Alzheimer's disease.

In addition, he had an ailment called spinal stenosis that rendered him unable to move his back and legs. It's a condition that squeezes the spine. Adding to this litany of horrors, he also had severe edema that involves a thickening of the ankles. To top it all off, he was incontinent.

My life became a nightmare as I scrambled to secure healthcare in the form of caregivers for my beloved husband of thirty-seven years. With the assistance of the VA, we secured six hours a day of professional help and three days a week of free adult daycare, which got him out of the house among other people for several hours each week.

In 2020, the pandemic brought all services to a halt. Adult daycare shut down, as well as respite care for the VA, which was like a vacation hotel for incapacitated veterans. The respite had enabled me to live like a normal human being for a week several times a year. Then, all of a sudden, Lee was home 24/7.

By Christmas week, I felt like I was losing my mind. My husband was uncooperative with the caregiver and had many accidents that had to be cleaned up. It became harder and harder to get him up and out of bed. And during the eighteen hours without professional help, I felt like my sanity was on the line.

It hurt bitterly to overhear a conversation between Lee and my older son, Brad, when Lee expressed how much he wanted to go out and buy me a gift like he used to.

"Don't worry. Maybe I can come up with something," Brad said, assuring Lee. But Brad finding something turned out to be unnecessary thanks to a new worker who came into our lives.

The week before Christmas, I hired a new worker who was younger than the rest. The woman had boundless energy and delighted in wheeling Lee a mile and a half to the nearest market.

One day, I watched her push him in the chair at her usual brisk pace as if he didn't weigh 190 pounds. Shaking my head and marveling at her energy, I settled down at my computer for a brief spurt of writing and awaited their return.

They were gone about an hour and a half, and when they returned, Lee was sitting up in his chair proudly holding four indigo blue bowls.

"It's a miracle we found these," the caregiver said.

"They were just the right gift for you," Lee said. "Blue is your favorite color, right?"

"Yes, I love blue," I responded, my eyes filling with tears.

It turned out the bowls had been left on the street because two of them were chipped, and therefore the set was unwanted.

But this amazing husband of mine remembered that blue was my favorite color. So, he asked his caregiver to set them in his lap and brought them carefully home to me.

Brad helped Lee wrap the bowls in bright blue paper before officially giving them to me on Christmas Day.

I still own those bowls to this day, two years after his death. They were the best Christmas gift I ever received.

— Lynn Sunday —

43

Box of Balloons

*If we experienced life through the eyes of a child,
everything would be magical and extraordinary.
Let our curiosity, adventure and
wonder of life never end.*
~Akiane Kramarik

One of the best gifts I ever received is also one of my favorite memories. When I was about three or four years old, all the little kids in my family got to unwrap a giant box of balloons.

We were overjoyed. Colorful balloons fell to the ground everywhere. My grandparents smiled. All my aunts and uncles laughed, and my parents were happy.

It is still one of the warmest memories of my life. My heart leaps just thinking about it.

When I became a mother, I wanted to give my children that kind of memory. I also wanted them to appreciate gifts like that — simple and inexpensive yet meaningful and filled with joy.

So, when my eldest daughters were five and three, I saved the biggest box I could get. I blew up so many balloons that my mouth went numb. And when it came to wrapping everything, I spent hours fighting with wrapping paper, ribbon, and tape to make it look perfect. But, when I finished, I knew my girls would have the time of their life.

When they raced to the tree and saw that present, their eyes shimmered. Their cheeks glowed. "You have to open that one last," I said. It was hilarious watching them open all the other presents. They really tried to mind their manners and were happy with the other gifts, but the time finally came to open the grand finale, and they ripped at my perfect packaging like wild hyenas.

Then, they opened the box and shrieked with joy. My eldest jumped in and sent balloons rushing everywhere in a rainbow of trapped air. My three-year-old attempted to climb in and dangled from the side.

Before I could help her, my eldest rushed to her aid. She walked her up the couch and pulled her in. Together, they swam in sheer joy. My living room housed that box of balloons for six months. It was like heaven. On bad days, we knew the balloons were waiting to make us laugh. Over time, they slowly lost air, but I replaced a few along the way just to prolong the magic.

That Christmas, my mom shared a secret with me. My favorite memory wasn't my gift. She laughed when I told her I was giving the girls a box of balloons like she and her side of the family gave to us children. She sat back and laughed.

Then, she leaned forward with a grin. "That was your uncle's present."

I cocked my head at her. "Why would anyone give a grown man a box of balloons?"

She laughed. "Mom and Dad got him a new fridge and put the manual in the box to trick him. It was your aunt's idea to fill the box with balloons as a prank."

"So that wasn't for us?" I asked.

My mom shook her head, but I just shrugged. "Well, it is still one of the best gifts I ever had. Unintentional or not."

"And now it's the best your girls have had," my mom added.

I now have three more children, and they're the perfect ages to enjoy a box of balloons. Their older sisters can't wait to help me get everything ready so we can swim in the joy of this silly, simple, and inexpensive gift. It has become a family tradition.

—Jessica Marie Baumgartner—

44

Chicken Soup for the Soul

I Love You

Inventing a toy isn't just about creating a plaything. It's
about giving birth to joy, laughter, and wonder.
~Patricia Kislevitz, co-creator of Colorforms

I still have the photograph that captured the moment — wrapping paper on the ground and my arms in the air, jubilant. I had received the gift I wanted most for Christmas!

It was a walking, talking robot. For 1992, it was a technological marvel. In my eight-year-old heart, it was the coolest thing ever created. His name was My Pal 2, and he had blue eyes like me and wore a red baseball hat. A basketball hoop came out of his belly, and a horseshoe stand popped out of his head. Whenever you scored a bucket or tossed a ring around the stand, you heard applause.

He could throw a baseball at warp speed and had a special button called "Guard Dog" mode. When you placed him next to your bedroom door, and the door moved, the robot started barking like a dog to scare off intruders. His nose also served as a flashlight. He had plastic pockets you could store money in and a tickle button on the side that made him laugh out loud. Other buttons enabled you to play the memory game or Simon Says. He wore the coolest royal blue and white tennis shoes with wheels on the bottom, allowing him to move around with ease, and his animatronic eyes and mouth moved while he talked to you.

Just as I'd heard in the commercial, he could say, "You're my best friend" and "Want to play?" For a young boy, what could be better?

But one of the phrases they didn't advertise was that My Pal 2 also said, "I love you."

The first time I heard my robot say "I love you" was the first time anyone had ever said that to me. For some reason, my family never spoke the words, "I love you." Hearing my robot say it gave me something I didn't know I needed. After a while, as I grew up, the excitement of the fast-pitch baseball arm or the applause lights and sounds from shooting the ball in his hoop wore off, but one function seemed to gain appeal.

I needed to hear those words. Not only did my family not speak them, but being an autistic child, making friends was nearly impossible. I was lonely and sad, and felt the stinging darts of rejection every time I left my front door. But every day when I entered my bedroom, even through high school and college, I would press the talking button of his heart and wait for those two phrases: "You're my best friend" and "I love you."

Even though they refer to it as "high-functioning autism," all that means is you can do the tasks of life without the bonds of friendships that make life full. I describe living with autism as playing a board game where everyone else knows the rules except you. People get frustrated by your moves, and you get frustrated trying to figure out what you're supposed to be doing but never seem to find the clues to the right way, and soon people don't want to play with you.

Luckily for me, my robot did. He told me every time I turned on his power button that I was his best friend — and, often, he was my only friend.

It's been thirty-two years since I unwrapped My Pal 2. I'm a teacher now, and autism is more abundant with children than ever. At the end of class every day, right before the bell rings, I tell my students the same phrase: "I love you big, giant, much!" Often, former students in the upper grades will pop in my class just before the bell rings and say quietly, "I really needed to hear someone tell me they loved me."

And my heart will grow because they don't know that I really needed to hear it too when I was a kid. I still need to hear it now. On my desk sits a robot with cool royal blue (my favorite color) tennis shoes with wheels that match his blue eyes, and on those tough days before I head home, I'll press the button on his heart. He still speaks, although I've had to replace his batteries quite a few times over the decades.

Right next to him is the framed photograph of a young Steve Schultz filled with joy, and unseen sadness, crouched down next to a Christmas tree, who had no idea the profound gift he was about to open.

And every so often, a student will see the robot and ask, "What's that?" And I say, "He's my best friend… and my favorite Christmas morning surprise." I'll press the heart button and watch my students smile as My Pal 2's nose lights up, and his eyes and mouth move as he speaks the three words that Christmas is all about: "I love you."

— Steven Andrew Schultz —

A Sister for Christmas

A sister is a gift to the heart, a friend to the spirit, a
golden thread to the meaning of life.
~Isadora James

My eight-year-old son Luke and I were sprawled on the living room floor. We were searching through what seemed like an endless pile of advertisements. It was time to make our annual Christmas wish list.

Luke was scrutinizing Nintendo 64 games and Nerf guns when he suddenly looked up at me. "What was the best present you ever received, Mom?"

I began reminiscing about the many magical moments when I had received a much-desired object. I could easily recall my parents surprising me with roller-derby skates. When I was a teen, my brother and his wife gave me the pottery wheel I'd dreamt of. There were many special presents, but one in particular stood out.

It was a week until Christmas. I was in fifth grade. Annie was my best friend. She had clear skin, a great laugh, and was always up for an adventure.

I lived above a store located on the main street in town. Our side of the city with the highway cutting through it was composed of working-class people. Our parents were employed as janitors, deliverymen, and bakers like my father. Many families received public assistance.

I was the youngest and the only girl. My father would wrestle with my brothers. My brothers would have contests to see who could hit the ball the farthest. I participated but longed for a sister to do some things my brothers wouldn't want to do.

It was with great excitement that I received the news that Annie would be living with us for a while. Her dad, who had battled alcoholism, had lost his job. He was headed into rehabilitation. Her mom could not afford the rent without his check.

She searched for safe havens to place her children. The plan was that Annie would stay with us; her younger sister would stay with her best friend. Her mom would be bringing the youngest sister and her brother to her mother's. As soon as she could find an apartment, she'd return for the two older girls.

Annie arrived the next day. Her mother always struck me as odd. Her hair was pulled back harshly. Her body was pudgy. She was always dressed poorly.

It wasn't just her physical appearance that repelled me. She talked very little. I was accustomed to my mom always explaining life to me.

Annie's mom only spoke when it was absolutely necessary. She would mutter short phrases like "Let's get going" or "We are gonna go eat now." She never teased or told jokes. Many times, she appeared to be far away, and she always fiddled with two long knitting needles.

But a desperate time for my friend's family was a joy for me. Having Annie around was like having a sister, one whom I liked. We stayed up late sharing secrets. We played records on my portable turntable. We laughed for hours and window-shopped the fancy stores as we snacked on Loft's ice cream.

For a while, Annie supplied my much-needed female bonding. Then, the inevitable occurred. Annie's mom returned for her. She had found a low-rent apartment in a neighboring town. Annie would be leaving in two days.

That night, I pleaded with my mom. I didn't want Annie to leave. I didn't think she should go. Her mom was so weird and always fussing with those stupid balls of yarn.

My mom assured me that Annie would be fine. She tried to explain that Annie's mom was a good lady who had just fallen on hard times. Her knitting was the way she kept calm.

On the Sunday when Annie was supposed to leave, her mom offered to take us all to the 10:45 morning Mass. She climbed up our three flights of stairs with her other children behind her. She lugged a big, green garbage bag.

It's probably a dead body, I thought to myself.

"Are y'all ready?" she asked in her barely audible voice. We nodded. She turned to my mom and simply whispered, "Thank you."

"Oh, it's the least we can do," my mom responded pleasantly. "You have become like family."

"I have something for you," Annie's mom said to Annie as she reached into the bag. She pulled out a well-crafted, colorful poncho.

Annie squealed with delight. She immediately slipped on the garment. Her mom handed out the identical garb to each of her other daughters. They were equally enthralled.

I felt my bond with Annie begin to disintegrate. I'd never felt as alone as I did that day watching the three sisters with their clothing uniting them. Then, Annie's mom turned to me. "Here is yours," she mumbled.

Our eyes met. I couldn't believe it. Even with all her troubles weighing her down, Annie's mother had still remembered the feelings of a scrawny, eleven-year-old kid. She had taken the time and money to knit me a poncho, too. I had misjudged her profoundly.

I will never forget that day as we walked to church together. I had received more than a poncho. I received the best gift ever that year. My eyes had been awakened to what was really important at Christmas, and it didn't come from a newspaper advertisement.

— Patricia Senkiw-Rudowsky —

46

Chicken Soup for the Soul

The Box

A wise lover values not so much the gift
of the lover as the love of the giver.
~Thomas á Kempis

I met Dan on a dating app. I was excited to get to know him, and we spent hours talking on the phone, learning about one another. I shared with him that I was in the process of finishing seminary. When I graduated, I dreamt of writing a novel based on stories from the Bible. I even mentioned my favorite biblical fiction author whose work I admired. Dan told me about his love of woodworking, which included creating furniture with his hands.

As our relationship progressed and Christmas drew near, Dan became excited about the gift he had planned for me. We hadn't been dating all that long, and I was at a loss as to what to get him, but he seemed to know exactly what he would be getting me. Gift-giving had never been my strong suit, so when he mentioned a woodworking book he wanted, I ordered it right away.

We exchanged gifts the day before Christmas. He thanked me for his book, and I couldn't help but feel pleased when his face lit up as he read my heartfelt inscription.

When Dan handed me my gift, I was surprised by how heavy it was. As I carefully removed it from the wrapping, I saw that it was a large wooden box. Dan quickly explained that he had handcrafted the box for me. My first thought was that it was a sweet gesture for him to gift me some of his own work, but he assured me that wasn't all of it and told me to look inside.

A book was tucked neatly inside along with several sheets of paper. I immediately recognized the name on the book's cover. Dan had remembered the name of the Christian writer I loved. Not only did he order her most recent book, but he contacted her publishing house and corresponded with her publicist to secure me a signed copy. He printed out all the e-mails between himself and Tyndale, the publisher, and placed them in the box. There was even an additional placard signed by the author to do with as I pleased. I scanned the pages of his e-mails and was so incredibly touched by all the trouble he had gone to.

But then came the biggest surprise of all…

"I made the box to exact specifications," Dan said proudly. "It has a special purpose."

I looked over the box as he explained. "It is your manuscript box. When you finish your first book, your manuscript will fit perfectly inside."

Dan had measured the paper I printed my stories on and crafted a box that would hold my very first novel. He remembered my favorite author's name — the one I told him I hoped to emulate someday — and included her in my manuscript box.

It is one of the top two most thoughtful Christmas gifts I have ever received, and Dan is the giver of both. This gift tells me that Dan believes in me. In this, I have no doubt.

Two years ago, Dan presented me with a second box, a beautiful jewelry box he crafted from zebrawood. My best friend and her husband stood nearby as I opened it to reveal an engagement ring.

If there is any doubt, I said yes.

— Melissa R. Bender —

Holiday Hijinks

47

Chicken Soup for the Soul

Moo

*Perhaps the best Yuletide decoration
is being wreathed in smiles.*
~Author Unknown

I should have known when I married him, but no one could have
been prepared.

It was our first Christmas together, just us in our little townhouse: a small, yappy dog, a couple of cats, and a lot of festive
decorations. Everything looked perfect — except the dining room table.

If I had it to do over again, I would never have touched it. Never
unleashed its furious power. Christmas would have been so, so different. I know that now. But then? It was just — a tacky, little thing. A
dumb, little item that didn't offend me during the rest of the year. But
I wanted to put together a lovely Christmas table centerpiece, and it
just didn't work.

It was a cow creamer.

You've seen them. Made of white porcelain with a hole in the back
to pour in the milk so they can puke it out into your coffee. Maybe you
repurpose one for thin gravy, or chocolate sauce, or something more
festive to spice up your eggnog. The sky's the limit with a cow creamer.

But it didn't work on my table.

So, I hid it.

I didn't throw it away. Andrew, my husband, had brought it into
our marriage, so it wasn't mine to pitch. I just hid it. I'm pretty sure I
nestled it in the branches of the Christmas tree. Festive, right?

Apparently not.

The next day, it was back on the dining room table, a reverse "Elf on the Shelf" but somehow even more sinister.

So, I hid it again.

Maybe it was on top of the kitchen cabinet that second time.

And the next day it was back, looking at me with those stupid, unblinking, white porcelain eyes.

I hid it again—in the toilet tank. (Note to the squeamish: We never actually used this creamer for cream, gravy, etc.)

He found it. He washed it (I hope) and returned it to the table.

We did not speak of this transaction. Not one word. It was a silent war and was carried out over the course of a month or so. As the blessed day got closer, my Christmas table continued to include a white cow creamer.

On Christmas Eve, she disappeared.

Victory!

Oh, if only that were true. Such was my underestimation of my husband.

Every year, we open our gifts together on Christmas morning, and since there's just the two of us, it's not a kid-fueled frenzy but an orderly giving where one opens a gift and then the other. They are given in a specified order, saving the best for last (assuming we remember what each one is, which is totally dependent on the amount of time since we wrapped them and has grown less accurate over the years).

So, we opened our gifts. I remember nothing else I gave or received that morning.

But one of my gifts was a small box labeled "Fragile."

Inside was the cow creamer.

I laughed. He laughed. I thought it was over.

Now, I know what you're thinking. *Wendy, don't you remember your birthday? When he asked you to tell him what you wanted, you couldn't think of anything, and he threatened to get you a Celine Dion CD. When you still didn't tell him anything, you got four Celine Dion CDs, and now your heart just goes on and on and… Did you learn nothing?*

I learned nothing. Not then.

But that Christmas morning, I learned.

There was one box left. Straight-faced, my husband handed it over.

Inside was *another* cow creamer.

That's not the scary part.

"Turn it over," he said.

Dear reader, I cannot adequately prepare you for the horror of the cow creamer's belly. Please, stop reading now if you are faint of heart. If the image haunts your nightmares, please know you were warned.

The cow creamer's belly had words written on it in Sharpie: "Christmas 2001."

Never has a date struck more fear into my heart because I knew what it meant.

Not more Celine Dion.

More cow creamers.

We've been together for over twenty years now. I have thirty-nine cow creamers. Some are not cows but cats, dogs, and one small dinosaur. Many are pure white; some are beautifully painted. One was a gift from our Realtor, which she had imported from her family in Poland because she heard I collected them.

I do not willingly collect them. And yet, every year on Christmas morning, they arrive.

I've heard of husbands who, knowing their passing is imminent, make arrangements with a local florist to have flowers delivered on his soon-to-be widow's birthday every year so she always has a bouquet from him forever. My husband is in good health. But I have to wonder if he's made a secret pact with the Cow Creamer People so that even his death won't stop the herd from growing.

They don't live on the dining room table anymore. They have a whole bookshelf in my office, and they're watching me type this.

And as Christmas approaches yet again, and we struggle to remember what's in the packages we wrapped for each other weeks before opening them, I know that at least one of them will greet me with the old familiar "moo," and Andrew and I will be once again newlyweds sitting on the floor of our little townhouse, creating our own tradition whether I wanted it or not.

You might think the moral of this story is "Never hide your husband's cow creamer."

But I think it's just the opposite.

—Wendy Vogel—

Chicken Soup for the Soul

The Naughty Parents List

Each day of our lives we make deposits in the
memory banks of our children.
~Charles R. Swindoll, The Strong Family

Our family had traveled out of town to visit my parents for Christmas. We had enjoyed a peaceful Christmas Eve and Christmas morning, but the atmosphere was about to change. Any minute, my brother and his family would arrive and join us for Christmas dinner. Although we loved them and looked forward to seeing them, their arrival was guaranteed to crank up the noise level.

In preparation for their visit, we told our three-year-old, Toby, to put his toys away before his young, rambunctious cousins arrived. At the last minute, my husband checked on him and found Toby still playing on the floor with his brand-new Christmas presents strewn about.

"I thought we told you to put away your toys before your cousins get here," my husband said.

Toby didn't look up but continued driving his new metal sports car down his pant leg. "Why?"

"We already told you why," I said. "If your cousins play with your toys, they will break them, and we'll have to throw them away. Do you want your toys broken?"

Toby shook his head.

"It's too bad," my husband added, "but your cousins don't take care of their toys the way you do."

"They don't?" Toby asked.

"No, they don't."

While it might seem mean to make Toby hide his toys from his cousins, my brother's children had earned a reputation for destroying anything they touched. That included many of our cherished childhood toys, which had not only survived our childhoods but my older children's childhoods as well. My mother had also confided in us that many of the toys she'd gotten for the grandchildren to play with at her house had been broken right away.

Most of all, we didn't want an awkward family scene with our child in tears because his toys had been destroyed. And so, against our son's wishes, my husband and I hurried and hid every last toy.

Shortly after we'd finished, the doorbell rang, and the house exploded with noise.

Amid the roar, we ate a delicious dinner and then settled in the front room to listen to my father play carols on the piano. It was also time to let my nieces and nephews open their presents from my parents. As I watched my brother's children sharing their new toys with Toby, I felt a twinge of guilt for not reciprocating. I pictured Santa scribbling our names on next year's naughty parent list for what we had done.

Once it grew late, my brother's family prepared to leave. Our family was heading for home in the morning, so we hugged them goodbye and wished them Merry Christmas. On his way out the door, my brother paused and stuck his head back in.

"Oh, by the way, I forgot to tell you. Toby and I had a fun uncle-to-nephew talk. I told him I didn't see any of his presents lying around and wondered if Santa had forgotten to bring him toys. He's so cute."

"Yes, he's a cutie," I said.

"Toby told me Santa brought him a lot of toys, but his mom and dad helped him hide his toys so his cousins wouldn't break them. He also said his parents told him his cousins don't take care of their toys like he does."

Wearing a cocky expression, my brother shouted, "Merry Christmas," and hightailed it out the door, leaving me standing there with a hanging jaw and a tomato face.

My husband and I spent the rest of Christmas night laughing at ourselves and our son's refreshing, innocent honesty. Toby's toys didn't get busted — but his parents sure did.

—Jill Burns—

49

Chicken Soup for the Soul

The Photo Prank

Sometimes we're a three-ring circus, but I
wouldn't trade my family for the world.
~Author Unknown

Every November, I take our family Christmas photo for our holiday cards. When our daughters, Sarah and Jenna, were little, I swore each time it would be the last, but the following year we would do it again. It was hard to get them dressed properly, sitting still, and smiling, while I fidgeted with the camera and tried to remember how to set the timer.

Each year, I picked a theme. When there was snow on the ground, we took the photos outdoors. Other years, we set up in front of the fireplace or on the couch.

One year, Sarah was looking through flyers and saw a picture of a family wearing matching plaid onesies.

"We should get some," she said.

"Better yet, we should take our Christmas photos in them," I said. And so, we did.

Another year, the girls sat on a sled pulled by our dog, Foster, a brown Aussie Doodle who wore reindeer antlers.

In 2020, my husband Al and I posed on the deck with our girls, wearing our masks and staring at our phones. Foster wore his Christmas bandana over his nose. The photo still makes me laugh.

One year, our annual photo shoot turned into more than just some goofy family snapshots. We were planning on taking our pictures that

Sunday when our friend Jay called.

"Charlie's hockey team made it to the finals, so we're not going to be back in time to feed Walter and let him out. Can you please look after him?" Jay asked. Walter was their friendly Golden Retriever.

"No problem," Al said.

"I was at Jay and Jill's last week, and they have their Christmas tree up already," I said. We're one of those families that abide by the no-Christmas-tree-before-December rule, so we never have a tree in our November pictures.

"We should take our photos at their house," I suggested.

Al donned a suit, and the girls and I wore fancy dresses before heading to Jay and Jill's. Al let out a happy Walter and fed him while I set up the camera. The girls admired their pet tarantula in its tank and asked if we could get one. Hard no.

We took our photos in a close-up shot in front of their Christmas tree with Walter. Walter was particularly excited because, apparently, he's not allowed in the living room of their beautiful historic home.

After our cards were printed, I dropped theirs in the mail without telling them what we'd done. I called them a few days later.

"Did you get our Christmas card yet?" I asked.

"We just got it," Jill said. "I haven't even looked at it yet." She went to get the card.

"Wait, that's not Foster…" Jill said. She paused, and then the realization hit. "Oh, my gosh, that's hilarious!" Soon after, I saw on Facebook the story of our holiday prank.

The annual Christmas photo struggles continue. Foster has since passed and been replaced by Smokey, a gray cat with little patience for being held during long photo shoots. We do our best to include her in the pictures without sporting cat scratches along with our Santa hats. Sarah and Jenna are teenagers. It's difficult to get them home from their activities and dressed for photos before sunset. Despite the hassles, we have happy memories of our years of family pictures, and one of our favorites is the one taken at our friends' house with their tree and their dog.

— Melanie Curtis Raymond —

50

A Half-Baked Idea

You will do foolish things, but do
them with enthusiasm.
~Colette

I want to start by saying that we didn't have to call the fire department. We were all fine. A little shaken but okay.

You're a little curious now, aren't you?

My family loves Christmas. We try to do all the fun holiday traditions. We go sledding, drive around looking at Christmas lights, go to our downtown Christmas festival where they light a massive tree, and even make a point to watch *Christmas Vacation* and *Home Alone*. My family is split on which is their favorite. I personally prefer *Christmas Vacation*, maybe because I feel a personal connection to Clark Griswold. We love Christmas and everything it brings, especially being together.

We've always made our kids wait until Christmas morning to open their presents. Some families allow them to open one on Christmas Eve and the rest the following morning. We aren't one of those families.

It's fun to wake up bright and early on Christmas morning. We can thank our youngest daughter, Ava, for that. We sit on the floor in a circle and watch everyone open their presents individually. I love seeing the smiles on their faces when they get the presents they want. I always play mind games with them to make them think they aren't getting what they asked for. I would think eventually they would have learned.

It was fun, but we needed to add something to spice it up a little, maybe add a new aspect to this tradition. So, we decided to make a game out of it.

Games are fun, right?

We decided to hide all the presents around the house after the kids went to bed on Christmas Eve. We would hide one present for each kid at each hiding place. At the time, we always made sure that we had the same number of presents for each of the three kids. This particular year, we had six presents for each kid, so I needed to find six hiding spots around the house. Luckily, we have a pretty decent-sized house, so finding places wasn't hard.

To keep it from becoming an all-out free-for-all, I made a clue list to lead them to the first hiding spot. They were going to have to work together to find it. Once they found that spot and retrieved those presents, they would have another clue to the next hiding spot. This would continue until they found all six, and then they would get to open them.

I hid all the presents the night before and was proud of myself. This was going to be awesome, and the kids were going to love it.

Christmas morning came, and no surprise, Ava was up at about 6:45, ready to go. You can't really go back to sleep when you have an excited eight-year-old bouncing on your bed, yelling at you to get up. So, we woke up the other two kids to get Christmas morning started. It didn't take much because, unlike on a school day, they are more than happy to get up to open presents.

Their big eyes and shocked expressions were priceless when they noticed all their presents, which had been under the tree last night, were gone. But they knew we had done something to them. Even when I joked about giving them away, they knew better.

I explained the rules of the game and handed them their first clue. It was amazing to see their faces light up. They worked well together to find the hiding spots. They were a real team.

Partway through tracking down presents, we noticed a burning smell. It was very subtle at first, but it started to get a little more notice-able. It was winter, so at first we thought maybe it was coming from outside — perhaps from someone's fireplace. We soon realized that it was coming from our kitchen — to be specific, our oven.

The oven was one of the six spots where I had hidden presents. Not knowing this, my wife had turned on the oven because she was making cinnamon rolls for breakfast. She turned it on to preheat it while the kids looked for their presents. We literally started to bake some of our kids' presents! You can't make this up. The best part was that, at the very bottom of the pile of presents, was a large art pad. A *paper* art pad!

Luckily, we caught on in time. We didn't set the house on fire and even saved the presents from being destroyed, including the art pad. It took minor damage but survived. It would have been ironic if one of the presents had been a superhero action figure. There wasn't, but it would have been funny.

The kids thought it was hilarious — and they still think it's hilarious today — eight years later. It will always be a funny Christmas memory for our family. There's no way I will ever live this down. My kids are going to love telling my grandkids about how their grandpa tried to cook their Christmas presents. My family doesn't need to recite "The Night Before Christmas" because we have "The Morning Dad Tried to Cook Our Presents." It's so much more entertaining.

Needless to say, that was the last time we hid the presents.

—Zach Fisher—

Chicken Soup for the Soul

The Extraterrestrial Nativity

*At the height of laughter, the universe is flung
into a kaleidoscope of new possibilities.*
~Jean Houston

No one knew when it had started. Or why. But everyone suspected who, and that's why no one attempted to change it. We called it the extraterrestrial nativity.

Behind the stage in my dearly loved church, we kept a closet of Christmas decorations. Only the Lord and possibly a retired custodian knew how long some of those items had been there or from whence they'd come. Deep in the recesses resided Joseph, Mary, and Baby Jesus. They seemed like perfectly normal lawn ornaments: pale plastic, hollow for illumination, and heralding from a decade the twenty-seven-year-old me had never witnessed. Every Christmas, they were posed front and center on the elevated stage from the week after Thanksgiving until sometime after the new year.

Their shining moment was the Christmas Eve candlelight service. You could always count on three things for the service: five carols, wax drips on the orange pews, and Joseph, Mary, and Jesus shining above all in a lovely green hue.

Yes, green. And not a pretty one either. A Kermit-the-Frog green radiated through every inch of them. They had no facial features painted on their forms, rendering their blank, verdant eyes the creepiest on this planet.

My favorite part of the service was when everyone left, and we unplugged the figures. Suddenly, Mary went from Martian to maternal. Joseph went from mutant to a muted cream. The figure of Jesus in the manger went from key lime to more like the Divine.

"Why do we have to light them up every service?" I often wondered. When the figures were unlit, we almost looked like a normal church.

What did new visitors think of our crowning holiday centerpiece? Did they wonder if we were some type of alien worshipers? That our church had roots in Roswell? Did everyone in town know us as the Church of the Green Nativity?

None of us church members ever said a thing about the Verdant Family from Venus. It was just expected that whoever put out decorations each year would place these almost life-size figures front and center. Every year, I'd notice some extra garland and props around the figures — sometimes, even costumes — but there was no distracting from that green.

Then, one year, I had an idea. My new position in the church office gave me the nerve I hadn't had in prior years. And the fact that I was a handyman's daughter also helped.

One day when I was working in the church office, Naomi, the beloved pastor's wife, chose to decorate the sanctuary for Christmas. She was well-respected but the one most suspected of implementing the green.

Christmas music began to radiate from the sanctuary. I hurried my work so I could help. Finally, I yanked open the sanctuary's double doors. The verdant family was scattered across the stage, fresh from their boxes, unposed and, best of all, unplugged.

My chance had come. Decades of church history had bottlenecked to this moment.

"I'll do the nativity scene, Naomi," I called, double-stepping to the stage. From somewhere under a moving tangle of garland, I heard, "Thank you, dear."

Immediately, I grabbed Joseph and turned him on his head.

In minutes, the family was void of wiring, and I had three light bulbs in hand.

"That's why they glow green!" I said, holding a light bulb before my face like *The Lord of the Ring*'s Gollum finally getting his hands on the Ring of Power. (Part of me also felt like Boromir marveling, "Is it not a strange fate that we should suffer so much fear and doubt for so small a thing?")

"Why?" I murmured. "Why would someone put green lightbulbs in them?"

Naomi had come up behind me and now looked over my shoulder at the perpetrator. Immediately, I regretted what I'd said, wondering if she'd heard.

"I don't know who thought that was a good idea," she said.

My stiffness eased. "Then you don't mind if I go find some regular light bulbs?"

"Please do!"

Off I sprinted for the utility closet. In five minutes, Joseph, Mary, and Jesus were restored to almost human representation.

When the office staff gathered to admire the decorations later that afternoon, we all felt as if we'd turned a corner in church history. It was a new era. A new light had dawned.

By the next time I was at church, word had spread. I had people taking me aside by the elbow and whispering, "Thank you!"

"My pleasure," I said, grinning. They never knew that the person they thought was insistent on green was just as glad as we were to have it gone.

Like Roswell itself, the history of the ghastly glow remains unexplained. But the nativity's future is bright. And that's because, when I replaced the light bulbs, I made sure no one could use the green ones again.

"Merry Christmas to all," I said from within the utility closet, "and to all a white light!"

— Meagan Briggs —

All Snug in Their Beds

*Laughter heals all wounds, and that's one thing that
everybody shares. No matter what you're going
through, it makes you forget about your problems.*
~Kevin Hart

'Twas the night before Christmas, and we gathered in the
living room of my fiancé Doug's childhood home, sipping spiked eggnog and peering at the tree as if it might
save us from the gloom. It was the first Christmas for
Doug and his siblings without their father, who had coached all their
soccer teams, done yardwork by their side every weekend, and acted
as their rock and cheerleader their whole lives. Six months earlier, he
had been rushed into emergency brain surgery and died two weeks
later. He was fifty-one years old.

This was also the first Christmas my future mother-in-law would
spend as a widow, at age forty-nine. For almost thirty years, she had
been a spectacular stay-at-home mom and holiday host. Her kids often
had home-baked cookies waiting for them after school. Easter brought
flags with baby chicks on the front porch, little clusters of pastel eggs,
and cookies shaped like bunnies with homemade frosting. Christmas
brought similar fabulousness.

Though I don't remember any Christmas decor that year, I'm sure
it is a lapse in my memory and not a failure of my mother-in-law's
dedication. Christmas wasn't something to neglect; homemade treats
were like air, twinkle lights like water.

The holidays also provided a good distraction. In this family, hard emotions were often shoved down deep or numbed by constant shopping, working, and doing. All the holiday events — even buying the tree, getting it straight in the stand, wrangling on the lights, and putting on one precious ornament at a time — distracted from the grief.

This evening gave us a rare moment of peace together: Doug and me, Doug's brother Dennis and his new wife, Doug's sister, and their mom. We had eaten a beautiful meal and sat around watching the fire, sad but stuffed.

All the kids had been caring for their mom in some way, mowing the enormous lawns, helping untangle the finances, and being a steady presence in a post-traumatic aftermath. Doug's sister had recently returned home after graduating from college. She had moved back to her room, still flowery and containing a twin bed with a trundle, although she often slept with her mom. Dennis had stayed at the house the night before Christmas Eve, probably helping his mom with making pies and wrapping presents. He had chosen Doug's old room because it had a queen-size bed and its own bathroom.

Dennis said goodnight first, with Doug close behind. The ladies stayed up a bit longer, savoring the eggnog and chatting. My sister-in-law and I were new to this family, just getting to know each other and the Brien women who would be our kin for the next several decades.

My sister-in-law went upstairs next. After brushing our teeth next to each other at the double sinks, we said goodnight. She went off to join her husband. And I was going to join my fiancé even though that was a bit scandalous. We were getting married in just a few months, so it seemed okay.

I wasn't going to push the limits, though, and put on a big, flannel, full-coverage pajama set and crawled into bed in Doug's room. His back was turned, and I cuddled up to him, spooning.

About 5:30 or 6:00 in the morning, he got up to use the bathroom. It sounded like an elephant walking through a pile of crinkled newspapers.

"Doug, could you be any louder?" I said.

"Shanti?" a strange voice responded.

"Dennis?" I squeaked out.

And then it was as if the world fell over and lay on its side, helplessly glitching. Dizzy with the remnants of the eggnog and the confusion of what was happening, I jumped from the bed and ran across the hall with Dennis. We looked down at his wife and my fiancé… spooning. They peered back at us, eyes exploding from their heads with surprise and confusion.

The guys hadn't told us that Dennis had taken Doug's room. Doug knew, but he hadn't told anyone. So I went into Doug's room, and my sister-in-law went into Dennis's room.

"AAAGGGHHH!" we yelled in unison. The North Pole surely heard us.

Doug's mom and sister came running in, expecting a crime scene or at least some blood. We talked over each other, trying to figure out what had happened. Did we really stay the entire night with the wrong person? How could that have happened? Who was the person most responsible? Most importantly, what had happened in those beds?

Nothing, it turns out. Doug and our sister-in-law had spooned back and forth in fits all night. He kept putting his arm under her head, and she kept shoving it away. Dennis and I slept peacefully. Still, we racked our memories for kisses, grabs, or touches. To this day, no one has confessed to such.

It was nightmarishly early to be up on Christmas morning, especially for a group of twenty-somethings and their grieving mother, and yet the adrenaline kept us chattering and laughing all day. It was just the relief we needed to get through the hardest holiday ever. It was a funny, unbelievable beginning for this broken but growing little family.

Now, it's a big family; my mother-in-law dotes on her nine grandchildren. Every year, she sews them each a set of Christmas pajamas. They pose in front of the overly decorated tree, matching and smiling. Many years, we have sat around drinking eggnog or hot cocoa and sharing stories. One of the most famous starts with "'Twas the night before Christmas…" and ends with "They slept, all snug in their beds, with the wrong person, all night long."

— Shanti Bright Brien —

Chicken Soup
for the *Soul*

A Rubber Chicken
for Christmas

My philosophy is: If you can't have fun,
there's no sense in doing it.
~Paul Walker

"**W**hat gifts are we taking to the Dirty Santa thing at church tonight?" my husband Eric asked.

"A board game and some Christmas decorations," I said. "I think these kind of gift exchanges are fun, but I almost always end up liking the gift I brought better than the one I take home."

Eric nodded. "Me, too."

"When I was a kid, I had a gift exchange at a Christmas party, and I really, really wanted the gift I brought," I said. "We drew numbers, and mine was the very last one. As each kid chose their package, I hoped they wouldn't choose what I'd brought. Nobody did, and I took my own present back home. I was pretty excited about that."

He shook his head. "It was supposed to be a gift exchange, but you didn't trade with anybody."

"I didn't care. I wanted that pencil cup."

"The thing you wanted was a pencil cup?"

"It was a purple pencil cup filled with pens and pencils. You know how much I love school supplies."

"Most kids would've wanted a toy."

"Don't laugh at me. I used that pencil cup until I went away to college."

Eric shook his head again. "I hope I don't come home from the party tonight with a purple pencil cup."

"Oh, if there's a pencil cup, I'm getting it. And that's a promise."

That night at church, we sat around a table with a group of friends, ready to play Dirty Santa. We decided that the oldest person would choose first. This put Eric and me in the middle of the group. The first friend chose a package and unwrapped it. It was a set of grilling utensils. Pretty nice gift.

The next person had the chance to steal the grilling tools or choose her own gift. She chose from the pile and opened a box of truffles. Everyone oohed and aahed, and no one was surprised when the next person stole the chocolates.

The replacement gift was the board game we'd brought. The next person stole it, and I was pleased that people liked our gift.

The next person chose from the pile and opened a small Crock-Pot, just the right size for my famous chili-cheese dip, and my slow cooker had just broken. I eyed the gift hopefully.

But after a few more people had chosen their packages, I knew it was not to be. We'd made a rule that each gift could only be stolen twice, and the Crock-Pot had made the rounds. It had ended up back with the first person, and it couldn't be stolen again.

When it was my turn, I decided to choose from the pile since I couldn't steal the truffles or the Crock-Pot. I could hardly believe it when I opened the package. My gift was a rubber chicken.

Literally. A rubber chicken.

I squeezed it, and it made an extremely loud honking sound. It was kind of funny, but what on earth would I do with it?

As everyone else opened their gifts, I tried to tempt them to steal the chicken from me. "You know you want this," I joked.

Not surprisingly, there were no takers for the rubber chicken.

Finally, all the gifts were chosen. I thought we were done and started to stand up.

"Hold on just a second," someone said. "The first person to go still gets the chance to steal a gift since they didn't have that choice during their turn."

The first person looked around the table, clutching her little Crock-Pot. I figured she'd steal the coffee gift certificate or just keep her Crock-Pot.

To my amazement, her gaze settled on my rubber chicken. "Can I steal that? I really want it."

As anxious as I was to trade, I couldn't help blurting out, "Why do you want a rubber chicken?"

She laughed. "I'm leading the teen girls' weekend retreat next month. That honking sound the chicken makes would be a great wake-up call to get the girls out of bed in the morning."

I pushed the chicken across the table, pleased that my friend actually wanted it. I was even more pleased to receive the cute little Crock-Pot in return.

The next morning, I received a text from her. "Who knew that our chicken friend was famous?" Her text included a link to a YouTube video. I clicked on the link and saw a rubber chicken — just like the one from the gift exchange — honking in tune to a popular Christian worship song. I burst out laughing at the pure craziness of it all.

The rubber chicken was known as "The Worshicken," a blend of the words "worship" and "chicken." To my amazement, the video had tens of thousands of views, and there were dozens of different songs. The Worshicken was an internet sensation.

I found it hilarious that I'd opened the rubber chicken and wondered what on earth I'd do with it. But my friend saw a creative alarm clock, and the people behind the Worshicken took it to a whole new level of crazy fun.

That Dirty Santa gift exchange was my favorite one ever. It was even better than the one with the purple pencil cup. Because now, every time I make my chili-cheese dip in my cute new Crock-Pot, I think about my sweet friend honking that rubber chicken as a wake-up call for a bunch of teenagers.

And, of course, I do this while listening to "Amazing Grace." Performed by the Worshicken, obviously.

— Diane Stark —

Pookie Goes to Paris

There is, incidentally, no way of talking about cats that
enables one to come off as a sane person.
~Dan Greenberg

I was busy packing my car with stuff to attend a conference in Paris, France just before the holidays. My husband always says that I take everything but the kitchen sink on road trips. I like to be prepared for any eventuality. Meanwhile, he was visiting relatives in Italy.

We decided to meet in Paris to spend our Christmas vacation together there. How exciting and romantic that would be! We hadn't done anything like that since our honeymoon because we were always working on endless home renovations and taking care of our growing family of rescue pets.

I was teaching university courses at the military base in Ramstein, Germany. Part of my professional-development responsibilities included writing and delivering papers at conferences worldwide. I would do them virtually whenever possible, but sometimes I had to travel to conference sites in person when internet presentations were not an option. I always tried to keep packing to a minimum but usually ended up filling the car with one thing or another that I thought I might need.

It was just a four-hour trip to Paris, where the trickiest driving would be maneuvering in the busy streets of the city. Thank goodness for the GPS system that would guide me through it all. I tried not to stack things too high in the car for this trip since I needed clear visibility when driving in Paris. I also had to leave room for my husband and his baggage, since he would be returning back home to Germany with me. Still, a little at a time, the car was filled to overflowing, especially since I was bringing wrapped Christmas gifts along with me.

My mother-in-law was staying at our home in Germany and would be babysitting our varied collection of rescue animals. She'd been raised on a farm in France, so she was somewhat of an animal whisperer. She loved anything with fur or feathers, and they loved her, so we knew our brood would be in good hands. That said, the animals missed us when we were on a trip and appreciated us all the more when we returned, especially if we were bearing delicious treats.

Pookie, a longhaired Persian cat, was far more domesticated than the rest of our ragtag bunch of rescue pets. She seemed to miss us more than the others and pined when I took out my baggage to pack. Often, she'd sneak into a bag to hide under the clothes laid out in the luggage, trying to pack herself in for the trip. Or she would roll around on my clothing, leaving deposits of cat hair, while whining miserably all the time I was packing. My overly cautious husband would check my luggage and even inside the car before I departed on any trip, making sure there were no stowaways. I always thought that was a charming waste of time.

Finally, I was ready to go. I waved goodbye to my mother-in-law and our brood and was soon speeding down the Autobahn. No speed limits in certain highway sections made the trip even more thrilling. The stereo was on high as I put the pedal to the metal and sang along at the top of my lungs.

After a while, I reduced speed, turned down the stereo, and stopped singing before I lost my voice. While I organized my thoughts, I heard a strange, tinny sound coming from the back of the car. I wondered if I had damaged a stereo speaker when I threw all my bags into the hatchback.

Checking my rearview mirror, I noticed that the Christmas packages had shifted and were blocking my view a little. I hadn't strapped anything down, so I wasn't surprised. I hoped that everything would stay put for the rest of the journey. I made a mental note to pack more tightly for the return trip home.

I stopped for coffee at a truck stop after a few hours of driving. As I walked out, a Good Samaritan approached me, saying he had noticed movement in the back of my car. He was worried that someone had hidden back there. Creeping up to the car together, we peered in through the back window, only to see a pair of ears partially hidden by the packages. Furry ears!

It would seem that, indeed, I had a stowaway. I would never mock my husband again for fussily checking out the back of the car before road trips. Too bad I hadn't followed his lead this time. It was too late to turn back now, so I went back into the service station to find some food for my feline. It was Pookie, of course, who had managed to tag along after all.

Taking her to the conference made her day, as well as mine. She was a total show-off, engaging with everyone she met. I won an award for presentation excellence, probably because she made both of us so memorable.

Afterward, my husband joined us in Paris and we purchased a leash for her so she wouldn't get away and into more trouble. She looked right at home in her fluffy fur coat, prancing around the city at Christmastime, where it seemed everyone was walking a poufy Pomeranian or Poodle. We got plenty of double-takes, curious stares and stifled snickers when others realized it was a cat at the end of our lead.

And so ended Pookie's accidental journey to Paris. She had the time of her life on her impromptu Christmas vacation in the fabulous city.

— Donna L. Roberts —

Grandma Gets Baked

If you obey all the rules you'll miss all the fun.
~Author Unknown

At Christmastime our entire family would gather for dinner at a relative's home. Dish after dish would be proudly carried in as everyone brought their signature dish to share. The main table basically became a trough, its entire expanse covered in dishes. Almost any dish you could possibly want was available, including turkey, ham, scalloped potatoes, corn, and, oh, the dressing! Most of the meal paled in comparison to the exquisite perfection of the dressings and gravy. Our family practically mainlined dressing, and gravy was nearly a beverage.

As always, the host was seated at the head of the table while the other end was reserved for the eldest among us. In the seat of honor, Grandma discovered to her delight, she now had almost unlimited access to the foods on each side of the main table.

The turkey wouldn't be the only gobbler at the table that day.

As a diabetic, Grandma had to be careful about what she ate but rarely was. We tried to monitor her for her own good, but she was slick, and we couldn't appeal to her logic because she also had dementia. If you weren't careful, she could consume a sizable amount of food in minutes. If we caught her, she was not only unrepentant, but her smile grew broader as her gaze continued to rove over the assorted dishes. She loved a challenge.

One or more of those among us had prepared an "herbal" dressing and discreetly placed it upon the young-adult table, more than likely with accompanying nudges and suppressed giggles for the privileged few who were privy to its secret ingredient. It was intended only for a few, but depending upon how you looked at it — fortunately or unfortunately — it was placed within easy reach of Grandma. It didn't go unnoticed.

Stealthily, Grandma surveyed the room. Then, slowly and subtly, she pinched a bite and sat happily chewing with clandestine pleasure. A bigger pinch, another bite and, before anyone noticed, she had created a moderate crater in the delicious, savory dish.

Grandma's happy chatter increased. She became positively euphoric, participating voluntarily in the conversations, which was unusual. She was usually content to sit back and listen. As everyone sat down to eat, the bowl was discreetly passed around among the informed few at that table. Perhaps one of the guilty parties noticed the large divot but attributed it to someone else at that table. After the blessing, it was like someone fired a starter's pistol, and she was off. Grandma dominated the conversation at the table that day, regaling everyone with stories from her past. To everyone's shock and some's delight, many of Grandma's stories were remarkably bawdy, and some were potentially prosecutable.

She told story after story that afternoon, as her children and grandchildren alternately gaped in shock and roared with laughter. No one left the table while she talked, enjoying a side of Grandma that none of us had ever known existed. But then, midway through the meal, someone at the young-adult table must have snapped to attention when they saw Grandma snag another wad from the nearly empty dish that had migrated back to within her reach. When she had helped herself to more, jaws sagged, and eyes bulged. To that table's occupants, there was now an obvious explanation for Grandma's uplifted mood: She had been surreptitiously eating from the private side dish for a while.

The "chef" was in a dilemma. That bowl had been meant for just a select few because the dressing had been prepared with a secret "herb" in addition to sage and oregano. In the seventies many foods were starting to be prepared with that particularly popular "herb." Instead of baking a pie that Thanksgiving, one of our enterprising young chefs had inadvertently "baked" Grandma.

Her elevated mood lasted into the evening until my aunt finally caught on. She had become somewhat familiar with those particular symptoms of euphoria from a late-in-life student career at a local college. A little bit shocked but giggling, she informed her siblings of her suspicions. After tasting the suspect dressing, she smacked her lips and determined that the dressing was "loaded." No one asked how she was familiar with that particular herb.

She and her siblings decided that the proper punishment involved ensconcing Grandma in the midst of the suspects where she rambled on and on through the evening as they tried to watch TV and play cards.

The guilty party was never identified because the young adults had quickly emptied the bowls after seeing Auntie tasting the dressing, but everyone had their suspicions.

After her buzz wore off, Grandma finally wound down and was tucked in for the night. Her lusty snores, like golf balls in a wood chipper, kept the household awake. Hopefully, the guilty party got very little rest that night.

We now know that medical marijuana has been proven to help relieve symptoms of depression. Perhaps our errant chef was simply ahead of their time, providing an inadvertent service that day.

And as for Grandma? We never looked at her quite the same way again. In relating stories of her youth, we all saw her as a young person like us who had made her own fun and mistakes.

She became more than just "Grandma" that day; she became one of us.

— Laurel L. Shannon —

Creative
Christmas-ing

Weekly Wisdom

*A good father will leave his imprint on his daughter
for the rest of her life.*
~Dr. James Dobson, Solid Answers

A s a college student in the 1980s, what I lacked in extra money, I compensated for with creativity. When it came to celebrating others, I often made cards, wrote poems, or baked cookies to honor milestones. One year as Christmas approached, I was at a loss over what to do for my dad.

I attended college 138 miles from my parents' home, a drive that typically took about two hours and twenty minutes from door to door. I didn't have a car back then, but any weekend I wanted to go home, my dad would begin work early on Friday and leave early, drive down to campus, and pick me up. On Sunday, at whatever time I chose, he'd drive me back to school. I'm sure I didn't express much gratitude, and I may have slept in the car, not even keeping him company.

All of this underscored the fact that I really needed to come up with a good Christmas gift for him that year. But what? More masking tape or duct tape? Some new tools? One year, we gave him light bulbs for a special lamp he had in his basement workshop where he repaired whatever we'd broken. While he seemed happy about the light bulbs, I knew I could do better.

I spoke to my parents every Sunday night at 11:00 p.m. while I was away at college because that's when the long-distance telephone rates were the least expensive. If our call was less than five minutes, I believe it was exceptionally cheap, so our chats became a true exercise in the economy of words. My dad asked about my grades, which I always reported were fine, and then told me what mail had arrived for me that week. Sometimes, he would read me a quote or a short, funny story from his *Reader's Digest* magazine.

The power of our Sunday night conversations inspired my idea for his Christmas present. I decided to collect fifty-two inspiring or humorous quotes, one for each week in the coming year, and give them to him for Christmas. I scoured books at the library and paid close attention to professors, my pastor at church, and friends' parents in an effort to gather quotes. This was before you could go on the internet and gather quotes in a matter of minutes.

I eventually had quite a collection of possibilities. As December started, I narrowed the list to fifty-two top choices. I spent a great deal of time curating quotes from U.S. presidents, authors, and comedians.

Among them was a favorite we both had always liked: "The harder I work, the more luck I seem to have." Though often attributed to coaches or Hollywood folks, I first heard it originated with Thomas Jefferson, and that's how I listed it among my dad's quotes. (Now that I can look it up on the internet, I see that Thomas Jefferson did not in fact say it, but no matter because it's still a great quote.)

I wrote the quotes on little slips of paper and rolled them into scrolls, each tied with a ribbon. Then I put all fifty-two of them together in a bag and wrapped it.

On Christmas morning, we all met at my parents' house for our traditional pancake breakfast and gift-giving. As my dad opened the package from me, I explained that I anticipated he would unroll one scroll each Sunday night when we spoke. His eyes lit up as he told me, "That's a great gift! And we'll keep talking every week."

I gave my dad a new set of quotes every Christmas for the next three decades, until his last one at age ninety-five. We spoke almost every Sunday night. He would grab a random quote to open from that year's supply and we would discuss it.

After my father passed away, my mother found that he had kept all the quotes I'd given him over the years. He had written the date he had opened each one on the back of the slip of paper, and sometimes added a comment, too.

I busily pawed through the slips of paper, some light blue, some gold-trimmed, some plain white typing paper with different versions of my handwriting on one side and his steady printed notes on the backs. I happily read the original quotes I had copied down and his occasional remarks on the backs of them, such as "Super Bowl Sunday" or "This was a repeat, we still enjoyed." It was as though my father was whispering right into my ear and holding me close as he had while he was still living.

Of all the gifts I've ever presented or made for anyone, I think "the Christmas quotes" are probably the best gift I've given to another person. But my father unknowingly returning the quotes to me is truly the best gift I've ever received.

—Jennifer Priest Mitchell—

The Treasure Hunt

When we recall Christmas past, we usually find that
the simplest things — not the great occasions —
give off the greatest glow of happiness.
~Bob Hope

With dread, my husband and I considered plans for that Christmas. Our four children were tiny back then, and so was our budget. If we spent beyond our means to put lots of gifts under the tree, we would regret it when the bills came due. The kids wouldn't even remember it. Besides, we honestly had more than we needed with plenty of toys already filling our home.

The problem was that our older two were just old enough to understand what was "supposed to" happen on Christmas morning. They had made their lists and excitedly talked about their hopes for what they'd receive.

Parents love to give to their kids, though, and we were no different. But with a small budget, we could only purchase for each child their one top wish. To complicate things further, those two oldest kids were hoping for a video-game system that would be shared! One gift to open for two boys sounded like a recipe for a disappointingly short Christmas morning.

My husband came up with a plan to stretch out our morning festivities. We would wrap a clue in the one box they would open. That clue would lead to another clue, which would lead to another, and so on. It was a Christmas treasure hunt to keep two young boys busy. We sent them all over the house, under sinks, and to the garage. The final gift was hidden in our home office with instructions to bring it back to the living room where we were waiting to watch them open it.

That day so long ago, we thought we were using a one-time strategy. However, they loved it so much that we've repeated it. Each year for the past decade or so, my husband has lovingly composed four different hunts with rhyming riddles of varying complexity.

By Christmas 2023, our kids were ages nineteen, seventeen, fifteen, and thirteen. We expected everyone to be too mature for a childish treasure hunt — especially our recent high-school graduate who had left home to join the Navy.

As we came to holiday-planning time, we approached the kids for their input. What would you like for breakfast on the 25th? Would you want to leave for the extended family visit early in the morning or the night before? At some point, someone mentioned, "And you're doing the clues, right?"

My husband and I looked at each other with surprise and asked, "Do you still want to do that this year?" Their answers shocked us. From the sounds of it, if we hadn't had a Christmas hunt, they might have mutinied!

After that conversation, we thought we'd better call our oldest son to double-check his expectations. He had been granted leave to visit home over Christmas break. To our surprise, his answer was the same as his siblings. "Of course I want a Christmas hunt!"

We happily began the work of shopping and writing clues just like all the previous years. Then, the wrapped gifts were snuck into position to wait for Christmas morning.

It was still early and relatively dark when we heard our bedroom door open on the 25th. Before we could turn on a lamp, one of our big kids flopped onto our bed to wake us up, just like they used to do when they were much smaller. There would be no rolling over and going back to sleep now. He told us that everyone else was already awake.

"Here we go. I'll get the coffee started," I mumbled to my husband as we crawled out from under the warm covers.

All six of us gathered in the living room — we parents with hot coffee in hand. The stockings had already been opened, and the kids were semi-patiently waiting for the gifts to be handed out. Once everything under the tree had been distributed, my husband started in with his usual routine. "Well, it looks like it's all over. Great job everyone. Make sure all the trash gets picked up." The cheerful chorus from these no-longer-small kids was, "No! It's not over! You still have our clues!"

My husband smiled, held up the color-coded clues, and reviewed the rules. "What do you do if you find someone else's clue?"

"Don't touch it!" came the chorus.

"And what do you do when you find your gift?"

"Bring it back here to open it!" they cheered.

With that, he gave them each Clue #1, and they were off. He took a seat, and we smiled at each other. They had gotten so big over the years — learning to use the kitchen, driving a car, and now the oldest having moved out. Yet they still delighted in the simple joy of being sent on a Christmas treasure hunt.

We looked out the windows and saw one of them run across the backyard. We heard someone moving boxes around in the basement. Shouts and cheers erupted when each next clue was found. Eventually, all four final gifts were discovered and opened.

By then, our coffee mugs were empty, and our hearts were full. Even though our Christmas tradition had started out of desperation, it had turned into one of our family's greatest treasures.

— Stacey Sisk —

A Grand Tradition

How can we expect our children to know and
experience the joy of giving unless we teach them
that the greater pleasure in life lies in the
art of giving rather than receiving.
~James Cash Penney

The grandchildren loved opening their gifts on Christmas morning, but they never waited to see me open their gifts *to* me, because those had actually been picked out and wrapped by their parents.

So, I decided to change this and I wrote this letter to my children, the parents of said grandchildren.

December 18

Dear Children:
You keep asking me what I want for Christmas, and now I've decided. Please take your kids shopping and let them choose a present for me. It doesn't have to be expensive — a fancy bar of soap will do — but I want it to be something they choose. Then, take it home, give it to them with wrapping paper, scissors, and tape, and leave the room. This way, it will always be from them.

I'd devised this idea one sleepless night a few weeks before Christmas when I remembered the excitement of my first-grade students the weeks before Christmas and Hanukkah. One of their favorite activities was making and then wrapping the holiday present for their parents. I asked each student to bring wrapping paper and a roll of Scotch tape. On wrapping day, I gave them a quick demo, and then I pretended to ignore them and became busy at my desk.

The kids helped each other as they chatted, but what I liked best was that their conversations were about how their parents would love their gifts and where they would hide them at home.

I hoped to instill the joy of gift-giving in my grandchildren.

Our son Chip and his family arrived midday on Christmas Eve. His wife Lauren greeted me with these words: "When I got your e-mail, I was furious. I told Chip, 'Now your mother tells us what she wants. I already bought her a gift, but I'll do what she asks anyway.'"

Uh oh.

"And," Lauren continued, "it was one of the best things we did all week!" She told me how she took each kid individually to Target to shop for Grandma. They pushed the cart up one aisle and down the next until they found the perfect present.

I had planned for the grandchildren to give me their presents on Christmas morning, but they had other ideas. Four-year-old Samantha was dancing with glee as she flung her coat on the floor to hand me a lumpy package slathered with tape. "Merry Christmas, Grandma." I carefully removed the layers of paper, murmuring a few times, "What could this be?"

"A surprise," she answered, and her gleeful bouncing intensified. I gasped when the paper fell away to reveal a ceramic Christmas tree music box. Samantha clasped her hands in delight and helped me wind it up to play "Silent Night" many, many times.

A few hours later, her older brother Jacob handed me a package wrapped in his favorite space-themed paper. He watched intently as I unwrapped a small, blue glass pyramid. "To help you remember your trip to Egypt," he said. How many seven-year-olds are that thoughtful?

My daughter's children were equally excited, and they couldn't wait for Christmas Day to arrive either. Four-year-old Jackson kept bugging his dad to get his gift from its hiding spot in the car. When he handed it to me, he was very serious about how fragile it was. I carefully peeled off the silver foil paper before getting to the four layers of newspapers that cushioned his gift: a rectangular ceramic plate he had made at school. I knew it was supposed to be for his parents, but my daughter said he insisted on giving it to me instead. He and I decided that this would be the plate for Santa's cookies.

Jackson's older sister, Isabel, waited until bedtime to give me her gift. We share a love of books, and she'd copied a part of one of her favorites. She proudly pointed out the parts she'd changed. I admired her effort at perfect second-grade handwriting, evidenced by the number of eraser smudges.

Of course, I lavished hugs, kisses, and high-fives on each child, thanking them repeatedly. They couldn't get enough of it. Throughout the next few days, they'd ask, "Grandma, did you *really* love my present?" Someone kept winding up the music box to play "Silent Night" again and again and again.

After all the grandchildren were in bed, I apologized to their tired parents for giving them such little warning, but I couldn't help adding, "Your kids know me well. Their presents couldn't have been more perfect." Now, it was time to hear their thoughts.

They loved the idea. My daughter-in-law said that she'll take her kids shopping for Daddy's gift next year, and he'll do the same for her. The others nodded their heads in agreement.

Surprisingly, this giving was remembered the next day, the next week, and for months to come. Jackson continues to tell me the steps it took to make Santa's platter. Jacob always looks for the pyramid on my desk when he visits and reminds me, "I gave this to you, Grandma," which prompts his sister to ask where the music box is. "Waiting safely in the attic for next Christmas," I tell her. The budding author, Isabel, just smiles, probably planning her next book.

— Polly Hare Tafrate —

59

Afghans for Christmas

A grandma is someone who plays a special part in all
the treasured memories we hold within our heart.
~Author Unknown

When my eleven grandchildren were all ages seven and under Christmas was a wonderful time for snuggling and reading a book together. But the kids complained that the afghans we had were too big. They would trip on them when they tried to carry them around.

So, one Christmas I made each of them a small afghan that was just their size. I hoped they would enjoy their very own crocheted blankets while we read a story or they watched their favourite TV shows.

Those little afghans served their purpose for many years, but eventually they became too small. One day, a few of the grandchildren, now all in junior high or high school, came over to visit. One of the granddaughters said, "Grandma, you know those little blankets you made us?"

I nodded, and she continued, "Well, they kinda don't fit us anymore."

"I wonder why," I joked with them. "Did they shrink?"

I got the look.

"Christmas is coming. You could make us new ones — big ones that we can wrap around us again." As we continued our discussion, she asked, "Can we choose our favourite colours? You will make them for us, won't you, Grandma?"

"Well, if I decide to make them, you will all have to tell me what colours you want. I think I know all your favourites, but I want to be sure."

I could sense the excitement in the room as the grandchildren contemplated what colours they would choose. I planned to tell the grandchildren who now lived far away about this conversation and see what they thought about new blankets. I had no doubt they would all agree.

In minutes, I had colour choices flung at me by all but the youngest grandson. Each time I asked him, he simply said, "Doesn't matter what colours you use, Grandma. I just want you to make me a blanket."

"Well, does that mean I could make yours last? I'll use all the leftover yarn from the blankets I make your siblings and cousins."

"Sure, that'd be okay. As long as I get a blanket, I don't care," he said.

His dad looked at him and said, "Dude, remember you have lots of sisters and mostly girl cousins. That might mean lots of pink and purple in your blanket."

My grandson's head jerked up. He stared at his dad, and then his eyes shifted to me. "Grandma, I want red and blue, okay? No pink or purple."

We all burst out laughing at his quick turnaround on colour choices. "Well, I'll think about making blankets for each of you, but no promises, okay?"

They nodded.

I had about six months until Christmas when I went yarn shopping. What a great idea those grandchildren of mine had. I could have presents they would love and all the fun of making them. I decided they would never outgrow these afghans as I bought yarn to make the first one. It would fit on a double bed.

I crocheted squares and more squares after I figured out how many of each colour I needed for that first blanket. My husband teased me to go faster and even timed how long it took for each square, egging me on to decrease the amount of time. Once all the squares had been crocheted, I laid out the pattern, joined them together and crocheted an edging around the giant project. It took me fifty hours to finish the first one. I knew I would never get all of them done in time for Christmas that year. The project needed to be extended for another year.

On Christmas Day, I watched the faces of my grandchildren as they opened their gifts. Those who had continually asked whether I was making afghans looked disappointed but quickly said, "Maybe Grandma will give them to us next year."

I crocheted and crocheted. I bought more and more yarn in all the right colours. I stashed them out of sight when the grandchildren came to visit. I loved their anticipation and hope. I enjoyed the hours of work to complete each one and looked forward to watching their faces on Christmas morning.

Eleven large afghans, taking fifty hours each, were completed and stored with great creativity in our small home. I had to make sure the secret remained hidden until Christmas morning as well as figure out how to transport four of them when we flew to another province. Blankets that large take up a lot of luggage space.

I enlisted the help of my children to hide the packages. I didn't want them put under the tree where it would be easy to figure out what they were. I planned for all eleven grandchildren to open them at the same time, some in Ontario and the rest in Saskatchewan. We would do it together via Skype.

I love when a plan comes together. The looks of happiness on the faces of my grandchildren as they opened their huge parcels made my Christmas wonderful. They wrapped themselves up in those blankets with smiles on their faces. One granddaughter even said it was like wrapping herself in a grandma hug. It made all the time and effort more worthwhile than I could have imagined.

— Carol Elaine Harrison —

Our Story Cloth

60

Always be on the lookout for the presence of wonder.
~E.B. White

I took two of us to carefully align Dad's hand, placing it just so over the tiny outline of a hand traced out in black marker. His gnarled, giant paw of a hand dwarfed the chubby little shape already on the cloth. As we gently traced around his fingers and hand, someone commented that nearly a century of experiences ran between these two prints. Dad was ninety-eight, soon to be ninety-nine, and his handprint is now preserved, resting over the handprint of his youngest great-granddaughter on our Thanksgiving tablecloth.

In 1993, separated from family, I was searching for a way to add something special to our Thanksgiving celebration. I bought a white twin flat sheet and a few colorful permanent markers. As a young military family, we had become accustomed to celebrating holidays, birthdays, and other milestones in the company of new friends or on our own. I was always looking for ways to make small celebrations extra special and create something memorable to carry forward, to build traditions we could call our own. On any given holiday, my husband, a pilot at the time, could be anywhere, and we learned to carry on as normally as possible, no matter what. This particular Thanksgiving, we would actually be together, and it was the perfect time to try something new.

I spread the white sheet, stark and plain, over our family table, smoothing it and finding the center. As carefully as I could, I wrote "…always giving thanks to God the Father for everything, in the name of our Lord Jesus Christ" (Ephesians 5:20). Thankfully, I didn't make any mistakes, and the words still mark the center of one of our favorite family traditions. I carefully set the table with our best dishes, which happened to be our only dishes, and made everything look as nice as possible, doing my best to disguise the fact that our tablecloth was a bedsheet. If you squinted, it could have been a lovely holiday table anywhere.

Thanksgiving dinner was turkey with all our favorite trimmings, and dessert couldn't have been anything except homemade pumpkin pie covered in clouds of whipped cream. After our children finished their "wine" (cranberry juice in special glasses) and my husband and I finished our coffee, we cleared what was left of the dishes from the table. Then the children were told that everyone was going to write on our tablecloth — something they were not typically allowed to do! Suggesting they write something special that they were thankful for or draw a picture to mark the occasion, I placed the jar of markers on the table. Cautious at first, they all got to work.

More than thirty years later, we are running out of room to write our words of thanks on that old white sheet. We have drawings and signatures, poems, and more from friends and family from Bonaire to Bosnia, boyfriends and girlfriends who are now spouses, and even a pawprint or two. You can find palm trees, a cornucopia, stories told in pictographs, baby footprints and cartoon self-portraits. One year, everyone wrote absurd haikus that still make us laugh. My favorites are brightly colored, hand-shaped turkeys of all sizes marking the growth of our children, and now our grandchildren. Our handprint flock is plentiful.

Throughout the years, our family had seldom been with my husband's parents on holidays and had only shared a Thanksgiving once or twice prior to 1993. We moved, they travelled, and holidays would pass without our paths crossing. Dad is the only one left now, and we celebrated with him in 2023, gathering together children, grandchildren, and great-grandchildren in a borrowed room at the care facility where he lives.

This was the first time Dad had been with all of us for Thanksgiving in many, many years, but, more significantly, the first time we traced his hand on our cloth. Those two hands — Dad's and a tiny baby's — separated in age by nearly a century are the highlight of this treasured piece of cloth that tells the story of our family.

— Susan Mulder —

A Christmas Gathering

When we have a circle of friends, we have more fun.
We get more done, we feel and are stronger, and we
really do celebrate the power of our "us."
~Mary Anne Radmacher

I was recently divorced, had a toddler, and was back in college getting a teaching certification. I had no money in my budget to host a Christmas party, but I took a leap of faith and sent out invitations anyway.

"You are cordially invited to a Christmas party at my apartment. Each guest is welcome to bring a favorite holiday snack and soft drink. In lieu of purchasing any gift, you are requested to bring a wrapped item which you already own that has a special meaning to you. This item will be exchanged with a guest during the activities planned."

I did not want the event to be a burden to anyone, as most of my guests were fellow students. I needed some joy in my life, and I knew that doing something for others at the holiday would make me happy. I also wanted my son to have a pleasant memory of our time on campus and in our apartment.

The party was scheduled for the weekend before finals started, so I wasn't sure that anyone would take time out of their studies to come. If only a couple of people showed up, we'd make the most of it.

My son followed me from room to room, bouncing around in anticipation of a "grown-up party." When the first knock sounded, he raced to the door before I could get there and flung it open. "Come

Creative Christmas-ing | 183

in!" he told them. His little face was lit up with excitement. He was generous with hugs for those who wanted one.

Guests began arriving. Several of the young ladies had made homemade candy, cookies, or brownies at their dorms. The young men brought no-cook items such as pretzels, popcorn, potato chips, or liters of soft drinks. When it was all spread out, I was relieved. There was plenty to share.

Once we had gathered, we sang Christmas carols, played charades, and shared Christmas memories. The gift exchange was saved until the end. I was more than a little nervous in anticipating how they had responded to my instructions about a gift. Had they thought my request was silly, or had they taken it seriously and put some thought into the gift they brought to exchange? Several had brought extra little gifts for my son. He was overjoyed by the small items he received, including a small teddy bear that someone had sacrificed from their own bed.

We assigned numbers to each gift. One by one, guests drew a corresponding number from a cup, with the only stipulation being that no one could receive their own gift. As numbers were drawn, we stopped to let the present be opened, and the donor shared their story of why they chose the gift and its significance to them.

Everyone had indeed put a great deal of thought into the process. The sincerity and generosity of the gifts were heartwarming, and the stories that accompanied the gifts were memorable. Even my small son realized the significance of what was taking place and insisted that he give one of his favorite stuffed animals (which had to be added discreetly to the pile of gifts).

As the evening came to a close, the guests were reluctant to leave. Several said it was the best Christmas party they'd ever attended.

My son fell asleep, curled up in a corner of the sofa, clutching his new (used) teddy bear. I tried not to wake him as I carried him to his bed.

During finals week, everyone was focused on finishing up the semester, but as we passed each other, there was a new depth to the smiles and greetings between those of us who had shared this Christmas gathering. We knew each other — and ourselves — a little better because of the evening we spent together.

In the years since, I've had many lovely Christmas memories, hosted get-togethers, and enjoyed holiday festivities with friends and family. That Christmas, however, when gifts came from the heart rather than the wallet or a shopping list, will always stand out to me as one of the most remarkable.

—Judith Victoria Hensley—

62

Never-Ending Gift

*An effort made for the happiness of others
lifts us above ourselves.*
~Lydia M. Child

It was Christmas Eve 1987. There was little money for gifts or a turkey dinner, which was a harsh reminder of how difficult the past year had been. No matter what we did to get ahead, we were thrown two steps back. We had taken a huge financial loss and had no income at the time. Jobs were scarce, and every day seemed to bring a new dilemma.

"Daddy hasn't had a job for quite a while, so there will only be a small present under the Christmas tree this year," I reluctantly told the kids. "But we are together and will have lots of fun, especially if it snows."

"Okay, Mommy," they said. They were young enough that fun was a priority.

When the doorbell rang, I was surprised to see our neighbors, who were farmers. They handed me a large grocery bag. "Phil and I want you guys to have a great dinner. We know you are going through a tough time, and our gift to you is our largest bird. Enjoy." They also gave us potatoes and carrots from their garden.

That kind gesture made me realize that the new year would bring many blessings. "We will get through this," I told myself.

My favorite spoon that I used for cooking was a long-handled, metal one with a rubber end to protect your hand. While preparing our Christmas Eve dinner, the rubber end broke off. Without warning, the floodgates opened, and I began to weep. All the pent-up emotion of our circumstances poured out. I sat down on the kitchen floor and cried. When my husband heard me, he came into the kitchen and saw the broken spoon in my hand.

Gently, he removed the spoon from my grip and laid it on the counter. He took me in his arms and held me. No words were exchanged. There was no need.

The next day was Christmas, and we woke up to snowfall. Perfect. We lived in a remote area surrounded by acres of woods. The beauty of the forest was breathtaking. What fun we had playing in the snow with our children. The freshness of the pure white snow confirmed the message that this year would be a new beginning. I found solace in that.

Although there were only a few presents under the tree, I was thrilled that the children had used their imagination to make a small token of love for each of us. Maybe they understood more about our struggle than I realized.

After opening the presents, I went into the kitchen to prepare Christmas dinner. Then, I saw it. On the kitchen counter was my spoon — my *favorite* spoon. I couldn't believe my eyes. It had a new wooden handle. I had no idea where my husband got it or how he did it, but he had found a perfect piece of wood to fit the spoon. My spoon. It could still be used. I got so excited that I wondered if my family was concerned that Mom had lost her faculties. I couldn't stop laughing.

The lesson the children learned that day was priceless. They witnessed the joy that comes when giving and receiving a gift from the heart. And what is important. What love means.

That was almost thirty years ago, and I am still using that spoon. And every day it reminds me that I need to find a way to make a gesture, no matter how small, to show appreciation to those I love.

— Carol Graham —

63

Faded Ink

You can't use up creativity. The more you use,
the more you have.
~Maya Angelou

"Oh, great! He made it safely once again." Aunt Treva pulled a red envelope from the stack of mail on her kitchen table and waved it at me.

"Who made it safely?" I asked.

"The Ol' Scotsman." She slit open the envelope and held up the card for me to see a bearded, cartoon-like character as she read the front. "Same old greetings year after year!"

I sat beside her. "He looks old."

"Yes. Back when I was a young mom, people didn't send lots of cards like they do today. I chose Christmas cards for only three special families. Bill and I picked out this funny one for his brother Mike and his family."

Though the paper was yellowed and the edges were frayed, the Ol' Scotsman himself looked rather chipper. He sported a red, plaid kilt with matching hat and socks, gold button-up boots, a black tailcoat, and a blue-checked scarf.

"I thought Uncle Bill's family came from Romania," I said.

Aunt Treva laughed. "They did. Scottish characters were just a popular trend at the time." I scooted my chair closer to hers for a better view. Ever so gently, she opened the card and read the verse inside:

Be very savin' of this card and
When Christmas next falls due,
The sentiment will still be good:
Merry Christmas from me to you!

"I signed it right here — Treva, Bill, Dale, 1946." She grew quiet for a few seconds, staring at the faded black ink. "I put a three-cent stamp on the envelope and sent the Ol' Scotsman on his first journey."

"I wish I could mail a card for three cents."

Aunt Treva handed the card to me and said, "Can you imagine how surprised I was the next December when he showed up in my mailbox again?" She pointed at the faded blue ink to the left of her signature. "Mike, Alora, Tommy, 1947. And that's how a tradition began. Every year since, the Ol' Scotsman has traveled between our home in Ohio and theirs in Arkansas."

"Do you pack him away with your Christmas decorations?" I asked.

"Oh, no. He wouldn't like that. He spends the year with us in our family Bible. And when he was at Alora's house, she kept him in her address book."

"1948, 1949, 1950," I said. My finger bounced around the card, locating signatures for all of the '50s, '60s, and '70s. "1980, 1981, 1982. Wait. Where is 1983?"

"Oh, yes, 1983," Aunt Treva said. "I received a troubling letter from Alora that Christmas season." She flipped through the family Bible and produced a folded sheet of paper.

Dearest Treva,

For several weeks, I have been trying to think how to tell you the sad news. I have been sick over it, but it must be done.

The Ol' Scotsman is hiding somewhere. I have hunted high and low, but he is nowhere to be found. No ransom demands have been received, so I don't believe he was kidnapped.

Please forgive me. I have tried to protect him all these years when he was in my care. If and when I find him, I will put him in the mail to your house, even if it is the Fourth of July.

Much love,
Alora

"The signatures begin again in 1986," I said. "Where was he?"

"Well, that's the curious part," Aunt Treva said. "After Alora died in 1986, the Ol' Scotsman mysteriously reappeared — and in his usual spot in her address book, no less."

"Really?"

"Yep, and her son, Tom, put him right back on the road to my house. Tom is carrying on the tradition for his parents, and someday Dale will do the same for me."

"Here's this year, 1998," I said, pointing at the freshest ink. "So that makes this card..."

"Fifty-two years old." She reached for the card and displayed it like a treasure in both palms. "I was in my thirties when I purchased the Ol' Scotsman, and now I'm pushing ninety."

Aunt Treva lived long enough to sign the card one more time. The Ol' Scotsman continued to travel between the two families for many more years. After seventy trips, he retired with honors to a special box for safe-keeping. He remains chipper in his festive plaid, ready to deliver Christmas cheer to future generations.

Simple traditions cost almost nothing, just a little intentionality to begin them and a bit of diligence to keep them going. Yet they provide a wonderful sense of something familiar year after year. I've started a few traditions of my own. I hope that, in seventy years, they are still proclaiming the message of the Ol' Scotsman: "Merry Christmas from me to you!"

— Becky Alexander —

A Kilimanjaro Christmas Conundrum

Do what you can, with what you have, where you are.
~Theodore Roosevelt

I feared for my life as the frigid, merciless, gale-force winds battered my unsteady, nauseated body, threatening to blow me off Africa's highest mountain. I should have been celebrating Christmas Eve with my family back home in America. Instead, I decided to break with tradition to scale Mount Kilimanjaro, towering almost 20,000 feet.

I knew I didn't belong there. I felt like a fifty-one-year-old imposter. I'd made a terrible, selfish mistake. Now, it was too late.

I'm a teacher, not a mountaineer; however, two years prior to my Christmas dilemma, a friend had talked me into trekking to Mount Everest's base camp in Nepal. I made it, vowing to forever leave such tortuous, long-distance, breath-stealing endeavors alone.

But then I took a teaching job in Zimbabwe. Since I was already in the neighborhood, I figured I might as well hike up another mountain.

Kilimanjaro in Tanzania is one of the so-called seven summits, a name given to the tallest peak on each continent.

Some climbers consider Kilimanjaro "easy" because no specialized equipment is required. A person can essentially walk to the top in as few as four days, but there's a major drawback — ascending so rapidly leaves little time to acclimatize, increasing the possibility of altitude sickness, a condition at higher elevations when the body can't get enough oxygen. Symptoms include fatigue, shortness of breath, headache, dizziness, nausea and, in extreme cases, death.

Kilimanjaro features several routes. Since I'm not a fan of camping, I chose a faster, five-day option to the apex, with huts for accommodation rather than tents, giving me only about a 44-percent chance of summiting.

The first three days of my quest went better than expected. I covered seventeen miles, gained 7,000 feet in elevation, and never lost my breath.

Day four, on Christmas Eve, wasn't as kind.

The trek turned into more of a mental challenge than a physical one. As I traversed six miles across an alpine desert, time flowed backward and forward. One minute, I was in Nepal, wandering the Himalayas. The next, I was fantasizing about summiting Kilimanjaro. The next, I was reliving past Christmases. I missed my family.

In the distance, I spotted a climber being rushed toward me on a one-wheeled stretcher. His name was Robert, a businessman I'd met earlier in the trek. He resembled a patient having just awakened from anesthesia — groggy, incoherent, disconnected from reality. The altitude had claimed another victim. I knew he'd recover as soon as he got to a lower elevation, but Robert's time on Kilimanjaro was over.

As disappointed as I was by his misfortune, I immediately blocked Robert out of my mind, concentrating on the job ahead, but the seeds of doubt had already been planted.

Around 3:00 in the afternoon, I arrived at base camp at 15,518 feet. My plan was to eat an early dinner, sleep, and awake before midnight to attempt the summit.

So much for plans.

While trying to fall asleep, I suddenly couldn't breathe. The pulse in my neck accelerated faster and faster, like a train racing out of control. I had dealt with the same sensation in the Himalayas and knew what to do.

Calm down. Take nice, slow breaths. It's just the altitude.

It didn't help. I felt as if I was suffocating.

I'd come too far to allow my body to stop me. I popped my first Diamox, a pill used to prevent and reduce the symptoms of altitude sickness, although the medicine itself can cause side effects similar to altitude sickness. The crisis passed, but my apprehension escalated.

And so, late on Christmas Eve — clad in four layers, encapsulated by a heavy, down jacket — I ascended the arctic tundra toward my prize, having slept just an hour.

My guide, Raphael, said it's best to hike at night because it gives climbers an opportunity to see the sun rise above the zenith. And, more importantly, darkness hinders them from fixating on the imposing challenge of the seemingly never-ending trail, getting steeper by the minute.

"We don't want you to lose hope," he said.

I peeked up and was immediately disheartened by what lay ahead. Still, I kept pushing forward until my nemesis struck again.

It began with a sharp pain at the base of the skull and quickly enveloped my brain, erupting into a full-blown, altitude-induced headache. As if on cue, nausea followed. My legs turned into rubber, and I tottered along the trail, surrounded by drops, appearing to disappear into nothingness. I knew the elements were conspiring to push me toward the abyss.

I dreaded the phone call to my elderly parents.

"I'm sorry to inform you that your son fell to his death on Christmas."

For the first time, I considered quitting.

"Do you think I have serious altitude sickness?" I asked Raphael.

"Only you know your body," he replied. "Let's go!"

Are you kidding me?

I was furious, having expected a pep talk or, at least, some stroking. I hesitated to move.

Rafael called my bluff.

"Do you want to go back?" he asked.

I found the motivation to continue. I'd show him.

Onward I battled, staggering like a drunk, suppressing the urge to vomit with each step, but I knew I'd make it, if only to spite Raphael for abandoning me.

Seven hours and thirty-four minutes from the moment I departed, I arrived at the summit. I didn't feel elated. I didn't feel pride. I just felt relieved I'd made it.

Upon returning to base camp, my irrational anger toward Raphael vanished. A guide's job is to get climbers up and off the summit as quickly as possible to minimize the effects of altitude, temperature, and winds. Raphael had adeptly accomplished his mission.

Without a doubt, rising out of bed in the middle of the night and topping Kilimanjaro was the hardest physical and mental challenge I ever faced, yet it was also, without a doubt, my favorite Christmas.

I didn't come across any chestnuts roasting on an open fire; instead, I marveled at the radiance of the sun bursting forth at the roof of Africa.

Santa never arrived on his sleigh, but so often those "must-have presents" end up discarded in the closet and forgotten just months after we tear through the wrapping paper. I received a gift that will last a lifetime—the satisfaction of overcoming adversity and achieving a goal that made me feel fully alive.

And even though I wouldn't be home for Christmas, it no longer mattered. Throughout the all-night struggle, I thought of my friend Jeff, who said he'd "push me upward" with his "secret mind powers." I recalled the note from Noleen, my school's human-relations manager in Zimbabwe, who wrote, "I know that you will represent us." I felt my mom's prayers from 8,000 miles away, reassuring me that everything would be well.

After the fact, friends worldwide told me they'd been sending out positive energy on Christmas Eve, knowing I might need it. Kilimanjaro wasn't a Norman Rockwell moment, but it was the profoundest sense of universal connectedness I've ever experienced, even though I was in one of the most remote places on Earth.

—Mark Dickinson—

Around the Table

The Dreaded Oysters

In every conceivable manner, the family is link
to our past, bridge to our future.
~Alex Haley

"Make sure you get some oyster dressing," my mom said, nudging my side just as I was trying to side-step past the dish.

I looked down at the collage of oysters, cornbread, and broth with about as much enthusiasm as I'd have looking down at my dog's vomit, but I dutifully grasped the large serving spoon and heaped what would be considered an acceptable mound onto my plate. Everyone was expected to eat a serving of oyster dressing on Thanksgiving Day. It was the only dish that eighty-seven-year-old Grandma Carol still made for the family celebration, and she was not about to quit. Nothing would ever stop Grandma from making her famous oyster dressing. Nothing!

Sitting down, I plotted how I might make my serving of oyster dressing disappear without taking one bite. Hide it under a thin layer of leftover mashed potatoes? Sneak it into my napkin? Work it into my hand where I could carry it into the bathroom and dispose of it down the toilet? All were valid options, but one look at my parents, and I knew that there would be no way around it. I was going to have to eat the oyster dressing. All while smiling.

My stomach did flips just thinking about it, which sent my conscience on a whirlwind of guilt when I looked over at my grandmother to see her beaming in my direction. It wasn't her fault. According to my family, the oyster dressing always tasted wonderful. If anyone could make oysters and dressing go together in a delicious combination, it was her.

There was only one problem: I hate oysters!

"Grandma, your dressing tastes amazing," my cousin Brian said after taking a bite.

"Thank you. I was worried it wouldn't taste as good this year…" my grandmother started to say, but a nudging from my mom had me turning away to look at her.

"Eat your oyster dressing," she mouthed.

Knowing that I was now under the watchful eye of my mom, I had no choice but to start eating it. Using my fork to section off the serving on my plate, I calculated that I could gulp all of it down in seven bites. With a strong inhale, I stabbed the first forkful and shoved it into my mouth. Without breathing, I chewed until it was mashed enough to swallow. Only then did I exhale.

"You know how difficult those oyster cans are to open…." My grandmother was still talking about making the dressing, so I tried to focus on her between bites. "Well, I was opening the first one and… slip! That sharp lid cut right through my skin and left a large gash right on my thumb."

Grandma Carol lifted her hand to proudly show everyone the large bandage. She turned her gaze down the line of family members to make sure that everyone saw her battle wound.

"Oh, no!" Aunt Ruth gasped.

Meanwhile, I had my mouth too full of the third bite of oyster dressing to do anything more than offer a cringe of sympathy. Only four more bites to go.

"Don't worry, I took care of my thumb and had it perfectly bandaged in time to finish the dressing." My grandmother lifted her chin, and I dutifully put another bite into my mouth.

Somehow, I finished it and sent up a little prayer of thanks that I wouldn't have to eat oyster dressing until next year. Four months later, however, Grandma Carol passed away. As much as I hated that oyster dressing, I started to miss it as I thought of her.

"Who made the oyster dressing?" I asked Brian at the next Thanksgiving.

"Aunt Sue."

Though Aunt Sue was a fantastic cook, I still said, "I think I'll pass."

He started to chuckle when I made a face. "Let me guess, you don't like it?"

"No, I don't."

"Me neither," he admitted, to which my jaw fell.

"Then, why do you always eat it?"

He shrugged. "It made Grandma happy. What better way to remember her than with her favorite dish?"

"Oyster dressing was her favorite dish?"

"Oh, yeah!"

I stared down at the dish of oysters and cornbread. Even though I cringed, I still grabbed the spoon and mounded a small portion onto my plate. My mom didn't even have to remind me to eat any. I finished every bite. I hated it and gagged the whole time, but I finished it. With a laugh, I realized that I would be doing the same next year, too. In honor of Grandma.

— Katrin Babb —

Pumpkin Pie Surprise

We must have a pie. Stress cannot exist
in the presence of a pie.
~David Mamet

"When is that boy going to marry you?" At the latest shot in a volley of personal questions from my ninety-year-old grandma, Pearl, I almost dropped the sweet-potato casserole I'd just removed from the overstuffed oven.

My mom and sister, Shelby, halted their preparations — Mom making gravy, Shelby mashing potatoes — and turned to hear my response.

"At your age, I'd been married half a dozen years and popped out two kids," Grandma added.

Instead of trying to explain — again — why, at age twenty-six and nearly three years of dating Steve, I still didn't have a ring on my finger, I set the casserole onto the trivet next to the plethora of foil-covered dishes. "Excuse me, I'm going to check on the turkey."

I raced to the back patio, where my grandpa, dad, Shelby's husband Bill, and *that boy*, aka Steve, were frying the turkey in an industrial-sized vat of oil.

As I got closer, I heard laughter and saw them patting Steve's back. The second I slid open the glass door, the joviality stopped, like a faucet had been shut off.

"You need something, honey?" Dad asked, his eyes bright, a soft smile on his face.

"Yeah, ETA on the turkey?"

"Just bringing it up now."

They were all staring at me like they were waiting for me to leave. I closed the door, with their eyes still on me. Clearly, they were up to something, but I had my own issues to deal with. Taking a deep breath to armor up, I headed back into the fire to the scent of something burning.

"Dad's bringing up the turkey now," I said and pulled the Parker House rolls from the oven, saving them from turning into hockey pucks.

"Well, it's about time," Grandma said.

Mom poured the giblet gravy into the gravy boat and handed it to me. "Let's start moving the food to the sideboard."

As we set out the numerous piled-high sides, Dad brought in the turkey and went to the kitchen to carve it.

Steve slid his arm around me. "You okay?" he whispered into my ear so I could hear him over Dad's electric carving knife, but no one else could. "You look a bit frazzled."

"Dodging prying questions is quite the workout," I whispered back.

"I know what you mean," he said, nodding toward the trio of men hovering around the turkey.

Ah, so that's what they'd been up to… an inquisition.

"Hope it didn't kill your appetite," I said jokingly. Steve had been gifted by the gods with a king-sized appetite and a metabolism to match — calories burned off as fast as they were consumed.

"I think I can force something down. Just to be polite."

Minutes later, everyone had loaded their plates and taken a seat at the twelve-person dining room table that saw use only during the trinity holidays of Easter, Thanksgiving, and Christmas. Grandpa said the prayer, ending it with: "And, please, Lord, give Steve and Stephanie the good sense to get married before I die. Amen."

My cheeks turned the color of the gelatinous cranberry blob in Grandma's prized Depression glass bowl. I glanced at Steve to judge his reaction.

If it had been totally up to him, we'd already be married. He'd been ready a year ago. I was the holdout. And I knew that hearing others, especially my family, question the delay made him feel like he was being irresponsible and disrespectful. Fortunately, at this moment, Steve was grinning. I was thankful he was taking Grandpa's statement as a joke and even more thankful when we got through the meal without any more mention of marriage.

After dinner and dishes, everyone waddled into the living room to watch football and enjoy the pies Grandma had made from family recipes that went back, she said, at least a century.

Steve served me a slice of pumpkin pie, with a healthy dollop of whipped cream, and sat beside me, his own plate laden with a slice of pumpkin and pecan.

At the third bite, I bit down on something hard in my mouth, and I used my napkin to take it out. Even with the bits of pumpkin and whipped cream clinging to it, I could clearly see that it was a ring.

My heart jackhammered in my chest when it came to me that there was only one reason a ring would be hidden in my slice of pie.

Other than the roar of the football game, the room had gone quiet, and all eyes were on me.

I turned to Steve. He looked a little shocked, eyes wide, mouth slightly twisted up in one corner. Nerves maybe? Over the enormity of the moment and the decision? Although I could be angry at him for using this family-centric moment to push a marriage that I'd said I wasn't ready for, I wasn't angry. I wasn't nervous. In fact, everything inside me had slid into alignment and was whispering, *This is right.*

A soft smile parted my lips and I quietly said a simple but heartfelt "Yes." Then, I hugged him.

That "yes" cracked open the silence in the room, and everyone rushed forward, hugging and congratulating us. Everyone except Grandma. She sat in her chair with an inquisitive look on her face, eyebrows drawn in. Then she grabbed her cane, pushed her way up out of the chair, and shuffled toward us. I stood, thinking she was going to hug me, too.

Instead, she snatched the ring from my fingers.

"Well, hello, I thought I'd lost you," she said to the ring. She slid it onto her finger and then shuffled back to her chair.

"Grandma?" I asked after I'd picked up my jaw from the floor. "That's your ring?"

"Oh, yes. It must have slid off my finger when I was making the pie," she said and took another bite. "Mmm. This is the best pie I ever made, if I do say so myself."

Shock faded into hilarity. I chuckled, and then laughed. Soon, everyone was laughing except Grandma, who was contentedly eating her delicious pie.

In the calm that followed, I felt Steve's gaze.

"Did you mean that 'yes'?" he asked.

To make sure my earlier "yes" hadn't just been me getting caught up in the moment, I tuned in to what my gut and heart were saying. The same peace was there.

"Yes, I meant it."

"Good." He stood, pulled a tiny box from his pocket, and knelt before me.

"Just so there's no confusion, this is me asking you to marry me." He opened the box. The simple solitaire was just my style. "With this ring."

I laughed, my heart overflowing with love and surety that this was absolutely the right move. "Just so there's no confusion, this is me saying yes. Again."

Serenaded by cheers, laughter, and tears from the family, Steve slid the ring onto my finger. It was a perfect fit. Just like we've been for going on twenty years now.

— S.M. Green —

67

Who's Coming to Dinner?

Blended families: woven together by choice, strengthened
together by love, and each uniquely ours.
~Author Unknown

"Are we expecting someone else for dinner?" my constantly hungry son inquired. There was, in fact, good reason for him to wonder since everyone seemed to be accounted for, and the mouthwatering aromas of our Christmas Eve feast were drifting into the family room.

"Yes, Kristi and Ollie are coming. Kristi said they were running a bit late, though," I explained.

Most of the group appeared to be happy to hear the couple would be joining us for dinner and our usual Christmas Eve festivities, with only one or two guests exhibiting slightly raised eyebrows.

Perhaps they were surprised that couples who shared a child but were no longer together could remain close members of each other's families.

When my grandson Elijah and Kristi had divorced, they continued to remain close, not only for their son but for each other. There were some hurt feelings at first between the couple as well as other family members. But most of us understood that ending a committed relationship is never easy, and with a little extra effort, it can have an amicable outcome — especially if there are children involved.

Elijah is not currently in a new relationship, so he spends the majority of his time working at his HVAC job and caring for Maze, who lives with him. This is more convenient for everyone involved since several family members are close by and can get Maze off to school in the morning and pick him up after school.

Maze visits his mother, who lives about an hour's drive from his dad's house, every other weekend during the school year and every other week during summer vacation.

When Kristi and her boyfriend Ollie arrived at the house on Christmas Eve, the merriment escalated — particularly for ten-year-old Maze, who loved having his parents together whenever possible. Ollie was tremendously good with Maze, which was an extra blessing.

It is nothing short of remarkable how well Kristi, Elijah and Ollie get along with one another. This was never more apparent than during that Christmas Eve celebration.

Opening gifts after dinner was a hectic but thrilling endeavor with all the children squealing in delight and the adults cherishing the precious moments while joining in on the fun. It wasn't long before Elijah and Ollie were tossing the Nerf football back and forth, playing Keep Away with the kids.

Ollie, Kristi and Elijah were especially fascinated with the plasma ball that Maze received as a Christmas gift. They tried a variety of scientific experiments, to the delight and amazement of both the kids and other adults, who eventually all wanted a turn touching the clear globe with their fingers to attract the multi-colored beams.

Later in the evening, a few of the men built a fire outside in the fire pit so the kids could roast marshmallows to make s'mores. Elijah and Ollie helped them find the perfect marshmallow-roasting sticks and patiently showed them how to safely whittle sharp points on the ends.

As the night wound down, we all bundled up and sat around the outside fire to enjoy adult drinks, hot chocolate for the kids, and lots of savory snacks and special Christmas sweets. The atmosphere was perfect for sharing stories about past Christmases — some funny and some a bit nostalgic. The night air was brisk, but I don't think it could have been more pleasurable.

If anyone objected to Kristi and Ollie taking part in our festivities, it wasn't apparent. In fact, everyone seemed to enjoy them and was exceptionally welcoming.

Following warm hugs, lots of thank-yous and Merry Christmas wishes, a sleepy Maze, his parents and Ollie were the last to leave the house.

As I watched both cars drive away, I thought a child couldn't receive a better gift than spending Christmas Eve with his two loving parents, even when the parents have chosen to live apart.

—Connie Kaseweter Pullen—

68

Because You Make It

The most important ingredient that goes into
a pie is the love that goes into making it.
~Sarah Weeks, Pie

Early in my parents' marriage, an older couple who lived across the street befriended them. The four of them often indulged in Euchre, Password, and other games while my sister and I played in the living room. This lovely neighbor lady stocked homemade pies in her freezer in case company dropped in, so each time we visited we indulged in a slice. These fruit, pumpkin, and other pies with their homemade crusts were so delicious that Mom asked her new friend how to make them. From that point on, my mother became our family's official pie baker for the holidays.

Every Christmas morning, my sister and I would enter the kitchen and find Mom already hard at work with a floured rolling pin in her hand, still wearing her pink chenille robe with the peacock design on the back. We breathed in the smell of freshly baked pie crusts as they cooled on wire racks. Mom spent hours making pumpkin pie for my dad, chocolate for the kids, lime for herself and my grandma, and mincemeat for my grandfather.

Mom said mincemeat was Grandpa's favorite, but if it weren't for him, she wouldn't trouble herself making it. Most everyone else in the family ignored Grandpa's pie and chose chocolate or pumpkin instead. Indeed, any dessert with "meat" in its name sounded gross to me. Mincemeat filling contains apples, raisins, spices, and sometimes minced beef—not usually a tasty combination for kids. Or adults, now that I think about it.

Mom made Grandpa's pie every Christmas. And each year, without fail, he served himself a large piece and complimented Mom on her effort. Grandpa's favored dessert became quite the family tradition.

Until that one year.

I don't recall the reason, but Mom didn't make the mincemeat pie. Perhaps she couldn't find all the ingredients, or maybe she ran out of time. She fretted that entire Christmas morning as we packed the other desserts into the trunk and drove the few miles to her parents' home.

"What's he going to say? Oh, he'll be so disappointed," she said.

"It will be all right," Dad said. "We have plenty of other flavors to choose from."

"But he likes that one."

Once we arrived, my sister and I carried gifts for my grandparents and cousins into the house while Mom and Dad brought the pies. The scents of roast turkey and baked rolls wafted toward us the moment we entered, and heat from the oven warmed the house. Christmas carols by Andy Williams, Perry Como, and Bing Crosby played on the stereo. And Grandma's silver Christmas tree gleamed with shades of red, yellow, and blue from a rotating color wheel that shined from the floor.

"I'm really sorry, Dad," Mom said as she handed the remaining pies to Grandma to put in the refrigerator. She shrugged out of her coat. "I didn't make the mincemeat."

"Don't worry about it," Grandpa said as he poured himself a cup of coffee.

My grandparents' tiny kitchen couldn't accommodate six kids and nine adults for dinner, so our Christmas celebrations always took place in their finished basement. Grandma, Mom, and Aunt Dorothy carried the food down from the kitchen. The ping-pong table near the base of the stairs served as our dinner table (minus the net).

During the meal, Grandpa entertained himself and everyone else with his antics. Grandma assigned him the job of mashing the potatoes, but he couldn't resist turning the task into comedic art. After he finished the usual steps of adding milk and mixing, he swooped the spuds into the shape of a giant, swirling mountain. Since the potatoes then looked like the top of an ice cream cone, he finished off his sculpture by dotting the peak with a maraschino cherry. And if someone asked him to pass them a roll during dinner, Grandpa put his former baseball skills to use and pitched one to the other end of the table.

When dessert time arrived, Mom and Grandma brought the pies downstairs with a pitcher of milk, whipped cream, and additional silverware. Mom looked at Grandpa. "Dad, I feel like I let you down by not making your pie, especially since it's your favorite."

"You already told me. It's fine." Grandpa reached for a fork, and it clinked against a pink-flowered dessert plate.

"I know, but I still feel bad. I promise you, though, you'll have it next year."

Grandpa looked at her with a twinkle in his eye. "Stop apologizing. To tell you the truth, I never liked mincemeat pie anyway."

I think all our mouths hung open.

"What do you mean? You eat a big piece every year. I only make it because you eat it."

Grandpa smiled and patted Mom on her shoulder. "I only eat it because you make it for me."

Mom stood at the table with wide eyes. "Then why did I think it was your favorite?"

"I have no idea. Now slice me a piece of the chocolate one, if you don't mind."

So ended one of our family's long-held Christmas traditions. My grandparents died over twenty years ago, and my parents are elderly now, but my sister and I make the chocolate and pumpkin pies so another generation can enjoy them. And occasionally we tell them all about their great-grandfather, his mincemeat pie, and the tradition that never should have started in the first place.

— Toni Wilbarger —

69

Chicken Soup
for the Soul

Instant Party

Never say, "Oops." Instead, say, "How interesting."
~Author Unknown

"It's all set." Mike sounded excited over the phone.

"So, we have the place and the date and the time," I said as my mind rolled through all the details of our upcoming Christmas party. "And everyone's been invited?"

"Yup. And everyone's looking forward to December 18th. It'll be a good time."

"How many are coming?"

Mike paused for a few moments as I heard him shuffling papers. "Thirty-six. Mostly couples, but a few singles as well. I know almost everyone pretty well. They're from seven different schools. We've told everyone to dress up for Christmas. I'm wearing a string of Christmas bells."

I knew Mike liked to put together odd outfits for various occasions. I could hardly wait to see what he'd wear to this party.

"Thanks for the info. I know it's potluck, so everyone's bringing a favorite dish. Do you think we'll have enough food?"

"No problema." Mike loved to throw his "Spanish" into conversations. "Talk later."

"Bye now."

I turned to my wife and smiled. "The whole party is organized, and it looks great."

Sue smiled back at me. "Only a week and a half to go!"

The next ten days seemed to race by, and the night of Saturday, December 18th, arrived for our annual teachers' Christmas party. Sue wore a long, black-velvet dress, and I wore a red sweater with a Santa pin. The nose lit up when I pulled a little string. My students loved the pin so I figured it was perfect for the party.

The drive was slow and snowy as we made our way over to the Simcoes' home for the party. We were the first people to arrive, and as we stepped in the front door, Nancy Simcoe looked a little puzzled but took our hot casserole to the kitchen. Both Nancy and her husband Bruce were dressed in jeans and old T-shirts. We shook the snow off our coats and stepped inside.

I noticed their Christmas tree was only partially decorated. The ornaments sat in boxes on the floor around the tree. "Bruce, I'll help you finish decorating your tree. I know how busy you must be just before Christmas," I said. I walked over and began to hang the decorations. Bruce looked a little flustered and then joined me as a thin smile spread across his face.

More guests arrived at the Simcoes' home, and the whole party turned festive. I stepped over to Bruce and Nancy and spoke in a low voice. "If you two want to change into your Christmas outfits, we'll look after everyone who's arriving."

Both of them looked a little awkward but quickly slipped upstairs to change.

Two of our friends, Lynn and Mike, found dishes from the kitchen cupboards and set them out on the dining room table. They also decorated the table with Christmas décor they found in a closet near the front door. Someone else found napkins and candles. It felt so good to be able to help the Simcoes decorate for the dinner and lower their stress level. We had the sense that they didn't entertain very much around Christmas, but that was okay.

Bruce and Nancy Simcoe soon reappeared in their Christmas outfits. As they stepped into the dining room, a look of amazement spread across their faces when they looked at all the food and holiday decorations. Everyone greeted them warmly, making sure to thank them for their hospitality.

Once all the guests arrived, we started the meal, and someone turned on Christmas music. The night was an amazing success.

When the meal was all over and before everyone started to leave, I clinked a glass and then made an announcement. "Thank you to the Simcoes for so generously opening your home to our Christmas get-together. We really appreciate it so much."

Bruce blushed and said, "Thank you," in a low voice.

A few minutes later, Bruce asked to speak to me one-on-one, so we walked together into the sitting room at the back of the house. Bruce looked down at the floor as he began to speak in a low, nervous voice. "It was good having all of you over tonight for the Christmas party, even though I didn't know a lot of the people." He cleared his throat and continued, "But it was a bit of a surprise for Nancy and me. We didn't know you people were coming here for a party."

The words hung in the air like smoke on a still day.

"Oh," I answered, not sure what to say next. "Didn't Mike call you and confirm everything with you?"

Bruce shook his head. "When you and your wife stepped through the front door, that was our first hint that anyone was coming over. We didn't know why you were coming, but..."

"I am so sorry," I sighed. "That's why you were dressed in jeans when we arrived at your front door and..."

Bruce awkwardly shifted from one foot to the other as he nodded his head.

My stomach began to twist in knots, and I felt awkward beyond words. My mouth suddenly went dry, and I had difficulty getting my words out. "We've got a small group who'll do the cleanup and straighten your house back to the way it was before we arrived."

"You don't have to do that," Bruce responded.

"We've already started." I smiled. I walked over to my wife and a couple of others and quickly explained that Mike hadn't told the Simcoes about the party. Everyone looked shocked, and an awkwardness hung in the air. We stood for a few moments, not sure what to do. Then, my wife said, "We've got a lot of cleanup to do. Let's get to it."

An hour later, we had washed all the dishes and cleaned up the main floor. Bruce and Nancy had stayed in the background as our team of six worked away. I suggested they join us in the living room for a glass of wine so we could all unwind a little from the party. We were all so embarrassed by what had happened that we hoped this time would help smooth the waters with the Simcoes.

When we were all seated, Nancy, who had been pretty quiet the whole evening, was the first one to speak. "As you know, this whole party was a bit of a surprise for us." She stopped talking and blushed.

I held my breath, not knowing what she was going to say next.

"We don't really entertain," Nancy continued. "But I have to admit that tonight was the most fun we've had at Christmas in years."

"Maybe ever," Bruce joined in. A broad smile spread across his face. "So, thank you for the surprise party. It really has made our Christmas this year very special. We loved every minute."

— Rob Harshman —

70

The Christmas of the Deep Freeze(r)

If baking is any labor at all, it's a labor of love. A love
that gets passed from generation to generation.
~Regina Brett

I t's a tradition that started way back, supposedly stemming from
our Italian heritage. My mom. Her mom and aunts. Okay, that's
as far back as I know, but it's a tradition all the same: baking
cookies for Christmas.

Now let me clarify. This is not your mother's Christmas cookie baking. (It's mine.) It involves old classics, from gingerbread and cornflake holly cookies, to intricate "hand-painted" cutouts. There are Italian pizzelles — the kind that require an appliance whose sole purpose is to make that specific type of cookie — and there are newer ones, like chewy toffee cookies and peppermint twists.

Each year requires the addition of at least one new cookie for my family to try. We judge whether the newbie is worth keeping in the Christmas cookie lineup.

I grew up baking these cookies with my mother. Specifically, my apprenticeship began as what I call an Accenter — putting the finishing touches on these bits of happiness: sprinkles on top of the icing, chocolate Kisses on top of the peanut-butter cookies, cinnamon dots on the hollies.

As I climbed the hierarchy of baking belts — Icing Spreader, Dough

Maker — I advanced to Piping Artist around my middle-school years. Yes, that intricate work involving multiple colors of icing, different piping nozzles, and just the right amount of pressure to get those tidy bows and buttons right. I knew I had made it, that there was a chance I could carry on the legacy, when family far and wide couldn't tell which cookies had been decorated by me or by my mom.

Onward into adulthood, I got married and moved to Tennessee. My husband and I alternated whose family we spent Christmas with, my childhood home in Ohio being visited every other Christmas. I looked forward to carrying out the cookie rite of passage with my children. Each year, I made my own set of cookies to share with local friends and family, while my mother made her batches over 500 miles away. My children helped of course.

After my mom's major back surgery, and hosting — and feeding — more and more grandchildren at her home over the holidays, it was time to step up. And honestly, I wanted to show the family that one of our most beloved traditions would carry on for at least another generation. I had something to prove and wanted to make my mother proud.

The Christmas cookies of 2019 would be provided by yours truly. I offered all of them, old and new, totaling seventeen varieties and numbering just shy of 1,000 cookies. I bought a deep freezer that year for my garage just to store the cookies. In order not to burn out, I started baking in early October, spacing them out, one or two types of cookies a week.

This was it. My big moment to shine. My black-belt test of honor. The plan was in place. We had a new third-row SUV that could fit our three kids comfortably, plus the luggage and cookies. The cookies would be stacked in the back of the vehicle, straight from the freezer. Our travel route involved traversing Ohio to its northeast corner. Luckily, the weather would be cold enough that the cookies wouldn't get too warm if we ended up breaking the trip into two days of travel.

I worried. Would they rattle in the back and break? Would the way I stacked them inside the containers make them stick to one another? Would the decorations fall off? So many aspects of cookie transportation to worry about.

Finally, the day came to leave. We started packing the car, and the usual chaos ensued.

"Where's my charger?"

"His pillow is taking up too much room!"

"But I want to sit in the back!"

"Is it actually going to snow this year? Do we need all the boots and mittens?"

We finally hit the road, with Christmas music playing over the speakers to set the mood. We were going to Grandma's house! Despite the packing hiccups, we were making good time. We had a full tank of gas. The kids had been fed. No one had to go to the bathroom.

And, then, it hit me, like Catherine O'Hara's character remembering Kevin on the plane to Paris in *Home Alone*.

"The cookies!"

The blood rushed out of my face. My stomach knotted itself, an unprecedented yet impressive feat of origami. The months of work. The tens of pounds of flour. The liter of premium vanilla. Not containers of cocoa, but special dark cocoa. An amount of butter that should require confession and atonement.

Sitting in the new deep freezer in the garage.

Forgotten.

My husband and I discussed the possibilities. We could turn around. But we were nearly to Louisville, which meant going back would add another six hours of driving. We could give our neighbor the garage code and have him ship them to Grandma's house. Not only would that inconvenience our neighbor, but it would cost a fortune, not to mention the odds of the cookies arriving looking like reindeer food.

There was nothing we could do. The cookies would remain at home over the holidays. I had to arrive at Grandma's with no proof of my months of work. No (unhealthy) fruits of my labor.

The one time my mom had entrusted me with such a responsibility, I had failed.

Of course, my mother felt terrible about it. She kept reassuring me that Christmas wasn't ruined. It'd be okay.

But... we had a few days before Christmas Eve. And, like John McClane in Nakatomi Plaza, I'm no quitter.

As we had done so many years over my childhood, my mother and I got to work. We made the gingerbread dough one evening, and baked and decorated them the next day. We whipped together holly cookies like a factory of Santa's elves. We pressed pizzelles, smelling up the house with the warm, sugary aroma that reminded us of Christmases past.

We didn't make seventeen different types, nor did we come close to 1,000 cookies. But we laughed together, shared stories of mess-ups over the years, and created a sense of Christmas spirit in that kitchen that we wouldn't have if I had remembered my cookies.

My brothers and their wives pitched in, bringing their own batches from their homes. We laughed at the rushed look of some of our cookies but ate them all the same. That Christmas wasn't spoiled. It became forever memorable.

And the added bonus? Christmas cookies for dessert at our family table clear through spring.

— Mary Shotwell —

71

When Thanksgiving Meets Christmas

Creativity is thinking up new things.
Innovation is doing new things.
~Theodore Levitt

The tantalizing aroma of a roasting turkey filled the air of the metro Detroit home that my sister and I shared. My boyfriend had just arrived for our Thanksgiving dinner. This was the man I hoped to marry, and as a divorcée with a grown daughter, I was long past seeking my parents' approval. However, I was introducing him to my parents at dinner, hoping they would accept him into the family.

I also needed to know if my Southern style of cooking could pass muster with my Vermont-raised boyfriend. What can I say? I'm a good cook, but he didn't know that yet.

Roger was also divorced, with a preteen son with whom I got along. I'm a blend of Southern and Northern manners and know that family connections are important in building a happy, cohesive family.

"Roger, I wasn't expecting you until 3:00," I said, surprised at his early arrival. I wasn't dressed for company. I looked a little disheveled from all the cooking, but he didn't seem to mind as he greeted me with a warm kiss.

"I came to help," he said, which made him a winner in my book. The only other man I knew who helped in the kitchen was my father.

He didn't hesitate to assist when needed, wearing the butcher-style apron he'd made for himself. When one of his male friends teased him about wearing an apron, he said, "I'm man enough to wear it."

Thinking my boyfriend would just be in the way of our carefully planned meal preparations, I said, "Roger, could you please iron the tablecloth, set the table for twelve, and put the floral centerpiece on the table?"

He completed the tasks without hesitation and then said, "I brought fresh cranberries to make a cranberry relish."

My sister and I looked at each other as she silently mouthed, "Cranberry relish?" That was something we'd never tasted. Our cranberry sauce came in a can in a solid clump of jelly.

I said, "Sure, that's so thoughtful of you."

With that said, he asked for a measuring cup and a saucepan, and started working. The popping sound of the boiling cranberries was a little disconcerting, but he seemed to know what he was doing.

When he finished, he commented on all the food my sister and I had cooked. "Wow! Did you cook for an army?"

I laughed and said, "We always prepare enough for our guests to take food home for the next day. We're expecting nine hungry relatives who won't have to cook tomorrow."

When family members arrived, Roger helped put the food on the table. Our menu consisted of my roasted turkey and cornbread dressing, green beans with ham, mashed potatoes and gravy, my sister's mac and cheese, her homemade yeast rolls, cranberry sauce from the can, and Roger's fresh cranberry relish.

On the dessert table, we put my sister's lemon pound cake and my specialty: deep-dish apple pie. There was vanilla ice cream in the freezer.

Our father carved the turkey, as always, and the many dishes were passed. I noticed that not one member of my family sampled Roger's creation. My mother even turned up her nose at the sight of the dish as she passed it on.

Of course, I put a spoonful of cranberry relish on my plate. I was hooked, but not only because I loved the man who prepared it. His sweet/tart dish was delicious. Later that evening after everyone left, I apologized to him because my family didn't even try his dish.

He said, "No problem. That just leaves more for me."

The man's a double winner, I thought.

After everyone finished dessert and the leftovers were refrigerated, it was game time. We all liked to play games, but Mother was a competitive word-game player and hated to lose.

I whispered to Roger, "Please let Mother win so she'll go home."

He said, "That's not in my DNA." I saw the competitive spirit in his expression.

We played her favorite word game until shortly after 10:30 p.m. when she beat Roger by one word.

I knew then she would accept him into the family.

The next step in our relationship was for me to meet his family. Roger, his son, and I traveled to freezing-cold northern Vermont the day before Christmas. I met his parents, brother, two sisters, and several in-laws. They were warm and welcoming to me.

On Christmas Day, dinner was held at the home of two of his aunts. We feasted on roasted turkey, squash, riced potatoes and gravy, tongue pickles, peas, carrots, and a gelatin fruit salad. Dinner was delicious, but I was most impressed at the sight of the delicious-looking variety of pies I had never tasted before. They had chocolate, maple, cream currant, raspberry, strawberry rhubarb, mincemeat, boysenberry, and blueberry pies. When asked which one I wanted, I couldn't decide.

One of Roger's aunts said, "Cut a sliver of each pie Barbara chooses."

I selected all the fruit pies and enjoyed every delicious bite.

I was surprised to learn that his family also played games after dinner. When I discovered that his mother was highly competitive, I felt right at home. She liked playing card games and hated to lose just like my mother. One evening, the family played her favorite card game until well after 1:30 a.m. because she refused to quit until she won.

Playing games each evening of our week-long vacation revealed my competitive spirit.

Roger and I realized that both our mothers were assertive and highly competitive, just as I am. Both our fathers were quiet, unassuming gentlemen respected by everyone who met them. Roger, like our fathers, is a well-respected gentleman.

When Roger and I looked at each other at the end of our fun-filled trip to Vermont, I said, "We were cut from the same cloth. That makes it easy to fit into each other's lives." He agreed.

We eloped the following May. Thirty-three years later, Roger and I still enjoy family meals, competitive game playing, and his delicious cranberry relish, which he prepares for me every Thanksgiving and Christmas.

— Barbara Pattee —

72

The Christmas Ham

You can't have Thanksgiving without turkey.
That's like Fourth of July without apple pie
or Friday with no two pizzas.
~Joey Tribbiani, Friends

I became a vegetarian during the summer of 2021. Postpartum hit me like a runaway train. As I sat on the kitchen floor playing with our cats, chowing down on one of the delicious ham-and-poppyseed sandwiches that my dad's lovely wife had made, I suddenly had this overwhelming feeling: *I'm eating someone's baby. Oh, no, I could be eating someone's mother! Or father!* Cue the waterworks and life-altering decision. Postpartum affects women in many different ways. For me, it stole my love of crispy bacon, grilled steaks, and any other previously tasty animal product.

I gradually grew accustomed to my new vegetarian lifestyle over the next few months. As the Christmas season finally arrived, I felt myself feeling downright giddy like I do every year. I have so many happy, funny, and sentimental memories that make Christmastime a cherished part of the year. This was our first Christmas with our newborn, so I was even more excited for all the new and special memories we would make as a family.

I fancy myself a decent cook, and I've always loved cooking for my family and friends. When I chose to become a vegetarian, I made it clear to my husband that I didn't expect him or our daughter to do so. She could make her own choices when she got older. That said, my husband is incredibly supportive and enjoys my meatless meals as much as any other meal. In the rare instances that he has a craving for a tender brisket or a smoked brat, I'm still happy to throw on my metaphorical apron and get cooking.

I informed my husband and our extended family that I was happy to make some traditional holiday foods, including meats like ham and turkey. I'd rather feast on the side dishes anyway; that's usually some of the best food. But my husband, the amazing guy that he is, wanted to support me for my first vegetarian Christmas. So, I started hunting for a new, main course that would be completely meatless but still mouthwateringly tasty.

Short story? I should've just made vegetable lasagna. Long story? In my infinite lack of wisdom and totally misplaced confidence, I decided to make a vegan holiday "ham."

A few days before Christmas, I strolled into our local grocery store with what turned out to be way too much faith in my culinary skills. This would be the best vegan ham ever. Vegetable broth? Check. Smoked paprika and liquid smoke? Check. Nutritional yeast? Got it. Ketchup, garlic powder, and salt? You bet. Extra firm tofu? Check! Refined coconut oil? Interesting. Our store didn't carry that. Oh, well. Surely this other coconut oil-like product would work! Vital wheat gluten? Hmm, the store didn't carry that either. But after doing a much-too-fast Google search, it looked like I could substitute flaxseed meal for that. Perfect!

Had I been more experienced in the art of meatless "meats," I would've realized that substituting ingredients for my first big holiday meatless meal was a terrible, awful idea.

One food processor full of tofu, a "kneaded" ham-shaped loaf, and one overfilled steamer basket later, and we had a vegan loaf! To top it off, I whipped up a glaze from scratch — vegetable broth, olive oil, smoked paprika, maple syrup, and just a few cloves. The smell was heavenly, a hint of smoky, spiced sweetness that reminded me of a hometown barbecue. After a positive, lip-smacking taste test, I spooned the glaze over our loaf. It actually looked like a bona fide Christmas ham!

My mother-in-law and father-in-law joined us for our Christmas feast that evening. We gave them warning that we were trying out a new recipe, but that there would be plenty of other delicious sides to offer: cranberry relish, honey-glazed carrots, mashed potatoes, dressing/stuffing, and green-bean casserole. Of course, I also prepared my great-grandmother's cherished grated sweet-potato pudding.

My husband's parents sang our praises over the savory, picturesque food. My poor, sweet in-laws.

The lights on our beautiful Christmas tree shimmered in the corner of our living room, the table was set with our fancy Christmas dishes and centerpiece, the warm aroma of spice and cloves hung in the air, and classic Christmas music played softly on our speaker system. Then, there was my daughter. My beautiful, giggly daughter with her contagious, toothless grin and a happy twinkle in her eyes. My husband put his arm around me, and a warmth spread in my chest. It was truly a picture-perfect moment.

My husband pulled out a carving knife and began to slice our vegan loaf while I collected everyone's plates to serve.

We noticed the odd brown color first. The inside looked porous and bread-like. It definitely smelled like ham, and we knew that the glaze was delicious, so surely it couldn't be too bad, right?

Everyone took an excited, albeit tentative, first bite... and froze. It had the faint taste of ham but in the way that a flavored potato chip only kind of tastes like its namesake. I chewed. Then, I chewed some more. The texture wasn't at all tender. Instead, it was a bit gamey. Not smooth but rough. It seemed to fill my entire mouth, even though I only took a small bite. It was difficult to swallow, even with the assistance of ice-cold water. I risked a glance at my husband's face to see his expression: an amused smile, with a hint of a grimace. He kept chewing but avoided eye contact. I turned to my in-laws. They kept their eyes focused on their plates.

I took another large gulp of water, as did the rest of the family, followed by an unnecessarily large drink of holiday wine. I laughed nervously, commented on the unsuspected taste and texture of our main dish, and continued to eat.

"This is really bad," I giggled.

My husband laughed but gently agreed.

My mother-in-law, husband, and I all finished our slices as quickly as possible, periodically grabbing bites of other foods and drinks to help flush out the not-so-ham-like flavor of the vegan loaf. My father-in-law, the saint that he is, persevered, even commenting that it wasn't that bad. He went back for seconds!

After many sympathetic smiles and a genuine effort by all to eat my culinary monstrosity, I spent the rest of the evening apologizing for my epic failure and ruining Christmas dinner. Blessedly, it wasn't actually ruined. We laughed about the whole incident while gorging ourselves on the delicious side dishes we thankfully had available. We devoured my granny's grated sweet-potato pudding, finished off our dinner with a tasty glass of wine, and proceeded to laugh and coo at my baby daughter's antics.

Our home was filled with laughter, smiles, and the innocent giggles of our beautiful little girl. So many new and wonderful memories were made that night, including my genuine promise that I would never make a vegan ham for a holiday dinner ever again.

— Whitney Kolba —

73

The Pecan Pie of Love

*I think I'm a lot like other moms out there who feel like
if we don't have the pecan pie we have every year,
then it just won't be Christmas.*
~Faith Hill

"**A**nd for Cecil, I've baked a pecan pie." After running through the menu of Christmas goodies she had prepared, my mother-in-law Ruth had a special pie waiting just for me.

Ruth and I had a complicated relationship. Said simpler, we didn't much like each other. I quit taking it personally when I realized she didn't exactly gush about anyone.

Ruth and her husband Russell lived in Indiana, and our family typically alternated holidays between Indiana and Texas, where Sara and I live. As the in-laws grew older, we would go north every year to visit them.

Typically, hospitable if not warm, Ruth played the role of good hostess by offering a slice of Texas Christmas in Indiana. She began a tradition of baking pecan pies. I'm the only one in the family who will eat pecan pie, so the annual pies were made especially for me.

Her first try was, frankly, the worst pecan pie I've ever had. Several things went wrong, but the most memorable was the presence of some pecan shells in the pie. A lot crunchier than anyone would want.

I gently tried to pass along via Sara that the pecans needed to be better shelled, knowing from family history that this wreck of a pie might be the first and last pecan pie Ruth made for me. When they were newlyweds, Ruth had baked a cherry pie for Russell, who pointed out to his bride that the cherries hadn't been pitted and watched in surprise as Ruth snatched the pie and tossed it, pan and all, into the trash can. She never fixed him another cherry pie in seventy-one years of marriage.

That storm didn't blow through this time around. Instead, Ruth kept trying to bake me a better pecan pie.

Now, you must understand that a pecan pie has three states: underdone, perfect, and burned. There is a very small window of time between these three states, which I personally have never gotten right, so I don't make pecan pies. Ruth kept earnestly trying to thread that needle.

Most years, the pie was burned. I would load on whipped topping to mask the taste and add moisture as I ate a slice of pie at every meal. There were other luscious options of pie and cake, but because the pecan pie was strictly for me, I saddled up and ate it throughout the holiday until it was gone.

On occasion, the pie was underdone, a gooey but tasty mess. One time, Ruth achieved perfection, which I welcomed and praised and never received again, despite her best efforts.

Now I have sweet-as-pecan-pie memories of our annual ritual. It wasn't torture but a truly touching reciprocal gesture with someone who was difficult to love and found it hard to express love. The most loving thing Ruth ever did for me was to bake that pecan pie. And the most loving thing I ever did for her was to eat it.

— Cecil Taylor —

Chapter
9

Giving & Gratitude

74

One Large Gift

*Concentrate on counting your blessings, and you'll
have little time to count anything else.*
~Woodrow Kroll

I t was my favorite day of the entire holiday season. Today was going to be even more special because, for the first time, my husband and I were taking our young daughters with us.

"Mommy, tell me again where we are going," eight-year-old Katelyn said.

"Today, we are helping at the Christmas store," I replied.

"So, we're going to Walmart," five-year-old Lauren said innocently. This brought laughter from my husband and me.

"No, it's not Walmart. It's not even really a store," Kevin replied.

I went on to explain that the Christmas store was located in the basement of a church. During the year, the church received donations of new clothes, toys, shoes, household items, tools and more. People who needed help at Christmastime could apply to "shop" at the store for themselves and their family free of charge.

When we arrived at the church, Lauren pointed and said, "Look at that line of people. Do we have to wait to go in?"

"No, Lauren, those are the customers. They are waiting for the store to open."

We entered through the side door. The drab basement of the old church had been transformed into a festive holiday shop. Carols played from the speakers, yummy smells filled the room, and lots of excited chatter and laughter could be heard. A kind, older woman with sparkling eyes greeted us and showed us where to put our coats and personal items. Turning to Katelyn and Lauren, she said, "Would you girls like a Christmas cookie before I put you to work?"

They both nodded and accepted the treat with smiles.

Kevin and I had worked at the store for many years, so we knew what to do. We were to be personal shoppers who escorted customers through the store and helped them pick out one large gift for each member of the family.

Katelyn and I worked together. Our first customer was a young woman named Maria. She was shopping for her mother, three-year-old son, infant son, and herself. After introducing ourselves and explaining the process, we began to shop.

Maria was very quiet and looked rather uncomfortable. I wondered how to break the awkwardness, but Katelyn had no such concerns. With her ready smile, she took Maria's hand and said, "Let's go look at the toys."

Maria seemed to relax, and off they went.

Before getting to the toy section, Maria saw all the household goods. She stopped and inspected each one, and then carefully pointed to a large Crock-Pot.

"For my mama," she said.

We loaded it in our shopping cart and continued on. As we neared the toy section, Katelyn pounced on a Hot Wheels racetrack. "Maria," she said, "your son would love this."

Maria carefully looked at the toy and smiled. She ran her hands lovingly over the box and smiled at Katelyn. "He would love this, but he needs a coat more." Then, she set it gently back on the table and moved toward the children's clothes.

Katelyn looked at me in stunned disbelief. "Mommy," she whispered, "clothes for Christmas? Why can't he have this *and* a coat?"

Gently, I reminded her that each customer got to pick out *one* large item for each family member. "A winter coat with hat and gloves will be Roberto's gift," I said.

"But he needs a toy for Christmas," Katelyn said as tears filled her eyes. I gave her a hug and reminded her that Maria knew best what her family needed.

At the children's clothes, Maria found a handsome, blue winter coat with a red stripe down the sleeve. There was a matching knit hat and winter gloves attached.

"This will keep him so warm this winter, and it will probably fit him next year as well!" she said with a huge smile on her face. "It's perfect!"

Katelyn nodded her approval, but I could still see that she thought Roberto needed the toy.

For the baby, Katelyn found a set of two winter rompers. Attached to the rompers was a set of plastic building blocks. Maria smiled at her and nodded her approval.

Now the only person left to shop for was Maria herself. She wandered through the aisles and looked at many items, but I noticed that she kept glancing back at the toy section.

Finally, she looked at me and asked, "If I don't get something for myself, can I get the racetrack for Roberto? He would love that so much."

"Of course," I said with a lump in my throat.

Katelyn jumped up and down with excitement, and then she ran over to grab the racetrack and put it in Maria's cart.

Soon, Katelyn realized that Maria would not be getting a gift. She pulled gently on my arm, and I bent over as she whispered in my ear. "Mommy, Maria won't have a gift to open on Christmas morning."

"It's okay, Kate. Her gift will be the joy she sees on her family's faces as they open their gifts. Mothers love to see their children happy."

"She must love Roberto a whole bunch," said Kate, looking unconvinced.

I gave her a big hug, and then we helped Maria finish her shopping.

Fast forward one year… We again took the girls out of school for our new family tradition.

The doors were just about to open to let in the first shoppers when we were approached by a familiar-looking young woman.

"Maria!" squealed Katelyn.

"Yes, it's me," she said, giving us all hugs.

"How are you and your family doing?" I asked.

"Very well. Last Christmas was a turning point for me. Your kindness and that of the other volunteers touched my heart. After Christmas, I was fortunate enough to find a good job. This year, I wanted to assist someone else, so I signed up to help. I know what it is like to need help, and now I will return the favor."

Katelyn asked, "Did Roberto like his racetrack last year?"

Maria's entire face lit up with joy. "Yes, it was the best Christmas gift I ever received," she responded as she winked at me.

— Mary Low —

The Little Girl Who Gave Me Christmas

*Some people arrive and make such a beautiful impact
on your life, you can barely remember what life
was like without them.*
~Anna Taylor

I sat in the old, creaky porch swing where my late husband and I used to sit side by side for hours. We shared everything in that swing, from laughter to tears and everything in between. With every creak of the swing, I could almost feel Bill's thigh against mine.

It was an unusually warm December day, and the sun had almost lulled me to sleep. Then, a commotion from the house next door jerked me to attention. There was a dented old green pickup backed into the driveway and a faded red Beetle parked at the curb. Trying not to look conspicuous, I took quick glances at the house. It had been a rental since the Millers moved away, and Bill and I never knew what kind of neighbors we would have. Some had been delightful, some had been disappointing, and a few had been horrible.

A very tall thin man and a small dark-haired woman were unloading the truck. I spotted a small face pressing against the window in the back of the Beetle. The woman saw the child at the same time and rushed over to open the door and help the child out of the car. A little girl with shiny blond hair falling down her back tumbled out of the car. The sun caught her hair and made her look angelic. "You can't get that in a salon," I muttered to myself.

The little girl laughed and skipped through the grass, throwing her hands up in the air. She broke into an impromptu dance. She spotted me watching her and stopped abruptly, looking at me curiously. After a moment, she gave me a timid little wave. Even the grieving should be courteous, so I flipped her a quick wave and averted my eyes. My aching heart wasn't ready to indulge a child.

After lunch, curiosity drove me back outside again. I brought my knitting with me as a decoy, so it wouldn't look like I was spying. The little girl was sitting on her porch steps with an assortment of dolls and stuffed animals around her.

I turned my attention to the scarf I was knitting. Out of the corner of my eye, I caught a blur of pink and turned my head to see what it was. The little girl was standing at the bottom of my steps, staring up at me, patiently waiting for me to notice her.

I laid my knitting aside and shook my head. "Should you be out of your yard? Your mother is probably going to be upset with you."

Ignoring my question, she climbed the steps and stood in front of me, looking at me curiously. "Are you a grandmother?" she asked.

"No," I said, picking up my knitting again, hoping that she would realize she was being dismissed.

Surprise filled her eyes, which looked too deeply blue to be real, like the eyes on a doll. "But your hair is silver like a grandmother," she protested.

"That's because I'm old," I said, keeping my eyes on my knitting.

She reached out and touched my hand. "But you're soft like a grandmother."

"That's because I'm fat," I said.

She stood silently for a moment before she spoke again.

"Can I sit in the swing with you?"

"I suppose so," I said. "But only for a minute. Your mother is going to be looking for you soon. She expects you to be in your yard."

Grinning, she climbed up into the swing and snuggled against my side. "You feel like a grandmother," she said as she leaned further

Giving & Gratitude |

into me. "I had a grandmother," she added with the bluntness typical of a young child, "but she died."

Looking up at me, she asked, "Why aren't you a grandmother?"

I pursed my lips, wondering how to reply. What could a child so young understand? Shrugging, I decided that it is always best to be honest and hope that she would stop asking questions.

"I can't have grandchildren because I never had kids. You have to have kids before you can be a grandmother."

She took my hand and held it tenderly as if to comfort me. "That's not fair," she said, her little face crumpling up as if she might cry.

Then, she brightened and gave me a big smile. "You can be my grandmother!" she said excitedly.

I shook my head. "I don't know how to be a grandmother," I said.

"That's okay," she said, giving me a sympathetic look. "It isn't hard. I'll teach you. Grandmothers sing and read stories to you. They don't get mad and fuss if you spill your milk or get crumbs on the floor. They bake cookies and make you macaroni and cheese whenever you want some. They hug you a lot, too. And they like to color with you, too."

Now, I was smiling. "Grandmothers like to color?" I asked.

"Yes, they do," she said emphatically. "Parents don't, but grandmothers do. But don't worry. I can teach you how to do that, too."

"I'm afraid your mother wouldn't agree to that," I told her.

In a flash, she jumped out of the swing and bolted down the steps, calling over her shoulder. "I'll ask Mommy right now."

I sank back into the swing, dreading the confrontation with the child's mother that I felt certain was coming. She would probably forbid the little girl to come near me again. I wanted to discourage the child from bothering me, but I didn't want her to think I was a monster.

In a couple of minutes, I saw the woman marching toward my house with the little girl in tow. I didn't look up at her until I heard her clomping up my steps. To my surprise, she didn't look angry. She looked embarrassed. "I'm so sorry if my little girl has been pestering you," she said. "She lost her grandmother, and she misses her terribly. And you, unfortunately, look a little like her grandmother. I'll try to keep her away from you."

I looked at the little girl and saw the hope and excitement drain from her face. Tears filled her eyes. I felt my frozen heart begin to melt. "You can't do that," I protested. "She promised to teach me how to color."

I opened my arms, and she fell against my bosom for her first hug from her new grandmother. I held her tight, feeling love swell within my heart. I whispered in her ear, "If I'm going to be your grandmother, I should know your name."

I thought that I was facing a lonesome Christmas, but now I had to get busy. I had coloring books and crayons to buy. And I needed to brush up on baking cookies, too.

And that's how I became Maisie's grandmother.

—Elizabeth A. Atwater—

76

That's a GOOD House

*The magic is in the Christmas lights; as the twinkles
spread, so does the Christmas cheer.*
~Author Unknown

My four-year-old son was nestled in the back seat next
to his Nana and Grampa. My wife was getting our
Christmas playlist going, and I was starting the drive to
a high-end neighborhood that puts on a light show for
charity every year. We didn't get too far before my son got excited.

"Whoa! Look at that!" he proclaimed as we passed by a small
home with a single strand of lights strung along the top of a chain-link
fence. "That's a GOOD house!"

We all chuckled because the house really wasn't very impressive.
A house down the road had thousands of lights and a front lawn full
of inflatables. If the last house was good, I wondered, what would he
think of this one?

"Ooooooh. That's a GOOD house," he announced.

We all took turns pointing out the decorated houses, and each
one was just as good as the one before it. When we got to the light
show, he was excited to see the thousands of candlelit bags that guided
us through a cluster of large, expensive homes.

Most of the houses were decorated, and they all had something
special to offer. The multi-colored homes were fun and creative. The
single-colored homes were sophisticated and serene. The homes with
animated figures were humorous and dynamic. One house had a large

Grinch that looked like he was stealing the lights. My son thought that was hilarious. As we took in all the amazing homes, every house was "a GOOD house."

I couldn't help but feel underwhelmed at one beautiful home that had nothing more than an unlit wreath on the door and some candles in the windows. My son wasn't underwhelmed in the least.

"Look at *that* GOOD house," he directed.

"That house doesn't even have any Christmas lights," I informed him.

"But it has candles, and those are pretty good," he replied.

On the way home, we asked him which house was his favorite. "All of them," he answered. When we asked why, he said it was because they all made him happy. He wasn't comparing one house to another or determining whether or not each of them met its subjective potential. He didn't care if there were a million lights or a hundred. He only looked at the brightness that each of these good houses brought into this world.

Somewhere along life's journey, we tend to lose sight of how significant the little things can be. Looking at lights with my son reminded me of when I would ride around looking at holiday lights with my parents. I don't remember ever feeling anything but excitement when I saw them.

When we were almost home, we passed a home with no outside decorations, but their Christmas tree was shining elegantly through large, arched windows. "Look at that one, bud," I announced. "That's a GOOD house!"

— Elton A. Dean —

77

The Last Noel

To ease another's heartache is to forget one's own.
~Abraham Lincoln

We found ourselves at the end of a long hallway. Every door was closed. My husband Gerald and I stood together, balancing our songbooks in our tired hands.

Christmas is a busy time for singers. Our caroling season had started in late November with lots of festive enthusiasm. Each day for the past month, we had donned full Victorian costumes, complete with scarves, capes, and a top hat for Gerald. People loved the classic look and complimented our vocal blend.

You see, Victorian caroling is traditionally performed a cappella, meaning "without accompaniment." The carolers simply choose a key and then sing together in harmony. Being instrument-free means we can literally sing anywhere, but without a guitar or piano to support the sound, it can also get vocally tiring.

This had been a particularly taxing day. Starting early that morning, we'd performed in three different seniors' homes. At each location, we'd strolled up and down the expansive floors, singing to residents in busy dining areas and crowded common rooms. Now, our voices were parched and our feet ached. The small of my back had a little knot from holding my heavy carol book all day. I could tell Gerald needed a meal and a good night's sleep. I looked at my watch: 7:00 p.m. on the dot.

"We're done." Relief filled our faces. Time to go home and rest up for the next day.

As we started to leave, a door at the end of the hall softly opened. A woman poked out her head and looked at us.

"Are you the carolers?"

She was in her early forties, with a long, heavy cardigan wrapped around her. She'd styled her hair early in the day, but now the curls lay flat around her face. Her gentle eyes were rimmed red from crying. Any other Christmas, she was probably the life of the party. Tonight, she was tired and spent.

"I'm Barb. My mother has been asleep since supper, but she just woke up. I know you're probably finished, but if you wouldn't mind, I think she'd love a carol." She sighed, her smile weary, her chest heavy. "We don't have much time left with her."

Gerald and I nodded and followed her into the room. Her mother lay on the bed, a homemade quilt draped over her. Barb, her husband, and their teenage daughter stood by the side of the bed.

"Do you have a favourite carol?" we asked.

Barb gazed at her mother, a flood of memories filling her eyes. "She always loved 'The First Noel.'"

We looked at the frail woman lying on the bed. Her eyes were watery, barely registering our presence in the room. She turned towards her family, and they towards her.

Gerald and I found our notes, took a breath, and started to sing, "The first noel the angels did say…"

As we sang, Barb gently reached her arm around her daughter, drawing her close to her side. One by one, the family laid their hands on their beloved matriarch. They smiled at her with a lifetime's worth of love. Tears silently flowed down their cheeks as their broken voices joined their beloved carol, singing about another loving family from so many centuries ago.

"Noel, noel, noel, noel. Born is the King of Israel…"

Something holy was filling the room. It was indescribable, but palpable and real. Our tired voices and fatigue fell away. Fighting back our own tears, we lifted our voices in harmony, offering our song as a gift to this family, a gift of peace and beauty in their tender moment.

The final note ended, softly reverberating in the stark room. For a brief moment, we were all held together in the echo of the song, that message of a new birth and a promise fulfilled on a long-ago holy night.

Barb and her family looked up at us with tear-soaked faces. Whispers of "Merry Christmas," "Thank you," and "God bless" drifted across the room. Gerald and I silently closed our songbooks and slipped out the door.

Back in the hallway, we held each other close. We lifted silent prayers for this family, for the honour of being with them on this night, and for the sacred moment we had just experienced together.

Since that day, we've spent many hours singing carols. Our voices get tired, and our feet get sore. But on those days when we are most exhausted, we remember Barb and her family. We give thanks for the power of music to draw strangers together in moments of comfort and joy.

Songs of hope. Songs of life. Songs of peace.

For us, there is no better gift we can give, or receive.

— Allison Lynn Flemming —

Unwrapped Gifts

The best of all gifts around any Christmas tree:
the presence of a happy family all wrapped
up in each other.
~Burton Hillis

I had been in Chicago on a speaking engagement and couldn't wait to get home to Tennessee. I had already decorated the house for Christmas, with a tree in every room. My three daughters would be home for Christmas soon, and I wanted to get gifts wrapped and under the tree. My husband said he would wrap them, but that would have been like trying to put a diaper on our cat. He could do many things, but wrapping gifts was not one of them.

My flight was delayed. And I didn't feel well. Surely, I wasn't getting sick. Not now. Not this close to Christmas, and certainly not here in O'Hare. I had not eaten anything all morning, so I reasoned that I just needed to put something in my stomach. I did feel weak from hunger. I hadn't eaten breakfast in my hurry to get to the airport.

Then they announced that my flight was being grounded due to mechanical problems. I groaned upon hearing this. An elderly lady who was sitting next to me patted me on the knee with a shaking hand. I could tell she had some kind of tremors. "It's going to be alright, dear," she said. Then, she opened a small brown bag, and with that same trembling hand offered me a sandwich.

"Here. You look like you don't feel well. I bought this sandwich earlier, and I have another one. Please, take it."

Her eyes were looking straight into mine. She kept insisting, so I took the sandwich, unwrapped it and took a bite. I thanked the woman, and she said something that surprised me. She said there was no need to thank her and just consider it a Christmas present from a little old lady who had nothing else to give. "You'll feel better after you've eaten," she said.

I was curious about the woman and asked her where she was going. She told me she was going to visit her daughter for Christmas. She hadn't seen her in a year. She explained how her husband had gotten sick the year before and died on Christmas Day.

After telling her how sorry I was, she told me I didn't need to be sorry. She said they had been married on Christmas Day when they both were eighteen. "He was my Christmas present, and I was his," she said, smiling.

Then, she told me that Christmas presents don't always come in pretty papers and bows. She said the best ones are those that don't need to be wrapped or unwrapped but are special enough that you want to keep them in your heart forever.

I listened as she continued to talk. She told me that there is so much ado about Christmas that it loses its real meaning. If you really want to celebrate Christmas, she said, find gifts you don't need to wrap such as the love of family and friends. She said that God has His love wrapped around us, and the only gift we need to give Him is to love Him back. No fancy wrapping paper or bows required.

Then, she said goodbye, and I watched her walk away slowly. Suddenly, she stopped and threw the brown bag into a trash can. My heart almost stopped. She had given me the only sandwich she had. I didn't even know her name. I felt ashamed that I had not asked.

I was given more than the gift of a ham sandwich that day. I had a long time to think about it while waiting for another airplane to replace the one with mechanical problems. Back at my house, there were decorations and a tree in every room. There would be wrapped gifts under a tree — as soon as I wrapped them.

But the most important gifts would be the ones that were not wrapped. Even as I watched my girls excitedly open their gifts, I would be thinking about an elderly lady who reminded me that the best gifts of all are the unwrapped ones.

— Carol Gentry Allen —

79

A Christmas to Remember

Trapped by reality, freed by imagination.
~Nicolas Manetta

It was my first Christmas after my husband left me. I was now the single mother of a three-year-old daughter, working multiple jobs to get by. I was nothing if not frugal. In the summer I cut firewood to lower the cost of heating our house with propane in the winter. I tended a garden in our backyard so we could have vegetables and berries to eat. Many times, I would skip meals so my daughter would have a full belly.

And, yes, at three years old, my daughter worked at my side. I had no money for babysitters or daycare. She was there every day while I was shoeing horses, working as a gas station attendant, and doing chores. While cutting wood, she would use a handsaw to cut kindling while I used a chainsaw to cut logs. She sat on the floor of the gas station coloring, learning to count change, or handing out Tootsie Rolls to customers while I worked the payment window.

These circumstances led me to make a difficult and heartbreaking decision. I had to pull my little girl into my lap and tell her that I was Santa's helper and there would be no gifts that year.

I felt so inadequate as a parent, and it was soul-crushing.

With the beautiful innocence of a child, my daughter said, "It's okay, Mommy. You can just wrap up some of my stuffed animals from my room and put them under the tree. I'll forget what's there by Christmas." I was amazed and humbled by her response to our situation. That evening after she went to sleep, I sobbed. The grace I was shown by my child dragged me to my knees.

Still heartsick, I did exactly as my daughter said. I wrapped up some of her stuffed animals and toys and placed them under the tree. She, as any child does, wanted to put presents under the tree for me. So, I had her go through my jewelry box and knick-knacks to choose items to wrap as presents for me, which she happily did. When Christmas Day came, she was smiling and staring at the tree with excited eyes, anticipating the moment we could open presents.

Our tradition was to eat the Christmas meal before opening presents. I managed to purchase a box of Jiffy cornbread and a box of Kraft Mac and Cheese for our Christmas dinner.

After we ate our untraditional dinner, we sang "Happy Birthday, Jesus" and several other Christmas carols. Knowing she was eager to open presents, I handed her the first one. As she ripped the wrapping paper off the present, she squealed with delight and exclaimed, "It's what I always wanted," and then giggled.

Her infectious spirit and joy were contagious. By the time we got to the last present, our sides were hurting and our eyes were watering from our uncontrollable laughter.

Later that night, after she went to bed, I reflected on the Christmas we had shared. I was so sad that I had to spoil some of her childhood joy in Santa, but I was grateful for the Christmas experience that we did have, free of commercialism but filled with our joy of being together in that moment.

The following year was little improved financially. Although prepared for another barren Christmas, I managed to set aside five dollars for each of us to buy presents. We went to the dollar store and picked out four items each to put under the tree.

My daughter and I went to the Christmas service at church before heading home to celebrate. When we arrived home from church and walked to the front door of our mobile home, I noticed a black garbage bag had been left on our front doorstep. Irritated that someone could be so cruel during the holidays to leave trash on someone's porch, I went to throw away the bag. But, as I reached for the bag, a label attached to the top caught my eye. It had my daughter's name written on it.

We looked at each other curiously. We carried the bag inside and opened it. To our surprise and her great joy, we found a new dress, an Easy-Bake Oven, several coloring books, and games. She jumped and squealed with delight to have such treasures. Between the gifts that we purchased for each other and the anonymous gifts that we received, my daughter was given the Christmas experience I had dreamt about giving her but could not provide on my own.

I have no idea who put us on the list to receive those gifts for my daughter. If you have ever wondered if the donations you make to toy drives make a difference, let me assure you that they do.

Twenty-plus years have passed. Since then, we have both been blessed greatly and have much more than we could ever have expected. Every Christmas, my daughter and I think back to that time in our lives and remember that first Christmas we spent with just the two of us. It is still one of our favorite memories. Anytime we have Kraft Mac and Cheese or Jiffy cornbread it reminds us of that time. We did not have much money, but we had love and laughter, which are all that really matters in this world.

—J. Nicolelli—

80

An Apple and an Orange

The orange has its place you know,
to fill each Christmas stocking toe.
~Roseanne Russell

Growing up, my mom always made sure that we had an apple and an orange in the toe of our Christmas stocking. And every year, after my brother and I had emptied our stockings of all their wonderful, hidden treasures and the only thing left to empty was the toe, we would think to ourselves, *Okay, maybe this is the year when there will finally be something different down there!*

We would dig our hands *waaaaay* down deep into the stocking, jamming our fingers into the toe, only to find the inevitable: an apple and an orange. And, once again, we would toss them aside, uninterested, and complain, "But we can have fruit anytime."

One year (after I realized Mom was Santa's official helper), I finally asked her about it, and I will never forget what she said. "Sometimes, growing up, that's all we would get for Christmas — the three of us — just an apple and an orange. But you know, I've never tasted anything so good and so sweet."

I never complained again.

Growing up, we did not have much money, but what we did have was lots of love. We also really enjoyed spending time together and still do. My parents always made sure we had a wonderful Christmas. Unfortunately, with my dad working at a large department-store chain, the retail "monster" claimed him for much of the season, but I always remember him being there when it really mattered. And when he was there, he was *really* there, in a big way. Every night, he read to me — fairytales and legends most of the year — but at Christmastime, it was stories like *Santa Mouse*, *The Gift of the Magi*, and *The Night Before Christmas*. And we always decorated the Christmas tree together, as well as the Christmas cookies. This is still one of Dad's favorite things about Christmas.

My mom would prep the dough and cut out the cookies using our vast array of cookie cutters. Then, she'd bake them and mix the icings. My brother, Dad and I would decorate them. We still continue this tradition every year. Our children now join in on the action.

I have always been fascinated by the ways in which other countries and cultures celebrate Christmas or their own winter holidays. I want to make sure that my husband and I not only include, but embrace, some of his family's cherished traditions and weave them into our own. I knew that some of my mother-in-law Pat's family had come from Slovenia, a country I knew next to nothing about. I wondered if trying to find common ground between my family's traditions and that of my husband's would be like trying to compare apples to oranges.

The Christmas before I married her son, I remember showing Pat a book that I had discovered, which featured a section dedicated to Slovenian Christmas traditions. I was intrigued to learn that Slovenia also celebrates St. Nicholas Day and St. Lucia Day. My mother-in-law was surprised and delighted to learn further information about the traditions that were so important to her family, and she was thrilled that I was interested as well. We talked about how we would share these and other customs with the children that her son and I hoped to have one day. We planned on making walnut potica (a special, traditional Slovenian holiday walnut roll) together with the children.

I can still remember that afternoon, and I am so thankful for it. A year later, she was gone — on Christmas Day, no less — making it all the more poignant.

As my husband and I share these special Christmas traditions — ours, as well as other cultures — with our daughter Elizabeth and our son

Nicholas, I realize something. Our celebration is imbued with an even deeper meaning now. It will be about more than leaving carrots for St. Nicholas's white horse in my old, wooden Dutch shoes from childhood that I've now passed down to them. Or even more than instilling in them a respect and compassion for others who may have beliefs, customs, and cultures different from their own. This is also about preserving my children's heritage — making it all the more important now that their Grandma Pat is gone.

Along with all the chocolates from our favorite cafe wrapped in brightly colored foil to look like ladybugs and butterflies, and all the other magical treasures that will be hidden in the children's stockings, I will be sure to include an apple and an orange.

And would you believe that, in Slovenia, St. Nicholas would leave children, not toys, but — you guessed it — an apple and an orange?

For all the many things that make us different from each other, at the very heart of it, we are still much more alike than we are different. We have more in common with each other than we think.

Sometimes, it comes down to something as simple — and as sweet — as an apple and an orange.

— Diane Dickson Shepard —

81

Santa Gifts Forever

We don't stop playing because we grow old;
we grow old because we stop playing.
~George Bernard Shaw

"**D**o you think you'll get a gift from Santa this year?"

I side-eyed my father. "I don't know. Is there a reason I wouldn't?"

"Santa only gives gifts to children. You're a college girl now."

Well, at least it wasn't because I'd been naughty. "That makes sense," I said, refocusing on the cookie dough churning.

I should have realized earlier that I wouldn't get an extra present under my stocking. I was nineteen. Santa didn't give gifts to adults.

And yet, when I trudged down the stairs after my younger siblings on Christmas morning, I had a gift from Santa. Wrapped in black paper covered in Santa hats, it matched the gifts under my siblings' stockings perfectly.

"Huh," Dad said. "I guess as long as there's a kid in the house, you all get Santa gifts."

I looked at my younger sister, who peered at me from under her sleep hoodie. At sixteen, she wasn't exactly a child either. But our brother was fourteen, and if that meant I got another four years of Santa gifts, I wasn't going to say no.

"Go on," Mom said. "Might as well open them at the same time."

My brother was already ripping apart the box, revealing a Nerf gun and foam target chest plate.

"Look at that!" Dad said. "Indoor laser tag."

My sis and I quickly got to work freeing our own Nerf guns.

Five minutes later, Mom boldly walked through the chaos of the fight spanning the open space from the living room to the kitchen, holding her coffee mug tight to her chest. All three of us couldn't resist the target.

"Hey!" she shouted when a fourth dart hit her. Dad stood across the open space near the couch, holding an extra gun.

She waggled a finger and continued to the kitchen.

"What did I do to deserve this?" she muttered, pulling her coffee cup closer as all three kids aimed our guns at Dad.

It was a Christmas miracle that foam ammo didn't land in the pancake mix.

***

"Do you think you'll get a gift from Santa this year?"

I swiveled my chair to look at my father. We sat gazing out the front windows of my parents' new house, watching the sun chase away morning fog. My sister was still sleeping, and my brother would make the hour-drive from his place on Christmas Eve.

"Is there a reason I wouldn't?" There were plenty of reasons, the most obvious being that I was thirty-one. Adults didn't get Santa gifts. Or they shouldn't. But Santa still left toys under the tree for me and my siblings every year. Nerf swords. Family board games. Grow monsters. At this point, it would be strange to not get a gift.

"We're in a new house. Maybe Santa doesn't know where we are. We also don't have a chimney anymore." My dad blew on his tea. He refused to look at me, but I caught a hint of a smile in his reflection.

"It'd be okay if I didn't," I offered. "I own a condo and everything. That's pretty grown-up."

Now, he did look at me. "Doesn't mean you're not a kid."

I huffed, hiding my own smile in a sip of coffee.

Lo and behold, Santa had no problem finding the house later that week. We'd been given bags of indoor snowballs, white pompoms with so little heft that they were hard to launch. It didn't stop us. My sister flung one at me. I hit my brother, who tossed one straight into our mother's lap. Dad reached for it, collecting ammo from around the room and from a bag he'd hidden.

Mom took that as her cue to leave, scurrying around the couch. She got hit with at least two snowballs.

"Children, all of you!" She yanked a snowball from between the back of the couch and a cushion and tossed it at my brother, grinning. He caught it.

"Gotta work on your throw, Mom."

"You monkey," she said fondly, heading to the fridge.

I also needed to work on my throw and knew when to give up. After aiming for and missing my brother, I left my siblings and father goofing around to refill my mother's coffee.

"I'm glad Santa brings joy for all of you," she said, accepting the mug and watching the morning chaos.

My dad pelted my sister with three snowballs in a row, causing her to drop her armful with a laugh. My brother scooped them up to lob at Dad.

"We're always gonna get Santa gifts, aren't we?" I said, leaning on my mother's shoulder.

She kissed my cheek. "You're my little girl. Of course, you will."

— Virginia Mueller —

82

Giving Thanks... for Christmas

Family is the most important thing in the world.
~Princess Diana

One Thanksgiving morning, I was busily preparing my assigned dishes to take to our daughter's home when my husband Dave shared that he wasn't feeling well. He complained of chest pain, asked for cough medicine, and decided to try and "rest it off." One hour later, his chest pain was worsening—and my patience was waning. Taking all decision-making out of Dave's hands, I contacted paramedics, who navigated a severe thunderstorm to reach us. As we hurriedly set off in the ambulance, I gamely reassured myself that the medics were acting out of an abundance of caution, and we would return home in a few hours.

Dave's admission to the emergency room was swift, and the tests were many. While awaiting the results and still convinced that everything would be fine, we held hands, smiled ruefully over the unfortunate timing of Dave falling ill, and discussing the myriad tasks that Hanukkah and Christmas would demand of us.

Our banter was suddenly interrupted by the doctor, who peeked through the privacy curtain and inquired of Dave, "Sir, you said that you don't have a history of heart problems. Is that correct?" When Dave answered yes, the doctor stated, "Well, you've had a heart attack... and it isn't your first one." When Dave informed the doctor that he hadn't wanted to spoil Thanksgiving and had every intention of seeking medical help the following day, the doctor bluntly replied, "You wouldn't have lived until tomorrow afternoon."

Dave and I looked at one another in shock, and I felt the room begin to spin. I was gently shuffled away by nursing staff as the area quickly filled with additional medical personnel. I was then advised by an attending cardiologist that Dave had indeed suffered two heart attacks, the first having taken place within the previous two weeks and the second one occurring after he was admitted. Meanwhile, Dave was whisked to intensive care in preparation for surgery. He underwent a procedure to remove two blockages and a blood clot. They put in five stents.

Discharged days later, Dave began his recuperation at home while I nervously hovered. When I meekly suggested that we cancel the traditional Christmas festivities, he wouldn't hear of it. He insisted that since we'd missed Thanksgiving, the remaining holidays would go forward as planned. My meekness quickly disappearing, I informed him that his typical holiday tasks would be severely curtailed and ignored his withering look of disagreement while I began compiling various to-do lists.

Cleaning, cooking, shopping, wrapping… It all had to be accomplished in a very short period of time. Five days before Christmas, things were going according to plan. Dave was recovering nicely while managing light activity. I'd completed most of the shopping and wrapping. Cleaning and food preparation would take place over the weekend, followed by our generally hilarious tree shopping and decorating.

About the time you relax and think that things are indeed going according to plan, life sneaks in without warning to upend those plans.

Just as he had on Thanksgiving, Dave again began having chest pains. We immediately summoned paramedics and returned to the emergency room. Dave was re-admitted to the hospital, this time with dangerously low blood pressure. After several days, many more tests and eventual confirmation that he did not have another heart attack, his medication was adjusted, and he again returned home.

At that point, our traditional Christmas simply wasn't to be. There was no time to purchase and decorate a tree. The time I would have otherwise spent cleaning and preparing favorite dishes had been spent by Dave's bedside, praying with everything I had that he would live. I once again fretted aloud as to what to do about Christmas, and Dave stubbornly insisted that Christmas go forward as scheduled. He wanted our family to be together in our home.

At that moment, I realized that we were going to have Thanksgiving for Christmas — a more meaningful experience than I could have imagined.

I gave thanks that Dave's life was saved twice within three weeks' time. I realized that no one would be concerned about absent Christmas trees, housecleaning or the missing favorite foods on the buffet table. The only thing that truly mattered was that we would be together as a family. Dave would video chat with our eldest daughter, son-in-law and toddler grandson, who lived overseas. He would open presents with me in the morning over coffee and pumpkin muffins, and get hugs and kisses from our family in the afternoon.

He would be home.

On Christmas Day, our home was filled to the brim with tears of happiness, hysterical laughter, and so much joy and love. A local barbecue restaurant catered a lovely, casual dinner that everyone thoroughly enjoyed. The day was wonderful holiday chaos, and not one person cared about carpets that weren't perfectly pristine, the non-traditional food, the missing tree or even the quart of barbecue sauce that I inadvertently dumped all over the kitchen floor.

As I often do during special occasions, I took a quiet moment to stand off to one side and survey the scene: our daughters gossiping and catching up with one another; happy grandchildren tearing into stockings and opening presents; gaggles of relatives deep in conversation over good wine… and my Dave, beaming with his incomparable smile, who has since recovered with an excellent prognosis.

There was — and is — no greater gift possible.

— Carole Brody Fleet —

83

We Can't Have Anything Nice

Any mother could perform the jobs of several
air traffic controllers with ease.
~Lisa Alther, Other Women

Christmas at home always drove me insane, and I attribute that fact to my mother. As the youngest of five children, I was keenly aware of how tight money was while growing up. That's how madness starts — through necessity.

As a simple matter of survival, my mom bought items in bulk, never threw out anything that could possibly be used later, purchased anything on sale in case someone might need it someday, and made coupons a way of life. This led to such holiday traditions as all of us kids trotting down to the grocery store and buying, say, two cans of corn each because there was a "two can per person" limit on the purchase. Or, on Christmas Day, we had to open gifts by neatly cutting the tape with scissors because wrapping paper is expensive and still in plenty good condition for next year's presents.

So, let's do some math. Between all the two-for-one coupons and the "buy $75 of groceries, get a free turkey" type of offers, my mom's garage is a veritable Costco of canned goods, paper towels, toiletries, pastas, rice, and cans of cat food for a pet that has never lived in our house. She also has three full freezers jammed with frozen free turkeys.

I don't want you to think we were poverty-stricken, but my mom was never quite sure if wrapping paper or canned corn would ever go on sale again. And, to be fair, she has adapted with the times. She now buys for eight adults instead of five children and three adults because we are all grown, after all. The only problem is that Nana and Dad passed on years ago, and all of us kids have moved out.

She's not, however, a hoarder. There's nothing suspicious growing in the unknown corners of the house, no rotten food or a forgotten dead animal, and items regularly cycle through the bedrooms to various charities. My sisters and I just call it OBSD: Obsessive Bargain Shopping Disorder.

Unfortunately, that blissful state of denial isn't possible during Christmas because all of my siblings, with their spouses and children, are at Mom's house. In order to get from one room to the next, we have to step over the pile of old VHS videotapes that Mom's going to give to the church at some point, but she has to go through them first to make sure there's nothing important on them like a Mary Tyler Moore special, *Murder, She Wrote* repeats, or a Carol Burnett reunion show that I recorded for her twenty years ago.

And, amidst all this chaos, my mother, who secretly wishes she could entertain like Martha Stewart and goes out of her way to make everything special, will break something in the kitchen and shout, "Dammit, we can't have nice things!"

That expression is the kicker. I mean, who's she talking to? God? Us? She says it like the chaos is our fault, but come on!

A couple of years back, I got a reprieve from the madness. I was working in Canada on a film and spent Thanksgiving with my friend's family. Let's just say, they're the antithesis of mine.

Derek's father is an architect like Mike Brady, having built the farmhouse they live in, and Derek's mother is so domestic that she's like Carol Brady and Alice combined. (That's *The Brady Bunch* for those of you too young to know!) We woke each morning to freshly baked muffins, eggs from the farm, and pancakes that Derek's mom wouldn't think of making with a boxed mix. Thanksgiving dinner was turkey and dressing, a potato casserole, fresh vegetables, rolls that Derek's mom made during the meal, and wine his father brewed in the barn.

And, no kidding, I was given some strawberry-rhubarb jam to take home as a lovely parting gift.

On that morning, feeling more rested than I've ever felt on a holiday at home, I thanked Derek's mom for all her hospitality and complimented her on everything for the hundredth time. She said simply, "It's how I find my joy."

Christmas soon followed, and as I arrived at my mother's house, with noises being emitted like the apocalypse had arrived, I was immediately overwhelmed. Inside, one sister was playing with the children, my brothers-in-law were talking about the hottest new stock, and it seemed like every TV, toy, and radio was turned up to full volume. The tension immediately rose from the base of my back and crawled along my spine.

Mom spotted me first. Her face lit up as she cheered in a singsong voice, "I get the first kiss! I get the first kiss!" and trotted over so that my nieces could beat her to me. But after the kids kissed me, Mom saw the look of intense, overwhelming exhaustion on my face. She grew concerned. "What's wrong?"

"Nothing," was all I could manage. "I just need an aspirin." What could I really say? She's my mom, and it was Christmas.

"I'll do you one better!" She grinned in victory and opened the cabinet above the microwave to reveal rows of Advil, Tylenol, Bayer, Children's Tylenol, Tylenol PM, Tylenol Cold, Aleve and Midol, which I didn't even know they made anymore. Rows and rows and rows of pain relief! She took out a whole box of Advil and handed it to me, proudly saying, "Keep it. Vons had a sale!"

Suddenly, I melted. When I saw Mom so excited about this little gift, I realized she had done what most people would consider a chore — feeding a family of eight on a very tight budget — and turned it into something she could enjoy. And amidst this house of noise and clutter — and watching where you walk for fear that you're going to crush something valuable — my mom was finding her own personal joy by taking care of everyone in the family in the only way she knew how.

Suddenly, none of it seemed insane at all; it just felt very nice. And with that understanding, I leaned forward and gave her a hug.

"What's this for?" she asked.

"'Cause I love you," I answered simply. And, as I let go, my arm knocked over a glass that broke in the sink with a crash like a chorus of screaming angels.

Mom whacked me on the arm, gave me a look, and muttered, "We can't have anything nice."

— Richard Andreoli —

Holiday Miracles

84

How a Combine Harvester Saved Our Christmas Tree

There are only two ways to live your life.
One is as though nothing is a miracle.
The other is as though everything is a miracle.
~Albert Einstein

Branches and needles. That's all I saw.

I was peering through my car's sunroof at the Fraser fir tied to my roof rack. The tree had been placed there moments before by a worker at the 4-H Christmas tree sale — emphasis on "placed." That's because he couldn't help me tie it to my roof rack due to liability issues.

But there was bountiful twine I could use for that purpose, he told me as he motioned toward a pile of skinny, plastic strings. I scooped up the twine and enlisted the humble assistance of my nine-year-old daughter. We started securing the tree to the roof rack with the twine, but the branches seemed impenetrable, and we struggled mightily to pull each piece taut.

"You'll want to go around the trunk more times than that, young lady," an elderly farmer commented from the parking lot where he stood watching us. I nodded my thanks and then felt jealous as I watched him toss his Christmas tree into an old trailer, climb into his truck and drive away, all in what seemed like twenty-nine seconds.

How did I get here? I thought. It was three weeks before Christmas, and I was trying, unsuccessfully, to bring home the family Christmas tree.

In the beginning, it hadn't seemed so nerve-wracking. My daughter and I were brimming with confidence that we could bring the tree home. Our usual compatriots, my husband and teenage son, were at an ice-hockey tournament all weekend. It was up to us to get the tree now or else we would lose our opportunity amidst all the other trappings of the season.

So, the two of us had perused the myriad Christmas trees for sale inside the barn at the county fairgrounds. Frosty clouds had escaped from our mouths as we "oohed" and "ahhed" over the fragrant selection before deciding on a bushy, six-foot tree with which to deck our halls.

Our cheerful Christmas tree shopping adventure ended with the liability issues and the twine, though!

With a sigh, I resumed my twine artistry, looping and tying the tree down as the branches and needles mocked and scratched me. When I thought it was good enough, I asked my daughter to stand in the parking lot and observe the tree while I cautiously drove a few feet.

Her eyes widened. She shook her head.

"It's too wiggly!" she cried.

Hmm. The tree did seem to bounce a lot. I applied yet more twine. The picturesque branches thwarted my every move, and the twine still refused to go as taut as I wanted. I did my best until my fingers cramped, and I reached an impasse. It was as good as I could get it.

I flashed a smile like a teenage girl taking a selfie and urged my daughter to get back in the car. They say that animals can smell fear. I think that nine-year-old daughters can, too.

"Mommy, it's not good," she said as we pulled out of the parking lot.

"I think it's okay," I replied, not looking her in the eye. "Deck the halls with boughs of holly," I started singing as I came up to the fifty-mile per hour speed limit on the two-lane road. We had a five-mile drive home.

Oomph! A bump in the road caused me to pause my caroling. It also caused the tree to bounce on top of the car. I braked lightly and then looked up through the sunroof to see the tree shift forward several inches.

My daughter saw it, too. "It's going to fall off!" she cried.

My smile faltered briefly. *Was the tree really that bad? Should I pull over? But then what?* I was no twine master. Perhaps if I could just go slower than the speed limit...

"Lord, help us," I whispered.

And He did. As I scanned the road ahead, I saw it.

It was a huge help, too.

"There's a combine harvester up ahead!" I exclaimed.

My daughter's face remained tense. She seemed perplexed by my enthusiasm for gigantic farm equipment.

"God sent us a combine harvester! Woo hoo!" I cheered, hope bubbling up in my voice.

The combine harvester was massive. Its giant tires turned slowly. It wasn't able to go more than twenty miles per hour. Cars crawled behind it. We joined the sluggish line, our tree no longer bouncing or shifting.

"Mommy, it's going to be okay," my daughter said.

I nodded in agreement as we inched toward home.

One mile down.

"Here's a country road, so it may turn off. Be prepared," I said to myself as much as to my daughter. In all my years of living in our town, I had never seen a piece of farm equipment on the main road for long stretches.

Still, the combine harvester churned straight ahead. I could see my daughter loosen her grip on the car door as we continued in the sedate line-up behind it.

Two miles down. Then three.

"Okay, here's another country road coming up," I reported. "It's probably going to turn on that one, but we'll be okay."

My daughter nodded ever so slightly before I saw her tighten her grip on the car door. But, to my surprise and delight, the combine harvester continued toward town.

So, we followed the giant piece of farm equipment until it peeled off mere blocks from our home. I was able to guide my car and its precious Christmas cargo slowly through our subdivision, easing into our driveway as if arriving home with a precious, newborn baby.

As I turned off the engine, the Fraser fir still present on our roof, my daughter and I looked at each other wide-eyed. We broke into smiles as we started giggling. We had done it. We brought home the family Christmas tree — with a little help from some twine and a lot of help from a very big combine harvester.

— Katy M. Clark —

85

Orbiting

She did not stand alone, but what stood behind her,
the most potent moral force in her life,
was the love of her father.
~Harper Lee, Go Set a Watchman

One year on December 25, I was e-mailing Christmas wishes with a group of friends online. Suddenly, an old e-mail attached itself to my thread. It was from my dad. But Dad had died ten years prior. How and why was an old e-mail from him appearing in this conversation? I was dumbfounded.

The date on the old e-mail from Dad was also December 25, the same date I was e-mailing my friends.

So, my Outlook program must have gotten its wires crossed and accidentally connected the old e-mail to this thread. But that had never happened before. Why now?

In the old e-mail, Dad made one of his classic remarks, highlighting his sense of humor, which no one in my family seemed to appreciate except for me. I "got" him and his humor.

I had noted in the e-mail that my sister's Christmas feast rivaled one put on by Martha Stewart. My dad replied to ALL, noting that Martha Stewart was a criminal who had been in jail.

I laughed, but I'm sure my stoic sister didn't appreciate the comparison.

Later, the e-mail appearing from "the beyond" reminded me how Dad used to insert himself into our conversations. It seemed like he wanted to be near us, within earshot, but not necessarily "officially" participating in the dialogue.

One Thanksgiving, at our after-the-meal board-game session, Dad started answering trivia questions from the living room sofa as we played our game at the dining room table.

"Do you want to come in here and play?" I asked him.

"Nope," he said, straightening his newspaper.

Those of us who were playing at the table shook our heads and rolled our eyes. Someone took another roll of the dice.

A friend told me her dad did the exact same thing. She even had a name for it: orbiting. He wanted to be around her but not exactly in the conversation or at the table.

Now, my dad seemed to be orbiting from beyond, chiming in on my Christmas e-mail.

Even though he'd been a difficult guy, I still missed his wit and dry sense of humor. Maybe the orbiting e-mail showed he missed me, too.

Why would someone "orbit" rather than participate? Was it because he didn't think we wanted him around? Was that the signal we sent him? Dad was, after all, in a household surrounded by women: my mom, three daughters and our dog Pepsi, who was also a girl.

Had our years of clothes shopping, girls' nights, and chumming around made him feel like he wasn't welcome? In retrospect, I'm sure we had excluded him at times. Maybe often.

According to one definition online, orbiting happens because of gravity. Objects orbit each other in a circular fashion because they are drawn to each other. My dad was drawn to us, causing him to orbit us, the way the Earth orbits the sun, never colliding or embracing but staying nearby and rotating in a consistent pattern.

I took a seminar once, and the speaker asked the class what we thought people wanted most from work and their families. The answer whittled down to appreciation. What would happen if we told our parents we appreciated them?

I called my parents' house that night, planning to talk to my mom, whom I felt was easier to chat with because of our close relationship.

My dad answered the phone with a gruff, "Hello?"

"Hey, it's Kris," I said.

"I'll get your mom," he said.

It struck me then that he never expected me to call and ask for him.

I responded, "Wait, I actually called to talk to you."

"Oh?" he said, surprised.

I took a deep breath. "I attended a class, and they made me realize how much I have to be thankful for. And I wanted to tell you that you did a good job raising me."

He paused. "Oh? Well, that sounds like a pretty good class." He laughed a little and beamed through the phone, the way you can tell someone is smiling just by the way their voice sounds.

I couldn't help smiling, too.

"And thank you for paying for my education," I said. I was on a roll, extending a plethora of appreciation.

"Ah... you're welcome," he said, his voice lilting up. "That feels pretty good to hear."

I had no idea the effect my words would have on him. That moment of appreciation, that short conversation that couldn't have lasted more than a few minutes, immediately changed the orbit we shared.

After that, when I went over to my parents' house for dinners, Dad no longer disappeared right away after we ate. Instead of going to his workshop, he would stick around and play cribbage or rummy. When I left at the end of the evening, he would loiter by the door waiting for a hug and goodbye.

Our relationship changed, and so did our orbit. The gravity of the relationship turned into a more positive force.

Several years later, Dad died.

Then, nearly ten years later, on that cold Christmas evening, an e-mail glitch placed Dad back in my orbit. It felt like a message from beyond, a miracle from the universe, a moment I'll always remember.

— Kristin F. Johnson —

86

The Stocking Stuffer

Dogs are miracles with paws.
~Susan Ariel Rainbow Kennedy

Quite frankly, I brought him home to die... in peace... and not alone. I was working as a cage cleaner at a local pet shop. It was Christmas Eve, and the store was getting ready to close. All the puppies had been sold except one, a small Boston Terrier, and he was quite ill.

The vet had stopped in earlier that day and said that the pup's prognosis was not good. In addition to being born with a multitude of genetic issues due to in-breeding, he had a serious respiratory infection. The vet told the owner of the shop that he could give him medication, but it was highly unlikely that he would make it through the night. Another option was to put him to sleep then and there.

Opting not to "waste his money," the callous owner told me to place the pup back in the kennel and he'd "take care of it" when he came back after the holiday. Hot tears came to my eyes. This was a time before twenty-four-hour vet services and emergency pet clinics in our area, so my only option was to take the best care of him I could while waiting for my miserable shift to end. I placed him on a warm heating pad and checked on him between tasks. He was no better and no worse.

I finished my work alone that night. Everyone had gone home for the next two days to enjoy family festivities. I looked in on my little friend. He was cold and unmoving, breathing heavily and unresponsive.

I made a split-second decision. "You're coming home with me," I said.

I wrapped his limp, fragile body in a small cloth and stuck him in a fuzzy blue, fur-lined Christmas stocking from the rack of unsold holiday gifts for pets. He slid down into the toe. I tucked him gently into my warm coat and out the door we went. I felt him relax a bit, nuzzled against me, and he began to snore. I drove around an extra hour on quiet, snow-covered roads listening to Christmas songs on the car radio just so he could sleep peacefully, all the while crying silently into my woolen scarf.

Once home and inside our cozy living room, I gingerly eased him from my coat, still sound asleep in the toasty stocking, and hung him low on our tiny, dimly lit tree. The cats had a sniff but seemed unconcerned with the newly added pre-packaged gift. They batted at a couple of ornaments and strolled away to find an interesting bit of fluff from under the bed. My husband came home shortly thereafter. I pointed to the snoozing bundle inside the fleecy sock and said with a sigh, "Don't get used to him. He probably won't make it through the night." He named him Boz.

We slept around the tree that night with six blankets, four pillows, and two cats piled high... never daring to peek inside the motionless stocking for fear of the worst. I asked anyone listening to please gift the little guy with an easy passing but allow him to make it at least to Christmas Day. I'm sure my husband asked the same. We dozed off knowing it was going to be a somber holiday.

On Christmas morning, we were startled awake by the cats hissing and yowling in the kitchen. Was someone breaking in? Was there a fire? Had they cornered Santa? Without checking on our small charge, we jumped up and gracelessly stumbled toward the uproar. My husband grabbed a baseball bat, and I snagged the fire extinguisher. We slowly entered the room, braced for the pure terror that surely awaited.

Both cats were perched on the edge of the kitchen counter in Mega-Angry-Whack-a-Mole Mode, spitting flaming sabers and glaring piercing daggers of hate... *at us!* Our eyes quickly darted down to the floor, and the cause of "The Christmas Fury of 1989" became crystal-clear. The tiny "Boston Terror" looked up at us, quite proud of himself, and grinned ever so slightly as only a Boston can. He then marched back into the living room. I looked at my husband and said, "Well, I guess he's decided to stay." I quit my job at the pet store the next day.

We had Mr. Boz for eleven years. The cats never did really forgive him, but a lifetime of tolerance is an acceptable compromise. He snored exceptionally loudly every night and wreaked absolute havoc during the day. His manners were atrocious, his smell unbearable at times, but he loved hard. And every year Boz got a little something extra in his worn, faded stocking for Christmas just for being Boz.

—Dorenda Crager Watson—

87

Entertaining an Angel

To cherish peace and goodwill, to be plenteous in
mercy, is to have the real spirit of Christmas.
~Calvin Coolidge

It is winter. Christmas is quickly approaching. I am sixteen. I have stayed too long munching on the one bag of fries that I share with my six best friends. None of us has much money, so we all pitch in for a snack. We are sitting at a booth in Junior Harvest House, our favorite local hangout.

I am troubled. I need fifty-five dollars for my yearbook next week. I have saved this money by working as a cashier in the local supermarket. I also need an additional fifty-five dollars for my share in a summer cottage that my friends and I have put a down payment on for the week following our graduation. I have signed the contract for our rental.

The thought of a week at the beach has been my incentive to finish school. I have allotted my money carefully, but one of my friends has suddenly dropped out. This has increased the rental fee for each of us. This has caused my immediate financial distress.

My parents are in a financial crisis themselves. They have purchased a new home. The stress has likely contributed to my father having a heart attack. He has had emergency open-heart surgery. The operation has left him unable to return to work. They are swamped with medical bills.

I consider all my options but realistically conclude that I will have to make a choice about which is more important to me: the yearbook or my week at the Jersey Shore. It feels unfair. I have worked hard, but

I am still ending up short due to my friend's departure.

On this day, I have missed my transportation. I will either have to hang around another hour until another bus arrives or walk. It is at least two miles to my new house.

I choose to walk. This gives me plenty of time to accept the fact that my dilemma, no matter how unfair, is not resolvable with such short notice. I will have to make a decision as to what is more important to me.

I am passing the huge, brick senior citizens' apartment complex in our community. I hear a disturbance up ahead. The traffic has halted. Someone is pressing on their car horn. A businessman has rolled down his window. He is leaning out, cursing. I am attempting to see what the problem is.

I step up my pace. I spot the source of the drama. An old man has fallen into the street. He isn't moving. His body is blocking the road.

He is dirty and dressed in worn clothes. The road is jammed with trapped drivers who cannot maneuver around his sprawled-out body. On the sidewalk, at least a dozen pedestrians are gaping at the helpless individual. No one makes a move to aid him. I am amazed at their lack of empathy.

I rush to the man. "Are you okay?" I inquire. He rolls over to face me. His face is gruff. He looks like he has had a difficult life. "I must have slipped," he mutters. He doesn't appear to be hurt, just shaken up.

I offer him my hand. He reaches for me. His hands are dirty and wrinkled. He smells pungent from perspiration and possibly urine. It repulses me for a moment, but my mother's voice echoes in my head. *How would you like to be treated?* I clasp his hand. "Ready?" I ask.

I give a tug. For a moment, I feel like I will be pulled down on top of him, but somehow I muster enough strength to ease him to his feet. Slowly, we step toward the curb together. I guide him onto the sidewalk.

I return to the street to gather his scattered food. There are only five or six items. I ensure that I've gathered everything. The roadway is empty.

I walk back to the stranger to hand him his bag. He looks deep into my eyes. His eyes sparkle. He thanks me sincerely. I am rewarded by his smile. After I am certain that he is stabilized, I continue on my way.

The next day brings a bizarre twist to this story. Once again, I am at Harvest House with my friends. This time, I am watching the clock to ensure that I don't miss my bus again. I leave five minutes early. As I am waiting for the light to change, I see my bus passing by.

"Hey!" I yell. "Wait up!"

"Sorry, I can't pick up passengers here. It's not a stop." The driver shrugs.

I glance down at my wristwatch. "But you're leaving too early."

He checks his wristwatch. "Yes, I am a little off schedule," he confirms, but he continues onward.

I run after the bus, but I cannot keep pace. He is gone. "What's going on?" I exclaim. I am feeling sorry for myself. I always try to do the right thing, but no one else seems to play fair.

My running has taken a big chunk out of my walk. I realize that I am within a few feet of where the man was lying the previous day. Today, the weather is different. It is much colder. The traffic is moving quickly. The sidewalks are empty. The wind is whipping. Garbage is flying everywhere.

I glance down to where the man was lying the previous day. I see what appears to be a small bundle. I lean over to view the item better. It is a twenty-dollar bill. I unfold it. There are three more bills: another twenty, a ten, and a five. It is fifty-five dollars. It is the exact amount that I need to obtain my yearbook and still have my week at the shore.

I look around to see if this could be anyone else's money. There is no one on the street. The wind is so powerful that napkins are being pressed against poles, yet this money has not moved. I am stunned.

A Bible verse pops into my thoughts, "Do not forget to show hospitality to strangers, for by so doing some people have shown hospitality to angels without knowing it" (Hebrews 13:2). I glance up to the sky. Somehow, I know that the money is meant for me. It is an early Christmas present. I give thanks and continue on my way.

— Patricia Senkiw-Rudowsky —

88

Chicken Soup
for the Soul

Christmas Miracle in the Newborn Unit

The giving of love is an education in itself.
~Eleanor Roosevelt

There is one Christmas I will never forget from my years as a teacher. I was assigned to sponsor a chapter of a club at my large high school in south Alabama. The nationally syndicated club had begun in response to so many young people being killed by drunk drivers, but it had expanded its reach to include other things of a philanthropic focus.

It was my final year to teach, and before I retired, I wanted my little group to make a positive impact on our community. So, at our initial meeting, I polled the students: "What do you think your club could do that would have the most positive effect on your friends and neighbors?"

The answers I received were as varied as the students with their different grades, backgrounds, and interests. "Wash cars and put the money toward a halfway house," one of them said. "Have a bake sale and put the money toward the local boys' and girls' ranches," another offered.

Finally, though, one student came up with an idea that everyone in the club could get behind. "Let's do something for the newborns of needy families here," a young girl shyly put forth.

The idea of doing something for a baby ignited the imaginations of the whole group. They even went a step further and decided to have gift bags for a baby boy and another for a baby girl. They enthusiastically dubbed this "Project Christmas Baby."

Just before Thanksgiving, I bought two large gift bags, one pink and one blue, and placed them in a prominent spot in the front office at school. Every morning, we made announcements, asking students to help fill the gift bags in time for the Christmas break.

During our weekly meetings, I had noticed a young man — I'll call him Sam — who always dressed in just-barely-acceptable bounds within the school dress code. He was always in neat clothing but, with his many piercings and dark expression, seemed to be screaming for attention — any kind of attention. One morning as the club was dismissing, I motioned for him to stay behind the others. "I get the feeling you don't want to be here," I told him. "I'm not judging you — I just want to help."

Sam frowned, and it seemed there was a dark, brooding cloud behind his deep brown eyes. "My dad made me join this stupid club," he said, "so you're right — I don't want to be here."

I smiled in an attempt to set him at ease. "Anything else you want to tell me?"

He frowned again. "My dad's getting remarried, and they're taking off for their honeymoon right before Christmas," he said. For just a second, it seemed I detected a small catch of emotion in his voice. "I won't even have Christmas this year. It won't be Christmas. Not for me."

I paused, and the bell rang. Time for the school day to begin. "I know you need to get to your first class," I said. "Let me think about this, and I'll see what I can do."

"Unless you can stop the wedding," Sam said, "there's nothing you can do." Then, before I could reply, he was gone, shoulders stooped, head down.

He's lost in his own misery, I thought to myself and found myself praying: *Please, God, show me something I can do to help Sam feel Christmas joy.*

Sam continued to show his misery. I encouraged him to start a journal, which I knew might help him vent his feelings and perhaps heal whatever hurt he was feeling. I even bought one for him to use.

A few days after I'd given him the notebook, he came to see me during my planning period. "I thought you might want to read some of this," he muttered, and was gone as quickly as he'd entered the classroom. I stuck the notebook in my briefcase along with some papers that needed grading that night.

After dinner, washing the dishes and walking the dogs, I remembered Sam's notebook. I felt humbled that he'd trusted me with his thoughts and feelings, and more than a little dismayed at the words he'd penned within its cover.

I'm so alone, he wrote. *No one cares about me, so I don't care about anyone else. But,* he added, *I want to feel something. A sense of belonging. A sense of something beyond myself. But I don't know how or where to begin.*

I closed the notebook and put it on the nightstand. *How can I get Sam to know that there's a purpose to his life?* I wondered, as I drifted off to a restless sleep.

Next morning, Sam came into my classroom again. Once more, it was my planning time, so it was just the two of us. "Did you read it?" he asked bluntly.

I paused before speaking as I handed him his notebook. "Yes, Sam, I did," I said gently. "I don't know if it helps you at all, but I care about you. Others do, too," I interjected. "Give it time; you'll see."

Sam just shrugged, turned and walked out of the classroom. Again, I wondered how I could reach him and make him understand that he was loved. *He'll know he's loved when he feels love for someone else.* That message flashed unbidden in my mind like a thunderbolt. Impatient as I was, I knew I had to just wait and see where, when and how Sam could begin to feel and see things differently.

Finally, the day arrived when my students and I planned to take the gift bags to the local neonatal unit at the hospital. I had a carload of students in my large SUV, and Sam rode with us.

When I had called prior to our coming, the head nurse had told us not to expect to see the babies or their families who were recipients of the gift bags. "You can see the babies in their little bassinets in the glassed-in newborn room," she told us. "That's all we can do, but thank you for thinking of these little newborns and their families."

Sam and another student, the shy girl who'd come up with the idea, handed the nurses the gift bags. Then, we went to look at the newborns and tried to guess which babies would be getting our gifts. As we turned to head toward the elevators, a young mother stepped out from her room in the unit. "Hey!" she whispered. "We got the baby-boy gift bag." Then, I swear, she looked at Sam, and only at Sam. "Would you like to see our little Emmanuel?"

I nodded to Sam that it would be all right with me and then motioned for the other students to take the next elevator. "We'll be along in a minute," I told them. "Wait for us in the lobby."

Sam and I walked into the family's room. The young dad stood by the window, looking down at his new son's face as he lay in his mother's arms. She looked up at Sam. "Would you like to hold him?" she asked.

"Sam," I said, "wash your hands first."

Sam went to the sink in the corner of the room, washed and dried his hands, and walked back to the new parents and little Emmanuel.

The mother motioned for Sam to sit in her rocking chair. She rose, holding her newborn, and had Sam sit down first. "Hold your arms out like this," she said, nodding to her own as she held her baby. As Sam did so, she eased Emmanuel into Sam's arms.

Sam held his breath for a couple of seconds, then we saw little Emmanuel stretch, yawn and go back to sleep. "Look," I whispered. "He likes you!"

For what seemed like a couple of minutes but could have been longer, Sam held little Emmanuel, rocking him gently. Then, Sam looked up at me, and I could see his eyes glistening with the healing power of tears.

Then he said something I will always remember. "This is Christmas," he said, and repeated, "This is Christmas."

A bit later, we said our goodbyes to the young family and left the hospital with the rest of the students. They were all elated over the joy they had brought others. To celebrate, I took them all out for milkshakes before heading back to school.

I had witnessed a Christmas miracle in seeing Sam with "his" baby and would soon learn there was more news for him. His father had postponed his wedding, so Sam, his dad and his fiancée wound up together for the holidays after all.

But seeing the change in Sam in just mere minutes had made my Christmas. He gave me an unforgettable experience, a lasting Christmas memory.

— T. Jensen Lacey —

89

Divine Intervention on Thanksgiving Eve

*Be not forgetful of prayer. Every time you pray, if your
prayer is sincere, there will be new feeling and new
meaning in it, which will give you fresh courage.*
~Fyodor Dostoevsky

T hanksgiving Eve was the night my mother was due to catch a
1:30 a.m. flight to Texas, bound for my grandma's house for
the holiday. I felt an urgent need to meet her at the airport, a
decision that would change the course of my life.

I was a twenty-one-year-old living independently, almost ninety
minutes away from my family. My afternoon work shift made visits
home to metro Detroit infrequent, but the prospect of missing the
chance to see my mother before Christmas was unbearable. I decided
to take the risk to drive home despite the winter-storm warning after
my shift ended at 11 p.m.

I called my family to share my plan. My father, however, expressed
concern, deeming the journey too risky. He implored me to stay home
until Thanksgiving morning after the salt trucks had cleared the highway,
ensuring a safe trip to spend the holiday with him. He assured me
that my mother would return before Christmas. Despite the caution, a
persistent voice echoed in my head, urging me to go home that night.
It was as resolute as my own determination, and I couldn't ignore it.

By 11:30 p.m., I was on the road, making my way down I-96,

battling the treacherous conditions. The highway was all but deserted except for the unfortunate cars that had succumbed to the black ice, resting in ditches on either side of the interstate. I felt the icy fingers of doubt clutching at my resolve, but the insistent voice drove me forward.

I came to an off-ramp and considered turning back. But the voice grew more urgent, practically demanding my compliance: "Go home tonight!" I became increasingly anxious, but I pushed on, determined to reach the airport in time to see my mother off safely.

As I continued on the treacherous road, I hit a patch of black ice, and my car skidded into the median ditch. The tires spun uselessly in the icy mire, and I was trapped.

Praying had always been my response when fear gripped me, and this time was no different. I fervently prayed for a snowplow or tow truck to rescue me from this perilous situation. Suddenly, out of nowhere, an old-fashioned truck appeared on the otherwise deserted highway headed in my direction. It was a sight to behold, resembling something straight out of the 1940s. The truck was bright red, with headlights that seemed to illuminate the entire night. It had an open back with wooden, fence-like railings. Three young men stood exposed in the back, cheering and whooping with excitement, while a driver sat inside the cab with his window rolled down.

Despite the frigid temperature and the snow, none of them wore coats, hats, boots, or gloves. At first, I was cautious, thinking they might be a group of inebriated revelers who had stumbled upon my car. However, I was desperate for help, so I cautiously cracked my window to speak to the young driver who approached. He wore an easy smile and had a calm demeanor. He tapped on my window and said, "Looks like you could use some help, miss."

I hesitated but eventually replied, "Yes, I could. I hit a patch of black ice, and my wheels are just spinning now. I was headed home. I'm stuck."

He called to his friends in the back of the pickup, saying, "Hey, fellas, let's help this young lady get home."

The three young men eagerly jumped out of the truck and swiftly reached the front of my car. Despite the treacherous conditions and their lack of appropriate winter wear, they pushed my car back onto the highway effortlessly. As they hopped back onto the truck, the driver smiled, saluted me, and then climbed back into the driver's seat.

I glanced down to shift my car from neutral into drive, grateful for an answer to my prayer by sending those kind strangers. When I looked in my rearview mirror to give them a grateful wave, the truck and its passengers had vanished. The highway was silent and dark once more.

I dismissed the inexplicable event, my primary focus being on getting to the airport before my mother's flight departed. I miraculously found a parking space at the terminal she was departing from. Spotting her, I ran to greet her. I hugged her tightly, surprising her with my unexpected arrival. "Surprise, Mama! Happy Thanksgiving! Where's Daddy?"

My mother informed me that my father had gone to park the car while she checked in and should have returned. I spotted him in the distance, walking through the skywalk from the parking garage, and I called out, waving and smiling. He saw me, waved back, and continued walking until he reached me.

But in a heartbreaking turn of events, my father suddenly collapsed. He had suffered a massive heart attack and he passed away right there in my arms. The joyous reunion turned into a nightmare of unimaginable grief.

If I had not heeded the inexplicable voice urging me to "Go home tonight," I would never have seen my father alive again. I couldn't help but think of the divine interventions that had guided me on that fateful journey.

Thankfully, Mama's flight had not yet departed, and we were able to spend precious moments with my father saying our final farewells. I shared the story of the mysterious pickup truck with my mother, and we both recognized it as a sign of divine intervention.

It was a bittersweet Thanksgiving that changed our family forever, but we were grateful for the inexplicable presence of those four young men who appeared when I needed them most. Their actions were a testament to the power of faith and the mysterious ways in which the universe can offer comfort during the darkest times.

—C. C. Foster—

90

Meant to Be

What's meant to be will always find a way.
~Trisha Yearwood

I couldn't believe it was happening again. I have a chronic health condition and have to work at staying well. But no matter how many extra precautions I'd taken to avoid anyone who was sick, I came down with a cough, congestion and fatigue during the Christmas season.

Besides staying hydrated and loading up on vitamin C, there was nothing to do but sit on the couch, watch TV and nap, hoping I'd be well enough to attend my favorite Christmas activities. But, as the days went by, I didn't feel any better. And each time I missed out on an event, a charity fundraiser, a Christmas party at church or our town's annual light parade, I felt a little more disappointed.

Thankfully, by the time December 17th rolled around, I was well enough to make the five-hour drive to Prescott with my husband to celebrate our thirty-eighth wedding anniversary.

The Hassayampa Inn, where we stayed, is just one block from the historic town center, close enough to walk everywhere we wanted to go. We enjoyed shopping in antique stores and thrift shops and eating at our favorite restaurants. In the afternoons, we lounged around in our room, reading or napping. Every evening, we bundled up and strolled around the town square as Christmas music played and thousands of colored lights on the courthouse and the trees in the plaza sparkled in the chilly night air. It was beginning to feel a lot like Christmas.

We returned home Friday afternoon with two events remaining on my list: a concert the next evening and Christmas Eve service the following week. The Yuma Orchestra would be performing "The Spirit of Christmas" at the Historic Yuma Theatre. For years, I'd wanted to attend, but something always kept me from it. This year, I hoped for a different outcome.

The concert had been on my mind for weeks. All along, I had the distinct impression that, somehow, everything would work out, and I would be able to go. But I put off buying a ticket, unsure if I would feel well enough to attend.

Now, on the day of the concert, I didn't have a ticket and had no real hope of getting one. It looked more and more like I would miss out on the concert this year, too.

All afternoon, my mind was preoccupied with thoughts of the concert. Voices in my head argued back and forth with one another. *Go! There will be a ticket waiting for you. Don't go! There are no tickets left.* I felt conflicted. What were the chances that a ticket would magically appear at the theater box office, reserved for me? It wasn't very likely. Still, I wondered, how would I know if I didn't go? There was only one way to find out.

It was already 6:00 p.m. when I checked the website and saw the concert started at 6:30. I rushed to get dressed and my husband wished me good luck. I drove the three miles to downtown and turned onto a back street to see packed parking lots. A block and a half from Main Street, I found a spot, parked my car and hurried to the theater. My optimism faltered when I saw an older couple turn and walk away from the theater box office.

When I got to the counter, I asked if there were any tickets for sale. The girl did not respond to my question. Instead, she looked down at a strip of paper, touched it and asked, "Are you alone?" When I told her I was, she hesitated and then said, "Well, there is this ticket. Someone got sick and couldn't attend. It was turned in so someone else could use it." She slowly slid the ticket across the counter toward me, and I picked it up.

What a serendipitous moment! Not only did I have a ticket, but

I didn't have to pay for it. I entered the theater beaming, thrilled I had followed my heart and the inner voice that encouraged me to believe magical things happen at Christmastime. It was an unexpected Christmas gift from an unknown benefactor, and I couldn't help but believe it was meant to be.

As I made my way to my seat, the woman next to me greeted me and told me the ticket I was holding had been for her husband. He hadn't been feeling well and stayed home. "You weren't charged for the ticket, were you?" she asked. "I wanted it to be a gift." I assured her the ticket had been given to me, and I thanked her for it. We chatted a bit before the concert began.

The emcee welcomed everyone and proudly announced the concert was a sold-out event. I had to smile. It was one more sign that I had just experienced my very own Christmas miracle.

The concert was everything I had imagined and more. Young children played simple Christmas tunes. Older ones played more challenging pieces. Then, the orchestra began their selections. It was wonderful. I quietly tapped my shoe and hummed along with all the songs. I couldn't help myself. Music makes me want to sing. The Christmas spirit was alive and well in this theater, and I was delighted to be a part of it.

I left the theater filled with joy and gratitude. That perfect, unexpected gift was more than just an evening of beautiful music. It was proof that miracles do happen at Christmastime. And some things are just meant to be.

— RoseAnn Faulkner —

91

Clara

It is Christmas in the heart that puts
Christmas in the air.
~W.T. Ellis

I n 2011, my husband's mother died of cancer. Our son, her only grandson, was just two and a half. We were devastated. She was the heart and soul of our extended family, and she was the only real mother I had ever known.

We spent every holiday with my husband's parents and brother, but Thanksgiving and Christmas were extra special to all of us. After Mom died four months before Christmas, none of us looked forward to the coming holiday season.

My husband and I decided we needed to start a new family tradition, something we could carry forward into our son's life that would become our own tradition. We needed something special we could look forward to together that would not be a painful reminder of Mom's absence. So, for the very first time in either of our lives, we decided to take our two-year-old son to see *The Nutcracker* ballet live on stage.

This was the fresh new tradition we needed! It was such a special night, and our little son was absolutely enthralled by the ballet, music, and story. We knew without a doubt that we had hit upon the perfect family tradition for us moving forward.

The next year, Christmas was not quite as hard to face as it had been the previous year. And we had our new tradition to look forward to — seeing *The Nutcracker*! This time, as we sat in our front-row balcony seats watching the show, my three-year-old son looked up at me and wistfully said, "I want a baby sister so I can name her Clara." I smiled sadly down at him, thinking how unlikely this was for our family, since I was already forty years old. I gently told him that I did not think God had that plan in store for us, but it was a lovely idea. I had no idea that night that this dream of his would change our lives and family forever.

My little son started praying earnestly to God every day, asking Him to send him the baby sister of his dreams so he could name her Clara like the little girl from *The Nutcracker*. Every day, I would listen to him pray, and my heart would crack just a bit more, thinking that there was almost no chance of this happening. Medically speaking, my son's conception and birth had been a miracle in itself, and the obstetrician had warned us then that we would never be able to have a second child. Until my son decided he wanted a sister more than anything, I had been fine with the idea of never having more children. Now, I found myself privately wishing his dream could come true, even though I never shared that with my son or husband.

After a year or so of daily prayer on my son's part, I found myself unexpectedly and shockingly pregnant! I knew, without any doubt, that this baby was the little sister he had prayed for, the one he wanted to name Clara. Without even waiting for the doctor's confirmation or any tests, I joyfully told my husband and son I was carrying his Clara, and that his dream would come true in about seven more months!

Clara Bonnie, named for the little girl in *The Nutcracker* and for my mother-in-law, Bonnie, was born in September 2013, perfectly healthy and the perfect addition to our little family. My son, now almost five, was there when she was born and cut the cord to "make her belly button," as he liked to tell people for years afterward.

The next December, we bundled up three-month-old Clara and took her with us to *The Nutcracker* ballet, in keeping with the joyous tradition that unexpectedly led to the most amazing blessing of our lives since Mom's passing. As my son watched his favorite story unfold on the stage below, he would lean in and touch his precious baby sister's head every now and then and say, "Clara," in a voice so saturated with joy that it would melt anyone's heart.

Today, my son is a teenager, and Clara is almost ten. Our family still goes to see *The Nutcracker* live on stage every December, continuing the beloved tradition that has more meaning for us than any other Christmas tradition we have ever known.

— Stephanie Schiano Wallace —

92

Chicken Soup for the Soul

The Cafeteria Ave Maria

Music is well said to be the speech of angels.
~Thomas Carlyle

As musicians, our entire December is full of songs. My husband and I spend the season of good cheer lifting our voices in concerts, church services, and festive community events. One of our most beloved traditions is singing Victorian carols for seniors. I pull out my crinoline skirt, full scarlet cape, and fur collar. My husband dons his top hat and a red-and-green wool scarf. Accompanied by nothing but a pitch pipe, we visit seniors' homes to sing a cappella renditions of "The First Noel," "Silent Night," and "White Christmas."

We sing in a variety of settings depending on the home. It might be a joyful concert for the full community, an intimate singalong on each floor, or a gentle carol by an ailing patient's bedside. Many of our audience members are suffering from the effects of dementia or Alzheimer's disease. Some haven't uttered a word in weeks. New staff members warn us, "You shouldn't expect too much. Most of these people don't even talk anymore."

But we always think the same thing: Don't expect too little.

The moment we begin singing "Away in a Manger," we see that flash of sweet recognition. These are the songs from their childhood, rooted deep in their memories. Smiles curl, and eyes light up. Their lips shake as they struggle to sing along. Tears flow down their cheeks as the songs bring back precious memories of Christmases long past.

We've seen that response many times. It's always incredibly power-ful. But one Christmas morning, we experienced something for which we were completely unprepared.

The large building contained three floors, so we knew we were in for a busy morning. As we put on the final pieces of our costumes, the staff shared their plan for us: visit each floor and sing to the residents during their breakfast hour. This was a terrible idea! Imagine a large cafeteria, filled with about forty residents plus staff members. There would be dishes clinking, hard-of-hearing residents asking questions, family members stopping by. Each dining room would be pure chaos.

And remember… we're only two voices, with no instruments or sound system. How would they even hear us?

Determined to try anyway, we found a semi-empty spot in the middle of the first dining room and started to sing. The people closest to us could hear, but we struggled to push through the noise.

After the first few songs, we stopped to sip some water before our next carol. It was then that she stood up.

The frail-looking woman with distant eyes needed two staff mem-bers to aid her that morning. She wore a thin, white nightgown, with simple slippers on her feet. Her unbrushed hair flew up at odd angles. Her pale face bore the strain of trauma and dementia. Someone had tied a jingle bell to her wrist with a piece of ribbon, an attempt at a bit of festive joy.

The woman staggered to her feet. She stared intensely at us as she took a faltered step forward.

And then, she opened her mouth…

"Ave Maria, gratia plena."

The purest soprano voice started to fill the room. Everything stilled. There was an unspoken agreement to hold our collective breath and just listen.

She didn't notice. She just kept singing.

"Maria, gratia plena,
"Maria, gratia plena,
"Ave, Ave Dominus,
"Dominus tecum."

The air was electric! Something divine was happening. We could all feel it.

"*Benedicta tu in mulieribus, et benedictus,*

"*Et benedictus fructus ventris,*

"*Ventris tui, Jesus.*"

She took one more deep breath, knowing the long notes were coming again.

"*Aaaaaave Mariiiiiiiiiiiaaaaaaa!*"

She looked at us, with clear eyes and a sparkling presence. Her world was on fire! She was alive, vibrant, the diva at centre stage singing one of the greatest melodies ever written! It was as if, for the briefest of moments, angels had breathed consciousness into her soul so we could all receive this incredible gift.

The final note echoed in the air, and the room basked in its stillness.

And then, as quickly as it had started, it ended. Her eyes glazed over, and her face went back to its sad, quiet state, the jingle bell dangling limply from her wrist.

A few people quietly clapped. No one wanted to be the one to break the spell.

Her care workers, still in awe, carefully helped her sit back down, wiping tears from their eyes.

We wanted to stop, to yell to everyone, "Do you realize what you just witnessed? How did this woman sing like that? How did that withered and suffering body produce that sound? Her high notes were clear as a bell! Her Latin was impeccable! Her breath support was perfect! How did that happen?"

But, instead, we took a deep breath. We chose our next song. We sang, smiled and marvelled.

As we finished our set and left the room, a staff member pulled us aside.

"She was an opera singer," he shared. "Did you know that? She spent her whole life on the stage. She never sings now, but I don't know, I guess it must still be in her somewhere."

We smiled and nodded, appreciating how the music of our youth can live inside us, even when we are too lost to remember it. Science tells us songs and early memories can live in those deepest parts of the brain, that they can actually survive age, trauma and all manner of struggle.

But what we experienced wasn't technical. This wasn't just the resurfacing of a long-held memory. This was something more glorious.

In that crowded, bustling dining room, we witnessed something holy, something pure. A moment that could only happen in the presence of the Divine.

That Christmas morning, an angel sang "Ave Maria" in a cafeteria, and we were blessed to be in her presence.

—Allison Lynn Flemming—

Chapter
11

Favorite Traditions

93

Chicken Soup for the Soul

Grandma's Red Christmas Sweater

*We think of our homes as places of warmth, familiarity
and love; of shared stories and memories,
which is perhaps why at this time of year
so many return to where they grew up.*
~Queen Elizabeth II

Every year my extended family gathers at my uncle's home for Christmas. It is a cozy little cottage tucked away in the woods. While the family members may change, and the food may vary, there is one constant: my grandma's red sweater, with gold beads that form flowers and diamonds.

"It was easy to get dressed because I wear the same thing every Christmas," Grandma says every year with a chuckle. She isn't one to make a big fuss about what she wears. She is very practical. Grandma received this sweater as a Christmas gift when I was very small and has worn it every year since.

No matter how much the world outside has changed, or how our family has grown and evolved, that sweater remains a steadfast tradition.

One Thanksgiving, after some family friends had passed away, we began the meal by remarking on the two we had lost that year. With my grandma in her mid-nineties at the time, I couldn't help but think that my holidays with her were numbered. Would she still be there for Christmas?

I thought about Grandma's Christmas sweater and what would happen to it after she died. I am not an overly sentimental person, but I decided I wanted that red sweater. I wanted to continue Grandma's tradition of wearing it every year.

But then, a thought popped into my head. *Why wait? How funny would it be if I showed up for Christmas in the same red sweater? While it is a unique sweater, decades old, it couldn't be the only one of its kind.*

After Thanksgiving dinner, as we sat around the table sharing stories of our lives, I quietly pulled out my phone. I searched on the internet for "Red Sweater Gold Beads." It took a few tries to get the keywords right, but I found some beaded sweaters that looked similar. I concluded they must be from the same designer. And then, knowing that designer's name, it only took me five minutes to find an online vintage shop.

To my astonishment and delight, there it was — Grandma's cherished red sweater. It felt like destiny had intervened. Without hesitation, I placed an order.

The sweater arrived just in time for Christmas, and I couldn't wait to surprise Grandma with it. When I arrived at my uncle's home, after the parade of hugs and hellos, Grandma was the first to notice.

"Oh my, that is my sweater," Grandma said, pointing to my outfit. She had to look down to confirm she was, in fact, wearing her version.

The joy and amusement on Grandma's face warmed my heart. It was a moment of connection, a bridge between generations, and a tribute to the enduring love within our family.

My uncle insisted we get a photo of me and Grandma in our matching sweaters. The whole family was delighted by the find.

The next year, I was asked if I would wear my red sweater again that Christmas. While it had been a fun joke the first year, would I actually make it a tradition? Not only did I decide that I would, but I was able to find the same sweater online in black, purple and white. So, while I save the red version to match with Grandma at Christmas, I like to wear the others at other family holidays. As Grandma is now ninety-nine years old, I know my worries about her being around for Christmas are now incredibly real. But even after she passes, she will remain in our hearts and will always be with us at Christmas in the form of my red sweater.

—Gertrude Daly—

94

Our Favorite Auntie

One's heritage and roots are something to be cherished.
~Author Unknown

Growing up, I didn't celebrate Kwanzaa. Each December, my white family decorated Santa-shaped sugar cookies and attended church a few extra times. I was completely unaware of the week-long recognition of African American traditions and values. This changed when my husband and I adopted Naomi, a wide-eyed, five-year-old girl from Africa.

She arrived in Minnesota in early December and saw snow fall for the first time the very next day. Our first year together was a steep learning curve, but the next holiday season we sought out opportunities to learn about Black culture.

We took in our first Kwanzaa celebration at the Minnesota History Center. The energy of a festive drumbeat rippled through the crowd in the main hall. As Naomi watched a dozen musicians in bright African garb, she was captivated by the precision movements of the traditional hand-held percussion instruments. Later, a volunteer painted a butterfly on her forehead, but we still didn't know much about Kwanzaa.

The next year, our public library advertised "Kwanzaa Stories with Auntie Beverly." Entering the lower-level meeting room, we were greeted by Natalie, the librarian. She invited us to sit around a circle. A Black woman sitting in a stuffed chair, which looked like it should have been in front of a fireplace, beckoned to us with a smile. "Come in, come in!" Auntie Beverly's voice was both soothing and authoritative.

Naomi was nestled on my lap as the story began. Auntie Beverly roared like a lion. Naomi giggled. "After hunting," she said, "the lion needed a nap." Auntie Beverly tilted her head to one side, rested her cheek against her prayer-position hands and snored. As she came to the part of "The Lion and the Mouse" fable where the tiny mouse climbs onto the lion's nose, Naomi pumped her arms up and down with excitement. The lion let the mouse go, and Naomi's body relaxed into mine. After the mouse chewed through the ropes, freeing the lion from the trap, the storyteller spoke to the children.

"You may be small, but that doesn't mean you can't do important things," she said earnestly, looking around the circle. "You have a purpose, things that only you can do. *Nia* is the theme of the fifth day of Kwanzaa, and *Nia* means 'purpose' in Swahili."

Between Christmas Day and New Year's Day, our family added the holiday tradition of celebrating Kwanzaa at the library with Auntie Beverly. She always greeted us warmly, commented on how much Naomi had grown, and taught us a little bit more about the Kwanzaa principles like *Umoja* (unity), and *Imani* (faith).

Almost five years after we adopted Naomi, we welcomed six-year-old Tutu, also from Liberia, into our family. She loved stories even more than Naomi, so we knew Auntie Beverly would be a hit. As we walked into the basement meeting room, Auntie Beverly's eyes lit up. "Who do we have here?" She bent down to take Tutu's hands in hers.

When everyone was settled in a circle, she showed samples of colorful fabrics that are traditional in the African culture. "Today, the story I have for you is *Seven Spools of Thread*, and it's about this colorful cloth. You see, there was a man in the country of Ghana with seven sons. And these sons quarreled with each other from morning until night." She shook her head and narrowed her eyes.

"One sad day, the old man died." Auntie Beverly paused to bring her hands together in prayer and raised her eyes to heaven. The children were riveted as Auntie Beverly told them that the chief of the village tried to tell the brothers about their inheritance but was interrupted by their arguing. "Finally, he got their attention. The chief told the brothers they would each receive an equal share of their father's property and possessions, but only if they learned to make gold out of silk thread."

One at a time, Auntie Beverly held up seven different colors of thread, one for each brother. "The chief also told the brothers they could not argue or be angry with each other, or all their father's wealth would be divided among the poorest villagers."

Auntie Beverly lowered her voice to tell her audience that the brothers were speechless. They returned home, made peace with each other and set to the task of turning the thread into gold. They wove the seven colors of thread into stunning cloth. At market, they were able to sell it to the king's treasurer for a bag of gold.

"Now, when the brothers returned to the chief with the gold, he asked them if they had been fighting," Auntie Beverly said. "They told the chief they had not. 'We have been too busy working together to argue or fight,' the youngest brother told the chief." She smiled as she told us the brothers were granted their inheritance and decided they would help the poor of their village by teaching them how to turn thread into gold.

"This story teaches us the seven principles of Kwanzaa. One of these is the principle of *Ujima*. *Ujima* is working together to solve problems. The brothers had to stop fighting and work together to figure out how they were going to turn thread into gold. Do we need to work together in our community?" The children nodded.

Auntie Beverly held up some *kente* cloth from Ghana, woven of silken threads. She invited the kids to weave paper into placemats. Tutu selected a yellow sheet for her mat. Auntie Beverly came over and told her, "You are doing important work."

As the years went by, we prepared traditional dishes of collard greens, black-eyed peas, and ground nut stew for our Kwanzaa celebrations at home. During the pandemic the story time moved to a virtual format, and we watched together at our dining room table. After that, our girls began to think they were too old to go to the library with the little kids.

In October, when Naomi was thirteen, we were surprised to get an e-mail from Auntie Beverly. She had been in the audience when Naomi sang "This Little Light of Mine" solo in a community youth choir performance. Auntie Beverly expressed what a surprise and joy it was to see Naomi singing. We had never corresponded, but somehow she had tracked us down.

The next December, we attended the Kwanzaa celebration hosted by the Midtown Global Market in Minneapolis. We enjoyed the food, dancers, spoken word artists, and storytelling by our favorite Auntie. Before we left, we found her sitting in a chair. She was in good spirits, despite having lost her husband the previous year. A few months later, we heard Auntie Beverly had suddenly passed away.

Beverly Cottman told us stories at Kwanzaa, and we know that she lived the principles she taught throughout the year as a leader in her community. Each year, we'll light the Kwanzaa candles and do our best to follow her example.

— Becky Hofstad —

95

Beyond Darkness

The spirit of Hanukkah, the Festival of Lights,
is shared by all people who love freedom.
~Norma Simon

Growing up, my brother and I weren't allowed to leave the table until the Hanukkah candles burned down — my mother's attempt to make the holiday meaningful to us. Those skinny, colorful tapers took their sweet time. Dan and I would sit across the dining room table from each other. Though it was sacrilegious to blow out the Hanukkah lights, we took turns subtly whooshing air in their direction. Not subtly enough.

"We are celebrating a story of religious freedom," my mother said sternly. "We are commemorating the miracle of one day's worth of oil keeping the temple's eternal flame burning for eight days. Surely, you can sit still for ten more minutes."

We sat. Even though I'd heard the Judah Maccabee story many times, the sense of the miraculous never sank in. What did an armed conflict in some ancient temple all those centuries ago have to do with me?

I grew up and got married. My husband was not Jewish, so we celebrated Christmas with his family. I enjoyed being part of their festivities, but after my daughters were born, I felt wistful for my own quiet holiday. Plus, I felt guilty. I was letting down my mother and disappointing my ancestors. Even though I hadn't connected spiritually with Hanukkah, it was part of my heritage.

My husband was agreeable to celebrating both holidays.

So, the next December, I unearthed the menorah my mother had given me years ago. It was plain and unadorned, much like the one my grandmother had given to my parents. My older daughter was seven; my younger daughter was four. This was the perfect year to celebrate the eight nights of Hanukkah.

The first night, I enjoyed lighting the candles and dutifully ate the soggy potato pancakes I had struggled to make.

The girls loved the candle lighting and wiggled about in their seats, eagerly awaiting their gift.

But the moment our meal was over and the girls had torn open their presents, I felt my old childhood restlessness. I was eager to clean the kitchen, get the kids ready for bed, and finish up the day's work. I didn't have time to sit around watching a bunch of candles burn.

However, as I contemplated blowing out the candles, I heard my mother's voice: "You can't sit still for one small miracle?"

So, I sat. Alone at the table, I gazed at the flickering flames, even as my thoughts jumped up and down, my children ran around, and my husband turned on the TV. The minute the candles went dark, I bolted.

Still, I lit the candles each night and vowed to make Hanukkah part of the season. I didn't love the holiday, but I liked my girls being part of this tradition. And I liked making my mother happy.

The years passed, and my daughters went off to college. I thought about letting go of Hanukkah, but when I talked to a Jewish friend about my inability to savor the holiday, she chided me.

"Hanukkah is about sharing your light with the world," she said. "Deborah, that should be a natural for you."

I'd never connected this holiday with my quest to help others and live purposefully. I began reading about modern celebrations. One rabbi suggested putting the candles in the window as a way to share light with the world.

Another rabbi encouraged families to invite non-Jewish friends to the festivity. But weren't they too busy with their own holiday activities? I'd always felt our Jewish winter celebration was a ragged Cinderella compared to the pageantry of Christmas. Still, the next year, I invited three friends to share the first night of Hanukkah.

I was surprised when each one said, "I'd love to come."

My parents were driving up, and my daughters and their boy-friends were joining us. Since "company" was coming, I created a small ceremony. I pared down the Maccabee story to its essence and added inspiring quotes about dispelling darkness. At the end of the meal, I asked everyone to write down three ways we could bring more light into the world.

I looked around the table at my parents, children, and friends as we read aloud our intentions: "Do something kind every day." "Be more patient." "Volunteer at the food pantry."

The candlelight illuminated their faces. For the first time, I was in no hurry to jump back into everyday life. I wanted to hear more about each person's ideas for a better world.

Today, my daughter Sarah continues our Hanukkah tradition. In fact, she has considerably improved our holiday experience. She makes crispy potato pancakes, treats us to her delicious matzo ball soup, and bakes a fantastic chocolate torte in the shape of a Jewish star for dessert.

We gather at her table, with her children and husband, other family and friends, using the ceremony I created so many years ago. Before dessert, we each share ways we can bring more light into our lives and into the world. As I listen, I watch the candles burn and contemplate the real miracle of Hanukkah: being together and taking time to let in the light.

— Deborah Shouse —

96

A Mother's Love

Life is uncertain. Eat dessert first.
~Ernestine Ulmer

I was raised an only child by a single mom. My mom always had food on the table. She always kept me warm and comfortable. And she always made me feel safe. But, as I grew older, I quickly learned we were not like everyone else. We didn't have what everyone else had. Other families had houses. We lived in an apartment. Other families had fancy cars. We didn't have a car at all. Other families would take vacations to Disneyland, the Hawaiian Islands, or some beautiful beachfront property. The first time I went on vacation, I was twenty years old.

But one thing she gave me was an abundance of love. There was so much love in that little apartment that neighborhood kids would flock to my mom just to hear the words, "I'm proud of you." And, more importantly, to hear, "Do you want something to eat?"

Coming from an Italian heritage, my mom's first love language was food. Smells of lasagna, pasta, and ravioli filled the house. The cookie jar was always full of fresh peanut-butter cookies, chocolate-chip cookies, and my favorite sugar cookies!

But a few times a year, we'd have a special treat. She would save up to purchase all the ingredients for homemade fudge.

There were a few epic nights each year that warranted such sweet treats: the annual TV event of *The Wizard of Oz*, the annual epic event of my birthday and, of course, Christmas.

I would wait and wait for those dates.

I'd ask over and over, "When is it fudge-making time?"

And then, finally, I'd hear her shout from the kitchen, "Diana, it's time!"

I'd fly out of my room to help. I'd watch her mix all the ingredients, feeling like a royal princess the whole time. She'd mix everything together and hand me the wooden spoon to stir. That was my job. I was the professional stirrer.

I had to stir the fudge for what felt like a lifetime, but it was really about fifteen minutes. It would boil and pop. It was a messy job, but someone had to do it. After it was done boiling, I had to dip the pot in cold water and stir and stir until I felt the fudge thickening. Then, I would pour it onto a plate and wait for it to cool.

I don't know if this is an East Coast thing or an Italian thing, but this was not the average soft fudge. This fudge hardened. It was not creamy soft. It was hard. Soft enough to bite into but hard enough that it confused anyone who tried it for the first time.

"This is fudge?" they would ask.

"Yes, isn't it good?" I would say with delight.

Most of the time, people would give me a confused look and put it back on the plate.

Right before my thirty-first birthday, my mom passed away. One of my first thoughts was I'd never have her lasagna again. I'd never have her peanut-butter cookies again. I'd never have her fudge again.

That first Christmas, I thought, *Why not try her recipes for the holidays?* I cried the entire holiday season that first year. And, honestly, sometimes I still do.

I decided at thirty-one to continue the family tradition of lasagna for Christmas. It was a success. I made her cookies. It was a success. I made her fudge… No one liked it. No one got it. They couldn't understand what they were eating.

Nevertheless, I continued to make fudge each holiday for my son and me. I didn't even bother trying to share it with others. It was just a little treat for us, and I was okay with that.

This past Christmas, twenty years after my mom passed, my dad called while I was making fudge.

He said, "What are you up to?"

I said, "Oh, I'm just making some fudge."

He said, "That sounds good."

I said, "It's not the traditional fudge most people are used to. This is hard fudge that my mom used to make when I was little."

My dad got quiet, and then he said almost in a whisper, "No way!"

I said, "You know what I'm talking about?"

He said, "My mom used to make that for me as a kid. It was my favorite! I haven't had that fudge in fifty years!" He added, "My job was to stir."

Growing up, my dad lived in another state. We missed out on a lot of opportunities to share life stories. To find out that we shared the same memories with our moms was almost too much. I felt the tears welling up. I couldn't talk.

He softly said, "Will you make me some fudge for Christmas?"

Tears filled my eyes. I said, "Yes, of course I will."

He said, "You know who would really love it? Your Aunt Donna and Aunt Debbie!"

I said, "Done. Be on the lookout, it's coming."

When we got off the phone, I went right to the store. I purchased all the ingredients for three batches of fudge.

As I stood in the kitchen stirring the ingredients together, I smiled and cried the entire time. Finally, someone who "got" it. Finally, someone who loved it. Finally, someone who truly understood it's not just about fudge.

It's about a mother's love. It's about connection. And now, I have this gift to share with my dad.

A new tradition was born this Christmas. It's probably the best Christmas gift I've ever received.

— Diana Lynn —

97

Chicken Soup
for the *Soul*

A Very Different Christmas

Call it a clan, call it a network, call it a tribe,
call it a family: Whatever you call it,
whoever you are, you need one.
~Jane Howard

I t was the holiday season of 1990, and my visions were less about sugar plums and all about gifts, but not the wrapped ones that normally are waiting under the tree or spilling out of the carefully placed stockings.

I was hugely pregnant with my first child, and my due date was December 31, 1990. Once I heard that, I set my sights on delivering the first baby of the 1991 New Year.

I wanted to have The New Year's Baby!

My then-husband, Max, and I were very young. We were just starting out, and our budget was tight. A year's supply of diapers — a prize for giving birth to the first baby of the year — would be a blessing. But it was more than that. I thought that having The New Year's Baby would make his or her birth more memorable.

That year, after Thanksgiving, my nesting instincts kicked into high gear. I became a cleaning and organizing machine. One day, while I was on my hands and knees scrubbing the baseboards in the small living room of our one-bedroom apartment, I came up with what I thought was a great idea.

Later that night, as we sat around our two-person table in our small, eat-in kitchen eating our dinner of Hamburger Helper, I told Max of my plan. "Since I won't be able to travel this year for Christmas, we should invite our families here for the holiday."

He agreed it was a great idea. Neither of us fretted that we lived in a cramped, one-bedroom apartment with only one bathroom, or that we only had table service for four.

The next day, we invited both sets of our parents, our three brothers and their girlfriends to our place for the holiday.

They all said yes. We would spend Christmas surrounded by family.

I spent the next weeks preparing our dinky place for the arrival of our crew. I planned menus and seating arrangements for the card tables we would set up in the sparsely furnished living room.

On Christmas Eve day, the defrosted turkey that Max's employer had given us was resting safely in the roaster pan in the refrigerator, and ingredients for several sides were ready. I padded around the steamy kitchen making chili and cinnamon rolls while I dreamed of our families gathered together to watch college bowl games, play cards, and eat way too much food — even if they had to do it off paper plates.

As I sang along with "The First Noel" on the CD player and marked things off my to-do list, I just knew that Christmas would be memorable for everyone.

As dusk approached, my mom and stepdad arrived, hauling in the air mattress they would sleep on, plus all the bedding to go with it. They brought a load of presents, which we put under the 36-inch Christmas tree perched on our wicker side table.

When everything was finally loaded into the apartment, they both remarked on how big I had gotten. I was barely fitting into the maternity jeans that Mom had given me for my birthday that summer. "It looks like the baby has dropped. It won't be long now," my mom said, beaming with happy anticipation at the approaching arrival of her first grandchild.

We spent the evening eating chili with cheese and crackers and cinnamon rolls, playing rummy, and watching *National Lampoon's Christmas Vacation*.

After everyone went to bed, I started having terrible stomach pains. I loaded up on my usual mint-flavored Tums, but this was way worse than my usual pregnancy heartburn.

I couldn't get comfortable. And then the pain intensified.

Finally, I woke Max. "I think I'm in labor," I said. I took a shower and grabbed the hospital bag I'd had packed for weeks. About 2:00 a.m., we snuck out the back door of our apartment, careful not to wake my parents.

My contractions seemed to speed up on the 25-mile trip to the hospital. We both got nervous when, at one point, they were two minutes apart.

We finally reached the hospital, only to have everything stop once they settled me into a birthing suite. As Christmas Eve gave way to the dawn of Christmas Day, Max called each family member to let them know they were still welcome to have Christmas dinner at our place, but we'd had a slight change in plans. We'd be celebrating at the hospital with a surprise guest, and it wasn't Santa.

Since our baby would be the first grandchild on both sides of the family, everyone loaded into their cars and made their way to the hospital to await the birth.

But as the hours passed and still no baby, we began to joke that we might still be in the running for The New Year's Baby.

Finally, at 1:50 p.m., with a big cry and a bit of blond hair, we had an eight-pound, five-ounce baby boy, a son we named Ross. His timing may have been a surprise, but something about holding that tiny bundle for the first time on the most special day of the year opened my heart in ways I'd never known before — I was a mom.

And I was in love in a way I'd never known before.

No, we didn't win the year's supply of diapers, and that Christmas didn't turn out quite as we expected. Everyone ended up having dinner in the hospital cafeteria. But Ross's birth would launch shared celebrations by our two families as we gathered on his birthday for years to come.

Today, that little blond baby is in his thirties and the daddy of two little blond boys of his own, Dax and Slayde. Every Christmas at

1:50 p.m. I tell him the story of his arrival—his birth story.

That very different Christmas taught me that the most special Christmases are about the small things, like togetherness, no matter where that takes place—and the surprise arrival of babies, too.

Yes, that's what the most special Christmases are about, aren't they?

Just as the first one was when innocent, helpless, sweet, saving love came down and was born in a manger—a baby for all of us.

—Amy Catlin Wozniak—

An Icy, Dicey Adventure

Every great story on the planet happened when
someone decided not to give up but kept
going no matter what.
~Spryte Loriano, *Artful Stories*

Christmas was always the big event for me when I was a kid. New Year's never appealed to me much as it always seemed anticlimactic. That changed, however, when I was fourteen years old. That was the year my dad suggested our family pack up and drive 500 miles north to ring in the New Year's holiday at our 600-square-foot lake cabin in northern Michigan.

At first, I was hesitant. The cabin was awesome... in the summer. It was our go-to spot for boating, fishing, swimming, water skiing, and tubing. Hanging out there in the dead of winter sounded boring and bleak.

I crinkled up my nose in disgust and asked, "What will we do?"

"There's tons of stuff to do," Dad replied. "We can spend the week skiing, snowshoeing, ice skating, and sledding! We can play games, sleep in, and explore northern Michigan in a different season. We can build a giant bonfire down by the lake and make s'mores, then come inside and drink hot cocoa."

Okay, I was in. My brother, Dan, was also intrigued.

A few days after Christmas, Mom, Dad, Dan and I piled into our red Chevy Blazer and hit the road. Five hours into our trip, my eyes fluttered shut. In my mind's eye, I imagined the scene that would welcome us when we arrived at the cabin. The bare tree limbs would be draped in snow and ice crystals. I suspected the lake might look larger in the absence of docks and boats. The one thing that I hoped would be like summer was that the sky would be a piercing bright blue.

Suddenly, I was jolted back to reality. Mom slammed on the brakes, my body flew forward, and my eyes popped open to find the highway ahead littered with police cruisers and smashed vehicles.

Our Blazer began to fishtail on solid ice. We spun 180 degrees, then slid backward down the interstate 1,000 feet before coming to an abrupt halt in the median. Our hearts raced as we realized how narrowly we had escaped crashing into the surrounding vehicles that peppered the freeway.

Soon thereafter, an officer approached our car to ask if we were okay. He told us the road up ahead was just as icy, so he instructed us to shift into 4-wheel drive and slowly head down the median until we were clear of the mess.

Several hours later, just as the sun was setting, we turned onto the cabin's gravel lane and were greeted by the familiar sound of crunching rocks beneath the tires, though slightly muffled from the snow on the ground. After the interstate fiasco, it felt good to be grounded and at our happy place.

We all jumped out of the car and ran to the cabin doorway. Like a giddy teenager, Dad stuck the key in the lock, but it wouldn't turn. Eyebrows furrowed, Dad took the key out, studied it closely, and then inserted it again. Jiggle, jiggle. Still no luck. The lock was frozen.

With no year-round neighbors nearby (and the invention of cell phones still years off), Mom and I drove to the local general store to use the payphone while Dad and Dan continued to fight the lock. As luck would have it, this was a Sunday, so no locksmith would help us until morning. The cashier suggested we buy a can of Lock De-Icer and spray it on the frozen lock to thaw it.

Back at the cabin, as Dad prepared to use the De-Icer, he announced, "Here goes nothing!" He was right. Two measly squirts of foamy air oozed from the defective nozzle before Dad hurled the can into a snowbank.

By now, it was after 7:00 p.m., the store was closed, and the temp was dropping fast; we needed a Plan B. Perhaps we could bunk in the car for the night. Mom opened the back window of the Blazer to see how many blankets we had packed. But when she tried closing it, it wouldn't budge. So, there we were with a frozen open car window and a frozen closed cabin door.

Teeth chattering, noses running, and fingers tingling and turning blue, Dad did what any freezing, frustrated, frenzied father would — he grabbed a big rock and heaved it through the kitchen window.

"We're in!" Dad proclaimed like Indiana Jones finding his way to the Holy Grail. And that's pretty much how we all felt — like we'd survived a perilous adventure and had at last found serenity and shelter in the much-sought-after and highly anticipated treasure (i.e., the cabin).

Although our first day of winter vacation offered more adventure than we wanted, we created plenty of great memories that week. We made more snow angels than I can count, fell down on skates more times than I care to admit, and sledded more miles than our knees appreciated. And to top off the warm, fuzzy holiday feeling, on New Year's Eve, we watched in delight as fresh powder blanketed the ground. Nineteen inches fell in total, enabling us to spend the remainder of our vacation frolicking in our own northern winter wonderland.

After that memorable trip, we thought it apropos to keep the infamous rock that Dad had used to smash the cabin window. It sits on our property just outside the kitchen window. Some call it a great piece of holiday history. We call it the spare key.

— Christy Heitger-Ewing —

A Heritage Lesson

Heritage is the bridge between generations.
~Nelson Mandela

I pull out the candelabra from its box. It will hold seven tall red, black, and green candles. My grandchildren help me place the *kente* cloth on the narrow living room coffee table with excitement dancing in their eyes.

"Tell us the story of Kwanzaa, Grandma," they beg.

"I grew up at a time when young actors were starring in stage plays like *Hair* that was celebrated as a musical protest on Broadway," I begin my story.

"Where's Broadway?" my energetic five-year-old grandson asks, turning in circles.

"In New York City, far away from Los Angeles," I tell him.

I always like to give them a bit of history with each memory I share.

"The play was about Black people wearing their hair 'natural' in Afros, and young white males letting their hair grow long. In those days, they called us 'hippies.' Parents were freaking out! They threatened to get the clippers and cut their teens' hair or grab the hot comb and straighten the natural, soft, fuzzy curls of their teenagers into straight locks."

"Like mine?" my ten-year-old granddaughter Maya asks, shaking her ponytail back and forth.

"Yes," I nod.

"It was a revolutionary time in this country. Young and old people of all colors were marching with Dr. Martin Luther King, Jr. for equal rights and civil rights."

"We read about Dr. King in school," chimes in Malakai, my eight-year-old grandson.

"Pulitzer Prize winner, Alex Haley, wrote a whole book called *Roots* in 1976. I met him once and his representative, Peter Long, in 1974. They told me I'd have to change the name of a column I was writing for a magazine called *Soul & Jazz Record*. My column was called 'Roots.' It was a historic column about famous black musicians. Peter suggested I change the name of my column because Mr. Haley was coming out with a book called *Roots*, and it would be a bestseller. He was right. Alex Haley also had a television series made out of his groundbreaking book."

My grandchildren stare up at me with interest from their seats on the carpet. I keep them after school each weekday until their parents come home from work.

"Anyway, it was a time before AncestryDNA and 23andMe existed. Those online ancestor-search companies weren't around. Black folks were interested in our heritage, our African family ties. We wanted to find our own Kunta Kinte. He was the main character in Alex Haley's book. What tribe were we from? Which part of the African continent did we come from? So, the concept of Kwanzaa grew more popular with that awareness. I grew up at a time when Kwanzaa was created," I told them.

"Really, Grandma?" Five-year-old Tré's saucer eyes stare at me in surprise. "You're really old, huh, Grandma?"

"Yes," I nod, laughing.

"It all started with a man named Maulana Ron Karenga, who introduced us to the seven principles of Kwanzaa. That's when we were changing our names to African inspired names, wearing dashikis, and wrapping our hair with turbans. He combined the idea of a first harvest celebration in Africa with our December holiday-season festivities. He called it Kwanzaa."

I take the candles out of their storage container. They are wrapped in white tissue paper. I tell my grandkids to put the candelabra on the *kente* tablecloth and then, one by one, we start putting the candles into place in the wrought-iron candleholder.

"These candles stand for the seven principles of Kwanzaa. Who remembers the name of the first one?"

My ten-year-old granddaughter, who is very smart, is the first to answer.

"The first principle of Kwanzaa is Unity," she tells me.

I nod at her proudly. "Yes," I respond smiling. "*Umoja* is the African name for unity. It stands for maintaining unity in the family, our community, our nation, and our race."

My grandchildren start chanting the word, like a little rhythmical choir.

"*U-mo-ja. U-mo-ja!*" They giggle, and I do, too. Music is a great way to teach children, so I join their singing game.

We unwrap the second candle. Malakai places it in its holder. This one stands for self-determination, and the African word is hard to remember. It's *Kujichagulia.* The kids don't sing that one. I laugh at Tré, the smallest child, who tries to repeat the long African word. It's joyful explaining this holiday to them. All the principles are positive, uplifting, and community-driven. They celebrate values that all human beings can embrace and appreciate.

Starting on December 26, the day after Christmas, we begin to light the candles, one day at a time. Each day, over seven days, we will light a new candle. Our family prays together for each new principle. The third day represents *Ujima.* This one stands for collective work and responsibility, building and maintaining our own community, working together. The fourth candle represents cooperative economics called *Ujamaa.* I tell the kids that stands for supporting our neighborhood stores and small businesses. Then comes *Nia,* which means purpose. Our purpose is to restore our people to their traditional greatness. We start by making our own lives purposeful.

We can't forget *Kuumba* that represents creativity, like dancing, singing, writing, drawing, painting and creating new things. We were practicing *Kuumba* when we decorated our Christmas tree.

The final principle is *Imani* representing faith. We must have faith in ourselves, our dreams, our parents, our teachers, and our leaders, and believe that we can accomplish whatever we put our minds to.

By this time, my grown children arrive to collect their kids. It's dinnertime. We light the first candle together and pray, holding hands.

"See you tomorrow," I tell them. "We'll light the next candle then."

We share hugs and kisses. Then, in a poof, they are gone. I miss their energy already.

—Dee Dee McNeil—

Strutting Through the New Year with a Pocket Calendar

A goal is a dream with a deadline.
~Napoleon Hill

Let me begin by stating that I am a very practical person. I carry an umbrella, wear a seatbelt, and dutifully charge my cell phone before leaving the house. My friends, depending upon their respective ages, view me as their "den mother," "big sister," or even "a super senior," now that the Gen Zers are entering the workforce.

Truth be told, I used to fantasize about adopting another persona when I was younger — a spontaneous, fly-by-the-seat-of-my-pants, free spirit. You know the type — a go-with-the-flow individual who lives in the moment, enjoys every headwind, and always ends up on her feet.

But that's not me, so it was no surprise when several of my former students from a journaling group I had facilitated approached me the day after Christmas, asking for my help in establishing a New Year's ritual. They were quite frank about their request. "We know you are a no-nonsense taskmaster, and we need someone like you to help us make this new year a better one," they stated. "In the past, we tried meditation, crystal healing, and energy balancing, but nothing seemed to help. Could you help us make this coming year more purposeful?"

Another person might have taken umbrage at their description of a "no-nonsense taskmaster" but I respected their honesty. "Give me a few days to think about it, and I'll get back to you," I responded. And, twenty-four hours later, I did.

Little did I know at the time that the "plan" I devised would become a New Year's tradition, and the only requirements were a pocket calendar, a working fireplace, and an open mind. Arranging the logistics was easy. Our journaling group had been meeting in a cafe that had been renovated from an old carriage house. Its focal point was a huge working fireplace. I reserved the large round table located near the fireplace, and the seasoned barista could handle the refreshments with more competence than anyone, especially me!

New Year's Day fell on a Sunday that year, so I chose the Friday before — December 30th — and reserved the table for 3:00 p.m. I e-mailed everyone with the specifics, asking them to bring a new pocket calendar, along with an open mind.

The Millennials in the group immediately texted back that a new pocket calendar was unnecessary as their smartphones were adequate for any type of scheduling. I promptly responded, telling them that the pocket calendar was non-negotiable. Bring one with you, and FWIW (for what it's worth), Walgreen's has quite a collection. I just hoped the open minds would accompany the calendars!

Having a Type-A personality, I arrived early but was taken aback to discover that I was not the first one at the table. All my former students were quietly examining their newly purchased pocket calendars, as if they had never seen such artifacts.

As I took my place at the table, the barista slipped my usual black tea at my place, and we were ready to begin. Just to get the proverbial ball rolling, I asked the group if they had any idea about what animal the upcoming new year signified according to the Chinese calendar. My only intention was to pique their interest, and the question was on-target.

Everyone in the group was familiar with the twelve Zodiac signs commonly associated with their respective birthdays. Some were even vaguely aware of the four elemental symbols such as fire, water, air, and earth. But when asked about the twelve animals coupled with the Chinese calendar, all eyes turned to me.

Taking a needed sip of my tea, I told the group that we were about to enter the Year of the Rooster, which brought about a few chuckles, exactly my intention. I continued reporting that the Year of the Rooster, like the other animals in the Chinese calendar, came along once every twelve years. Like their namesake, those born under this sign are considered to be honorable, upstanding, good leaders, confident and eager to let others know about their many accomplishments — much like the animal itself crowing its own praises.

That said, this coming year should be good for all of us, I continued. Now, how could we make that happen in our own lives? Attempting to add some humor to the situation, I added that we should channel our inner rooster and apply those positive traits so we'd have something to "crow" about at the end of the year.

We spent the next few minutes flipping through the empty pages in the pocket calendars, pointing out the sheer gift of time. I said, "What an opportunity before us — four beautiful seasons, twelve delightful months, divided into fifty-two weeks and 365 days. How are we going to use them to make this year our best one yet? Let's concentrate on specific activities, not on generalities, like losing weight or saving money. What is something specific that we would like to accomplish? And when we look back on this gift of time a year from now, how will we know we were successful?"

I hadn't expected an answer, so I was surprised when a Baby Boomer responded that he had always wanted to try cross-country skiing, but had never even put on a pair of skis. A Millennial sighed that she had never traveled outside the United States and wanted to visit the Caribbean. And a Gen Zer confessed that she had never read a *Harry Potter* book, which prompted a discussion on sports, travel, and books.

By the time that discussion concluded, everyone had a goal for the month of January written in their pocket calendars, along with specifics on ways to accomplish that goal. When someone came upon a potential roadblock, the group chimed in to assist, and the conversation continued until we reached December.

Looking back, some of the goals were quite complex and would require a lot of planning, time and effort, such as researching a specific grant opportunity. But these more complicated aspirations were interspersed with easier goals, like expanding one's palate with sushi, and I reminded the group that the process itself—regardless of the outcome—was a valuable experience.

Finally, I passed out a small Post-it note to each student. I asked them to close their eyes and celebrate the exercise we had just completed. I applauded their courage, creativity, and determination. Then, I asked them to think about that critic who lives inside all of us—that voice in our heads that tells us we are not smart enough, brave enough, or good enough. We would need to silence that voice.

As a final step, I asked them to write every negative adjective associated with that critic on that Post-it, crumble it up, and toss it into the fireplace. As those Post-its caught fire and turned to ash, I watched the faces of the students reveal astonishment, a smile, and then a fierce look of determination.

"You're ready to make this year—the Year of the Rooster—the best one ever," I told them. "Now, go strut your stuff!"

And, I'm proud to report, they did just that!

—Barbara Davey—

A Life-Changing New Year's Tradition

I am happy because I'm grateful. I choose to be grateful.
That gratitude allows me to be happy.
~Will Arnett

I come from a long line of pessimists. Our unspoken family motto is "If anything bad can happen, it will." I've spent most of my adult life fighting this tendency to expect the worst, with mixed results.

For example, I tried keeping a gratitude journal where I wrote five things each day for which I felt grateful. The practice did help me appreciate the blessings in my life, but I still spent most of my waking hours focused on the negative.

I never imagined that practicing a new holiday tradition could change that.

But then, one December, I saw an online post about creating a "Good Things Jar." The idea was simple: Whenever something good happened, you were supposed to record the event on a piece of paper and place the note in a jar. At year-end, you emptied the jar and re-read the notes. Then, you started the process all over again on New Year's Day.

The idea appealed to me immediately. I pulled a clear, plastic container from the recycling bin to use as my jar. I wrote the phrase "Good Things" on an index card and glued it over the old label. On the first day of the new year, I began watching eagerly for good things to record. I made notes about events both small and large, from getting a coupon in the mail for a favorite restaurant, to having a fun chat with the desk clerk at our health club, to taking a long-planned vacation. My husband added his own good things, such as finding a quarter on the sidewalk, and besting his younger brother at golf.

Every time I saw the jar sitting on our kitchen table, I smiled at the growing stack of notes. They were tangible evidence of the good things in my life. Seeing them also reminded me to keep a constant lookout for more good things. Gradually, I got better at noticing all sorts of blessings. And I felt a lovely, little jolt of joy whenever I stopped to record one.

As the months passed, we watched the jar fill. By November, adding another note meant we had to squish the others down before screwing the cap back on.

On New Year's Day, I emptied the jar, dumping the contents into a large pile on the kitchen table. My husband and I took turns reading the notes. We were amazed at how many of the good things we'd completely forgotten. For some of the ones we did remember, it didn't seem possible they'd happened less than a year before. But every single note made us smile all over again. The process was more than a fun year-end review — it filled me with joy and gratitude. I'd never had a happier start to a new year!

From then on, the Good Things Jar was a permanent addition to our home. After that first year, we added the date to each note to help jog our memories when we later read it. We eventually moved the jar to a special spot in the living room. We also started using neon-yellow notepaper. As the slips of paper piled up, they brightened the room, both visually and emotionally.

Our New Year's Day review became a highlight of the holiday season. And with each passing year, the practice of treasuring all the big and little blessings was helping to shift my negative outlook. I was beginning to almost expect good things.

Then, Covid-19 hit. In March 2020, our governor issued an order to "shelter at home." Our favorite restaurant closed. Our health club closed. And our planned trip to Scotland was postponed indefinitely.

In the living room, the Good Things Jar sat with only a few yellow slips at the bottom. The nearly empty jar seemed to mock me. I could almost hear it whisper, "There will be no more good things." My pessimism returned in full force. I felt sad, depressed, and lethargic.

But the habit of looking for good things must have been ingrained by then because I began to notice blessings in the midst of the pandemic. While countless people were sick and hospitalized, my husband and I were healthy, and so was everyone in our extended family. As spring arrived, our daffodils and tulips bloomed once more. The warmer weather meant we could get our exercise by walking outdoors. We began visiting new-to-us forest preserves. There, we encountered birds we'd never seen. I found an online group where people posted photos of birds spotted in our state; that helped us not only identify the new birds but also learn about others to watch for. We enjoyed this new hobby together even as the pandemic raged on.

I added notes about these and other blessings to our Good Things Jar: We had plenty of food (and toilet paper!). Our church was technically closed, but the staff found a way to livestream Mass on Easter morning, and we were able to watch on the "smart" family-room television we'd bought just the Christmas before. We couldn't celebrate the holiday with my eighty-five-year-old aunt as usual, but we were able to video chat with her. I would never have imagined such a thing a year earlier!

The pandemic dragged on, keeping us from gathering for our usual family celebrations that Christmas. Even so, by the end of 2020, we had again filled our Good Things Jar. Reading the notes on New Year's Day 2021 was a bright spot in an otherwise dismal winter. I realized then that this annual tradition was one of our best "good things." It had taught me to constantly be on the lookout for blessings and silver linings instead of focusing on the negative.

And that's a big lesson for a born pessimist.

— Carmela A. Martino —

Meet Our Contributors

Kristi Adams has enjoyed sharing her stories in numerous magazines and publications, including eighteen books in the *Chicken Soup for the Soul* series. A kid at heart, Kristi especially loves regaling readers with tales from her mother, particularly during the holidays. Learn more at kristiadamsmedia.com.

Becky Alexander is a tour director, leading groups in Charleston, New York, Toronto, and other destinations. When not on the road, she writes magazine articles, devotions, and inspirational stories. She loves volunteering year-round with Operation Christmas Child. Send Becky a "happy" message at www.happychairbooks.com.

Carol Gentry Allen is an inspirational speaker and published author. She is also a dementia and Alzheimer's practitioner. Carol enjoys traveling, writing, inspiring others to be the best they can be and enjoying their lives to its fullest. She lives in South Carolina with her four-legged pets.

Teresa Ambord was an accountant for many years before becoming a full-time writer and editor. She writes from her home in rural California, surrounded by her posse of small dogs that decorate her life. Teresa makes a living writing for business, but her heart is in writing about her family, faith, and pets.

Raised in San Diego, **Richard Andreoli** moved to Los Angeles to attend UCLA. He's produced stand-up comedy shows, written for magazines, websites, and TV programs, and launched multiple content websites. His newest novel, *Battle at the Comic Expo*, came out in May 2018. In his free time, Richard performs on a trapeze and teaches circus arts.

Violetta Armour is a former English teacher and bookstore owner. She has published five novels, including *Mahjongg Mystery* and *A Pickleball Poison*. She spends her days between Sun Lakes and Flagstaff, AZ with her little rescue dog, Lola.

Elizabeth A. Atwater lives in a small town in North Carolina where she raises standard bred racehorses. She loved books and reading at a very early age, surpassed only by her love of writing.

Katrin Babb lives with her family on a small farm. When not writing for her blog, "Mission Log of the Diabolical Baby Brigade," or for various magazines, she can be found training for her next triathlon.

Phil Baisley was born and raised in Canarsie, Brooklyn, New York. He is a seminary professor, pastor, musician, and reptile enthusiast currently residing in Richmond, IN.

Susan Bartlett is a Registered Nurse with almost forty years cumulative experience in various specialties. She has a daughter living in Manhattan who she loves visiting. Susan's writing has appeared in nursing magazines, the *Bellevue Literary Review* and FWA short story publications.

Jessica Marie Baumgartner is a homeschooling mother of five who writes for *Mid Rivers Newsmagazine*. She is the author of *Reclaiming Femininity* and other titles, as well as a four-time Missouri Writers Guild Award winner. Her work has been featured in *Missouri Conservationist*, *St. Louis Post Dispatch*, and many more.

Karen Beatty can no longer drive but she can still body surf. She was reared in an impoverished family in Eastern Kentucky. She served in Peace Corps Thailand in the 1960s, and then settled in New York City, where she trained as a trauma-informed counselor. Karen's first novel, *Dodging Prayers and Bullets*, was published in 2023.

Following a career in nuclear medicine, **Melissa R. Bender** is joyfully exploring her creative side. She recently moved to the Texas coast where she and her husband are renovating a thirty-year-old former Parade of Homes fixer-upper. Follow her home renovation at www.facebook.com/chicvintique.

Gail E. Bierschbach lives in a suburb of Detroit, where she has raised her two children and enjoys spending time with her grandchildren. She has recently retired after a lifetime of working with children of all ages and is looking forward to writing about faith and inspiration.

Theresa Brandt is a writer who lives on a farm and shares her life with her wonderful husband, three grown sons and lots of furry friends. She loves to write, cook, garden, sew and do crafts. She is blessed to be surrounded by supportive friends and family and is always working on her next writing project.

Shanti Bright Brien is an author, criminal defense attorney and co-founder of Fogbreak Justice. Shanti's memoir, *Almost Innocent: From Searching* *to Saved in America's Criminal Justice System* (Amplify, 2021) was named one of the "Best Memoirs of the Year" by Kirkus Review.

By day, **Meagan Briggs** is a communications manager at a non-profit. By night, she writes historical fiction, devotionals, and humorous stories pulled from the day-to-day. She lives in Tulsa, OK, and can rarely be caught without plans for her next travel adventure. You can keep up with her via her website meaganbriggs.com or social media.

Karla Brown has been a flight attendant, a nursery school teacher and a certified TEFL teacher. She lives in Philadelphia and dreams of Ireland. Her family constantly amazes and delights her. She published her first novel, *Miss Darling*, under the name Robbie K. Brown. E-mail her at mscherry9392gmail. com.

Alice Burnett is a retired teacher. Her children are now grown, and she spends her time with her four youngest grandchildren. In addition, Alice reads, sews, plays tennis, writes God stories, bird watches, and travels with her husband mostly on volunteer projects.

Jill Burns lives in the mountains of West Virginia with her wonderful family. She's a retired piano teacher and performer. She enjoys writing, music, gardening, nature, and spending time with her grandchildren.

Katy M. Clark is a writer and mom of two who lives in Michigan. By day, she works in academia. By night, she enjoys writing about motherhood or the 80's. Her work has been published on numerous websites and in her blog ExperiencedBadMom.com, where she shares her imperfections as a mom.

Steve Coney has been a freelance writer since graduating high school in 1992. His wide and varied publishing credits include *REPTILES* magazine and *Chicken Soup for the Soul: Tough Times Won't Last But Tough People Will*. A widowed single dad, Mr. Coney lives in Endicott, NY with his daughter, Maybellene.

Kim Cook studied technical and professional writing at the University of South Florida and has been a professional copy editor and managing editor of national specialty automotive magazines. She creates engaging written content, poetry, visual arts in watercolor and acrylic, and delicious culinary creations and baked goods.

Tracy Crump dispenses hope in her award-winning book, *Health, Healing, and Wholeness: Devotions of Hope in the Midst of Illness*. Her articles and stories appear in numerous publications, she freelance edits, and her blog encourages caregivers — our unsung heroes. But her favorite job is doting on five grands. Learn more at tracycrump.com.

Gertrude Daly is an experienced writer and blogger. In her day job, Gertrude writes operation and maintenance manuals for automated guided vehicles used in factories and warehouses to move goods. In her free time, Gertrude runs "Gert's Royals", a blog about European Monarchies. Gertrude has also contributed some short stories to anthologies.

Barbara Davey is a frequent contributor to the *Chicken Soup for the Soul* series and views the staff and contributors as extended family. For forty years, she honed her writing skills drafting corporate communications, and is now enjoying retirement. She and husband, Ron Becker, live in Verona, NJ, where she does her best to avoid the kitchen.

Elton A. Dean is the author of *A Yeti Like Freddie: Talking to Kids About Autism*. He is a husband and a father, a leader and teacher in higher education, and a retired soldier. Among his awards is the Military Outstanding Volunteer Service Medal for over 1,000 hours of direct community service.

Mark Dickinson is an international instructor currently teaching in the United States. Before beginning his career in the classroom twenty years ago, he worked for almost a decade as both a television and newspaper reporter. In his free time, Mark traveled to more than eighty countries.

Elizabeth A. Dreier is a retired teacher and freelance writer who lives in Poland, OH with her husband, Jerry, of forty-three years. When she isn't writing or tending to her garden, Dreier likes to engage in shenanigans with her two grandsons, aged five and two. She thinks that her mother, aka Skinny Santa, would be proud.

RoseAnn Faulkner is a retired elementary school teacher. Her stories about family, faith and everyday miracles have been published in the *Chicken Soup for the Soul* series and *Guideposts* magazine.

Zach Fisher has been married to his amazing wife, Alisha, for twenty-six years. They have three outstanding kids: Shelby, Tyson, and Ava. They motivate almost everything he does, including his writing. With no formal writing education, he leans on his creativity and crazy life experiences for his stories and loves it!

Carole Brody Fleet is a multi-award-winning author, media contributor and nine-time contributor to the *Chicken Soup for the Soul* series. An expert in grief and life-adversity recovery, Ms. Fleet has made over 1,300 radio appearances and has appeared on numerous television programs as well as in worldwide print and web media.

Allison Lynn Flemming is drawn to the power of story to grow hearts and communities. Singer, songwriter and worship leader, Allison and her husband, Gerald, form the award-winning duo, Infinitely More. Publications include *Guideposts*, *The Upper Room* and six previous titles in the *Chicken Soup for the Soul* series. Learn more at www.InfinitelyMore.ca.

Claudia Flisi has written for *The New York Times International Edition*, *Fortune*, *Newsweek*, *Variety* and other publications. She has visited 105 countries, fallen off horses on six continents, and raised her sons — and dogs — in three languages. Her children's book, *Crystal and Jade*, was published in 2016. Learn more at www.paroleanima.com.

C. C. Foster holds a Master of Arts in Education, with honors, from Western Michigan University. A published poet and YouTube Baby Sensory Content Creator, she lives a serene life in the Midwest. C. C. enjoys writing, tutoring ELL, and practicing daily meditation for self-care.

Carol Graham is an author, podcaster, YouTuber, teacher, speaker, prayer coach, certified health coach, wife, mom, grandmom, and dog rescuer. Carol received the Woman of Impact Award and the Author of the Year award for her memoir, *Battered Hope*, and the global award One Woman — Fearless.

S.M. Green received a Master's in English from University of New Mexico and began a career as a corporate writer and editor. She enjoys hiking, yoga, movies, reading, baking, and spending time with family and friends. Her alter ego is a published author of more than a dozen romance novels and stories.

Carol Elaine Harrison has her Bachelor of Education and is a writer and speaker from Saskatoon, SK, Canada who has always loved to hear and tell stories. She also enjoys reading, spending time with family and friends, family history, and paper crafting. E-mail her at carol@carolscorner.ca.

Rob Harshman taught high school for over thirty years and has written numerous Geography textbooks. Recently he e-published his first volume of children's short stories. He plans to publish more in the near future. Rob loves spending time with his four grandchildren as well as traveling, gardening and taking photographs.

Wendy Hobday Haugh's short stories, articles, and poetry have appeared in dozens of national and regional publications including *Woman's World*, *Highlights for Children*, and WritersWeekly.com. This is Wendy's twentieth story to appear in the *Chicken Soup for the Soul* series.

Christy Heitger-Ewing is an award-winning author who has published more than 2,500 magazine articles and contributed to twenty-seven anthologies.

She loves to run, practice yoga, and snuggle cats. An Indiana native, she dreams of one day opening a cat sanctuary. Learn more at christyheitger-ewing.com.

Judith Victoria Hensley is a retired middle-school teacher. She was a columnist for the *Harlan Enterprise* for over twenty-five years and has been involved in dozens of book projects, magazine articles, and freelance writing projects including the *Chicken Soup for the Soul* series, *Samaritan's Purse*, and other notable publications.

Becky Hofstad writes about faith, special needs, adoption, and transracial family parenting. Her work is published in *Chicken Soup for the Soul: Get Out of Your Comfort Zone* and *Guideposts* publications, including as a regular contributor to the magazine *Strength & Grace* for caregivers. She enjoys active outdoor adventures.

Stan Holden is a commercial art director who has parleyed his creative expertise into a successful sales and writing career. He is the author of four books including the critically acclaimed best seller *Giving Candy to Strangers*. Stan is currently working on his next book, *Don't Lie Down In The Aisle*.

Kristin F. Johnson received her B.A. from Gustavus Adolphus College, and M.S. from Metropolitan State University. She has published more than ten books for kids, including her middle-grade novel *Fearless*. She lives in Minnesota with her family and their rescue dog. Learn more at kfjbooks.com.

Denae Jones is a middle-school teacher and mother of six. She has authored *Love, Joy, Peace*, and co-authored devotionals *Everyday Grace for Teens*, *Everyday Grace for Mothers*, and a novel *But, Even Now*. Her writing has also been in *Chicken Soup for the Teacher's Soul* and *A Second Chicken Soup for the Woman's Soul*.

Suzannah Kiper is a graduate of the University of Louisville and a seventh generation Kentuckian. She has been married to her husband Tim for twenty-seven years and has two amazing kids (Daniel and Lydia) and a Maltese dog (Chloe). She has previously had three stories published in the *Chicken Soup for the Soul* series.

Alice Klies is a member of an International Word Weavers chapter in Northern Arizona. She is the Board Chair of the Verde Valley Humane Society, a retired teacher, and hopes her stories bring laughter, tears, and encouragement to others. She is married to Raymond, and has three children and a rescue dog, Lola.

Wendy Klopfenstein likes sunshine, sweet tea, and a good book, preferably all together. She enjoys putting the stories in her head on paper for others to enjoy. To sign up for her newsletter visit www.wendyklopfenstein.com.

Laura Knoy was founding host of New Hampshire Public Radio's "The Exchange" which for twenty-five years was the state's most widely recognized and respected radio news program. Today, Laura is an in-demand interviewer, moderator, and narrator. She's also a fitness instructor and host of two podcasts. She lives in Concord, NH.

Whitney Kolba is the author of "The Epiphany" in *Chicken Soup for the Soul: The Joy of Christmas* and "Thanksgivings with Grandpa," in *Chicken Soup for the Soul: The Wonder of Christmas*. She has fourteen years of publishing experience and works as a Senior Editor. Whitney's greatest gift is her family — her husband and her daughter.

T. Jensen Lacey is the author of twenty-three books and nearly 900 articles for newspapers and magazines. This is Lacey's eighteenth story to appear in *the Chicken Soup for the Soul* series. Besides writing, she enjoys cooking and the outdoors. Lacey lives with her husband and dogs in Fairhope, AL. Learn more at TJensenLacey.com.

Lisa Leshaw is humbled and overjoyed to have her words published in her twelfth book in the *Chicken Soup for the Soul* series. She's currently writing a picture book for women about being their authentic selves. Lisa has everything crossed, hoping and praying that someone likes it enough to give it wings.

Mary Low earned a Bachelor of Arts in Elementary Education and went on to earn a Master's in Curriculum and Instruction. She taught elementary school for years and currently substitutes in special education classrooms. Mary loves spending time with her family and traveling to new places.

Diana Lynn is a small business owner and freelance writer. This is her thirteenth published story in the *Chicken Soup for the Soul* series. She is the daughter of Joyce and Mike. She is a mom to her son Kenny. She feels this story honors her relationship with both her parents and is deeply important to her.

Lisa Mackinder received her Bachelor of Arts at Western Michigan University. A freelance writer, she lives in Portage, MI with her husband. When she isn't writing, Lisa enjoys being outdoors, reading, spending time with family and being around animals. Learn more at lisamackinder.com.

Cheryl Maguire holds a Master of Counseling Psychology degree. She is married and the mother of twins (son and daughter) and a daughter. Her writing has been published in *The New York Times*, *AARP*, *NatGeo*, *The Washington Post* and many other publications. She is a professional member of ASJA and an active member of SATW.

Carmela A. Martino is an author, poet, and writing teacher with an MFA in Writing. Her credits include two award-winning novels: *Rosa, Sola*, for ages ten and up, and the YA historical novel *Playing by Heart*. Carmela's poems and short stories have appeared in numerous magazines and anthologies. Learn more at carmelamartino.com.

Laura McKenzie is a retired kindergarten teacher living in Abilene, TX with her husband, Doug. She enjoys traveling and spending time with her children and grandchildren. Laura loves reading, writing, and volunteering at the local food pantry. Laura is thrilled to be a part of the Chicken Soup for the Soul family.

Dee Dee McNeil is a published poet, singer, songwriter, and freelance journalist for six decades. Her music has been recorded by icons like The Four Tops, Gladys Knight, Diana Ross, Nancy Wilson and Edwin Starr. Her original music is on albums she recorded at CDbaby.com. She contributes to LAJazzscene.buzz and MakingAScene.org.

Jennifer Priest Mitchell holds a B.A. from Capital University in Ohio and an M.A. from Arizona State University. She has published poems and articles and is currently completing a collection of essays. Jennifer enjoys researching her genealogy, baking, hiking with her husband and dogs, and traveling to visit family.

Virginia "Ginny" Mueller is a travel fanatic who loves to take advantage of living near a large international airport. Her travels are a constant source of inspiration as she uses her B.A. in Communication and Media Studies for nonfiction essays and travelogues.

An artist and writer, **Susan Mulder** teaches workshops from her studio, gardens, and gets into mischief all while adoring her grandchildren. Married to her high school sweetheart, she lives and works tucked away in deep woods somewhere in Michigan.

Sandra R. Nachlinger enjoys reading, quilting, writing, lunching, travel, and hiking in the beautiful Pacific Northwest. She has written two novels (so far!) and her short stories have appeared in several titles in the *Chicken Soup for the Soul* series, including *Age Is Just a Number*, *Get Out of Your Comfort Zone*, and *Too Funny!*

Brian Narelle, graduate of USC Cinema, is an actor, screenwriter, cartoonist, and puppeteer, having starred in the cult classic *Dark Star* and The Learning Channel's *Bingo & Molly*. He created the San Diego Chicken and has taught cartooning at the Charles Schulz Museum. E-mail him at Briannarelle@comcast.net.

J. Nicolelli has a Bachelor of Science degree in Business and Computer Science. She has one daughter and loves the outdoors and spending time with her family.

Barbara Pattee received her master's in teaching middle school mathematics. An avid reader, writer, and amateur genealogist, she writes short memoirs, one of which was published in *On the Shores of Detroit*. She received honorable mention in the Writer's Digest Short Story contest in 2023. She's currently working on a novel.

Brittany Perry is a resident of the beautiful mountain state, West Virginia. She is a West Virginia Governors School for the Arts alumna and attended Concord University. She has been published in two other books in the *Chicken Soup for the Soul* series. Her hobbies are hiking and tending animals with her two sons and husband.

Connie Kaseweter Pullen lives in rural Sandy, OR, near her five children and several grandchildren. She earned her Bachelor of Arts degree at the University of Portland in 2006, with a double major in Psychology and Sociology. Connie enjoys writing, photography and exploring nature. E-mail her at MyGrandmaPullen@aol.com.

Melanie Curtis Raymond has a Master's in Clinical Psychology. She lives in Ottawa with her amazing husband, Al, her two sweet daughters, Sarah and Jenna, and their quirky cat, Smokey. She enjoys reading, writing, and running. She hopes to publish her romance novel. E-mail her at melaniecurtis@yahoo.ca.

Donna L. Roberts is a native of upstate New York who lives and works in Europe. She is a tenured university professor who holds a Ph.D. in Psychology. Donna is an animal and human rights advocate, and when she is not teaching, researching, or writing, she can be found at her computer buried in rescue pets.

Steven Andrew Schultz is the FVSD School Board President. He won Teacher of the Year twice. Steven's stories are published in multiple books in the *Chicken Soup for the Soul* series and other national publications. He also wrote a monthly magazine column for eleven years. Learn more at leadloveelevate. com or via e-mail him at personalbest22@gmail.com.

Patricia Senkiw-Rudowsky received an English degree from Kean University. She lives at the Jersey shore. She is dedicated to writing about all of the amazing miracles that she has encountered. She is blessed to have a wonderful family including two adorable grandchildren and her dog, Clayton. E-mail her at Storyteller1012@aol.com.

Laurel L. Shannon is the pseudonym of this NW Ohio author. She lives with her rescue Australian Terrier, Trixie, and two formerly feral cats, Pongo and Shy. She is on Facebook under Laurel L. Shannon.

Diane Dickson Shepard is a poet and writer with a B.A. in Journalism. Diane is passionate about poetry, nature, animal rights, North Carolina mountains, her family of really cool humans, really warm cats and underdone brownies. She lives authentically — marching to the beat of her own drum — even when it's out of tune. E-mail her at dianeedshepardwrites@gmail.com.

Mary Shotwell is the author of small-town romance including *The Christmas Catch* (Harlequin Special Release) and *Waverly Lake* series (City Owl Press). She lives in Nashville, TN with her husband and three children and loves holidays — especially Christmas. Learn more at maryshotwell.com.

Deborah Shouse is a writer, speaker, editor, and dementia advocate. She has an MBA but uses it only in emergencies. Deborah is the author of *An Old Woman Walks Into a Bar*. Her latest book is *Letters from the Ungrateful Dead: A Grieving Mom's Surprising Correspondence with her Deceased Adult Daughter*.

Stacey Sisk and her husband Chris parent four ever-growing children. They enjoy living in mid-Missouri near family and also traveling to exciting destinations. Giving gifts is among her favorite pastimes... especially for Christmas. You can find her writing professionally for marketing clients at CSDesign.Online.

Billie Holladay Skelley received her bachelor's and master's degrees from the University of Wisconsin. A retired clinical nurse specialist, she is the mother of four and grandmother of three. Billie enjoys writing, and her work crosses several genres. She spends her non-writing time reading, gardening, and traveling.

Karen Kipfer Smith earned her Bachelor of Education from the University of Toledo in 1972 and Master of Counseling from Bowling Green State University in 1992. She was a school counselor for twenty-five years, retiring in 2010. She is working on a collection of personal essays. She lives in South Carolina with her husband and near her six grandchildren.

Diane Stark is a wife, mom of five, grandma of one, and freelance writer. She is a frequent contributor to the *Chicken Soup for the Soul* series. Diane loves to write about the important things in life — her family and her faith.

John Stevens resides in St. Marys, Ontario. He has worked in many professions including teaching, radio and television, and association management. He has also visited over thirty countries, which has given him a unique outlook on life. E-mail him at stevens.john@zohomail.com.

Lynn Sunday is an artist, writer and animal rights advocate who lives near San Francisco, CA. Her stories have appeared in twenty books in the *Chicken Soup for the Soul* series and numerous other publications. She lives with her son and dog, Biscuit. E-mail her at Sunday11@aol.com.

Polly Hare Tafrate spent twenty-five years in the classroom teaching first graders how to read. Retirement brought the joys of welcoming seven grandchildren. She began a second career as a successful freelance writer to fill in the gaps between visits with her grandchildren.

Cecil Taylor founded CecilTaylorMinistries.com to teach Christians how to live a seven-day practical faith life. He is author of four books on Christian living and parenting. Married with three adult children, Cecil graduated from the University of Texas and later added an MBA. He enjoys sports, music, travel and gardening.

Venus Velvet started reading and writing almost before she could talk. Due to autism, she didn't speak until age five. In 2024, she retired from a forty-year career in television, architecture, teaching, and theatre. Now, she writes full-time including poetry, novels, plays and screenplays.

Wendy Vogel is a veterinarian, author, playwright, and cancer survivor. Her novels include the *Horizon Alpha* sci-fi series (Future House Publishing) and *The Risen* (Outland Entertainment). She lives in Cincinnati, OH with husband, Andrew, and a houseful of special needs cats.

Stephanie Schiano Wallace is a minister who writes about the experiences that have shaped her and her faith. She lives in Lexington, KY with her family. She loves to read, write, walk her dog, and spend time with her husband and two children. This is her second story published in the *Chicken Soup for the Soul* series.

Dorenda Crager Watson is a writer specializing in humorous essays, whimsical children's poetry, and simple living anecdotes. In addition to the *Chicken Soup for the Soul* series, her work has appeared in the children's magazine *Root & Star* and the Minimalism Life Journal. E-mail her at dcwatzworld@gmail.com.

Toni Wilbarger has been previously published in the *Chicken Soup for the Soul* series, *Guideposts*, and *The Upper Room* and published her first novel,

Out of Grace. After serving as office manager for her church for twenty-one years, she retired in 2023. She also enjoys singing, coffee, and chocolate. Toni and her husband live in Curtice, OH.

Amy Catlin Wozniak is blessed to share her life with her soulmate, four children, three grandsons, and a Great Pyrenees named Scarlett O'Hara, who has absolutely no problem living up to her namesake. She's living her dream of sharing her stories of faith and hope with *Chicken Soup for the Soul* readers.

Annie Yorty writes and speaks to encourage others when life hits hard. She, along with her sweetheart, parent three grown children and a furry beast Labradoodle. She co-hosts Empowering Homeschool Conversations and has written *From Ignorance to Bliss* and *Find Jesus in 25 Symbols of Christmas*. Learn more at AnnieYorty.com.

Meet Amy Newmark

Amy Newmark is the bestselling author, editor-in-chief, and publisher of the *Chicken Soup for the Soul* book series. Since 2008, she has published 201 new books, most of them national bestsellers in the U.S. and Canada, more than doubling the number of Chicken Soup for the Soul titles in print today. She is also the author of *Simply Happy*, a crash course in Chicken Soup for the Soul advice and wisdom that is filled with easy-to-implement, practical tips for enjoying a better life.

Amy is credited with revitalizing the Chicken Soup for the Soul brand, which has been a publishing industry phenomenon since the first book came out in 1993. By compiling inspirational and aspirational true stories curated from ordinary people who have had extraordinary experiences, Amy has kept the thirty-one-year-old Chicken Soup for the Soul brand fresh and relevant.

Amy graduated *magna cum laude* from Harvard University where she majored in Portuguese and minored in French. She then embarked on a three-decade career as a Wall Street analyst, a hedge fund manager, and a corporate executive in the technology field.

Her return to literary pursuits was inevitable, as her honors thesis in college involved traveling throughout Brazil's impoverished northeast region, collecting stories from regular people. She is delighted to have come full circle in her writing career — from collecting stories "from the people" in Brazil as a twenty-year-old to, three decades later, collecting stories "from the people" for Chicken Soup for the Soul.

When Amy and her husband Bill, the CEO of Chicken Soup for the

Soul, are not working, they are visiting their four grown children and their spouses, and their five grandchildren.

Follow Amy on X and Instagram @amynewmark. Listen to her free podcast — Chicken Soup for the Soul with Amy Newmark — on Apple, Google, or by using your favorite podcast app on your phone. You can also find a selection of her stories on Medium.

About Toys for Tots

Toys for Tots, a 77-year-old national charitable program run by the U.S. Marine Corps Reserve, provides year-round joy, comfort, and hope to less fortunate children across the nation through the gift of a new toy or book. The gifts that are collected by Marines and volunteers during the holiday season, and those that are distributed beyond Christmastime, offer these children recognition, confidence, and a positive memory for a lifetime. It is such experiences that help children become responsible citizens and caring members of their community.

Since 1947, the program has evolved and grown exponentially, having delivered hope and the magic of Christmas to over 301 million less  fortunate children. The Marine Corps Reserve Toys for Tots Program also provides support year-round to families experiencing challenges and exceptional circumstances, thus fulfilling the hopes and dreams of millions of less fortunate children nationwide. The Marine Toys for Tots Foundation is a not-for-profit organization authorized by the U.S. Marine Corps and the Department of Defense to provide fundraising and other necessary support for the annual Marine Corps Reserve Toys for Tots Program.

You can learn more about Toys for Tots by visiting their website at https://www.toysfortots.org.

Changing your life one story at a time ®
www.chickensoup.com